BROKEN CASTINGS

John Woolmer

Pen Press Publishers Ltd

First published in Great Britain by
Pen Press Publishers Ltd
39-41, North Road
Islington
London N7 9DP

ISBN 1-904754-91-0

Printed and bound in the UK

A catalogue record of this book is available from
the British Library

Cover design by Jacqueline Abromeit

To my daughter Susan,
for her constant encouragement.

About the author

Following grammar school and an engineering design apprenticeship, John Woolmer worked at the London Docks, designing and drawing plans for refitting ocean going liners.

Later he was a technical illustrator at the Royal Aircraft Establishment, Space Department. This work included scripting and drawing for animated training films for the Armed Forces.

There followed a period designing Air Safety Posters for The Fleet Air Arm for use on aircraft Carriers.

Now retired, he can spend more time writing.

Contents

PART ONE

Chapter 1
The Return

The walk from the station seemed unfamiliar, bearing little resemblance to his recollections. Perhaps he should never have returned.

Confused, he hesitated, but when the traffic cleared, he crossed the road. He had the face of a man always deep in thought, with bright blue eyes that seemed to show an inner sadness. To him, the traditional market town had seemed permanent, indestructible. But now, where the old works had once stood, a massive faceless structure sprawled before him. He thought of the design office where he had worked in the 1940s, so different from his London-based commercial art studio, where computers had mostly replaced the drawing board and bore little resemblance to his memories. He was now in his late sixties and casting his mind back more than fifty years.

A wave of sadness washed over him. He had expected changes, but there was no way he could have imagined what would eventually happen to the old factory. Bureaucracy had permitted such changes. To Tom, it was vandalism in the name of progress. New owners would be blinded by the developers' plans for a great new world formed in concrete and glass, to generate ever greater profits. The town planners' had authorised a mass demolition. The past had been gouged away, leaving only a vast prime site. As the dust settled, architectural mania had produced this huge new shopping centre. Just a place to spend money – no room for individual creativity, or skilled craftsmanship. A way of life which had taken many years to evolve had gone for ever.

He paused before entering the great artificial area. There was a seat near where a small tree had been planted, and an inscription carved on the back rail read: '*In memory of Charles Fenton, Engineer.*'

He sat there, closed his eyes and drifted back in time. For a brief moment, he saw the workshops, the machines and the men in overalls and caps so clearly that he imagined he could even smell the oil. Awoken briefly by the shrill sound of children, he opened his eyes. But he was soon back with his thoughts.

In the year 1941, the works had constantly pounded to the sound of industry. Its gentle hum could be heard reverberating at the street entrance and even in the offices, which were part of the same sprawling factory buildings. These extended over a large area of the town from one street to another. The old buildings in the main street had been a house from a long gone age; the entrance leading to the works had been bridged over after the old family house was made into offices. Once, large horses had clattered through this same entrance, hauling wagons for more than a century. The first floor that extended over this wide passageway was the main area of company business, where the old man, a direct descendant of the family who had founded the firm almost two hundred years earlier, ruled through the management down to the most humble apprentice.

Tom sighed as he remembered.

'I want you to put your best foot forward,' said the chief designer, with his strong Scottish accent. This was Tom's first day, and the first of many a long lecture that he would have to endure. 'Your father was very wise in bringing you here. Your next five years are sealed, you must take full advantage of those years, do you understand?'

'Yes,' Tom said, doing his best to adopt an air of confidence.

From the works passage, the old front door led into a dimly lit hall where the floors were covered in a dark green but well polished linoleum. The pay office had a hatch that was opened when the men queued up in the main entrance on payday. The typing office sat at the foot of the stairs that led up to a landing surrounded by doors to the various offices, and a steep stairway ascended to a storeroom above, a secret hideaway under the roof, full of old books and files.

The room where the chief designer worked had two drawing boards and shelves loaded with reference books. Piles of drawings and blueprints lay on a table near a dark intriguing cupboard. The long drawing office, with a roof of north lights above the cream painted roof trusses, extended from a once large bedroom in the old nineteenth century family home. A designer, deep in thought, formulated his ideas, with slide rule at hand, while a woman traced on cloth from pencilled drawings. In this room, apprentices were trained and operated the blueprinting machine that stood in a recess on the left with a window from which one could see the chief designer. He in turn could see the back of the machine and catch sight of misconduct by a high spirited apprentice; he was a man obsessed!

'I'll not put up with this kind of noisy behaviour, you'll go home for a week!'

'But it wasn't my idea, I...'

'What was that? I saw you playing around!'

'Yes... sorry Mr Glenn... but.'

'No buts, you'll go home for a week.'

Old Mr Fenton, the managing director, was nearly always in his office. A product of the Victorian age of heavy creative engineering and still hanging on to hopeful but fading progress, he was deeply immersed in memories of past achievements but sad about the inevitable failures. Every Saturday morning, he shook hands with each of the staff in turn and wished them a nice weekend.

In a tiny washroom, which had once been the smallest bedroom, there was a little cast iron fireplace. A few steps led up to a bare-boarded long room, built over the main entrance passage. This was called the print room. There was an old fashioned blue printing contraption, sometimes used as a stand-by. A drawing and blue printing paper were wrapped round an upright glass cylinder while a carbon arc light was lowered with an adjustable speed governor into the cylinder then hauled up quickly. Tom smiled when he recalled his struggling with the antiquated machine.

There were north lights and a whitewashed window from which the workshops could be viewed through a small pane left clear. It was Tom's job to develop the prints in a large shallow tank near this window, by hosing them with water, which removed the chemical from areas unexposed to the arc light, leaving the lines white on a background hardened to a dark blue. The place was heated by creaking steam radiators that quickly dried the prints. Shelves in this room were full of old working drawings on strong canvas, beautifully drawn, shaded and coloured, though yellow with varnish. They reminded Tom of ancient scrolls and were originally sent into the workshop before blueprints were invented.

A dark passage led to a room with a large window across the full width over the entrance, giving a good view of the street up to the market place. There were long wooden boxes of glass photographic plates – hundreds of them. They were negatives of marine engines, boats, some of buildings being constructed, very early cars and machinery that must have dated from the last century. Fascinating archives for a young apprentice to scrutinize, especially the ancient cars. Tom made prints from the plates on blueprint paper.

The drone of the machinery was largely unobtrusive, but in the works it became much louder where two huge diesel engines pounded. They were started by putting a heavy bar into one of several holes in a gigantic shining flywheel. One hard pull downwards, and the first engine burst into life, *boom, boom*, quickly speeding up. Then the second engine was started. Together, they drove two generators that powered all the machinery in the workshop. Very large electric motors with belts up to long shafts in the roof drove a forest of slapping belts driving the machines. Some of these were huge, and so robust they looked made to last for ever.

Who could have known how soon those awe-inspiring machines would end their days? At some unknown date, they were switched off for the last time and fell silent, their operators gone forever. A dead factory, groaning in the wind, where the buildings had become obsolete, the roof leaking and the rust starting to form on the machinery quietly waiting to be taken away as scrap. A few may be seen in museums and looked upon with wonderment.

Tom pondered how time had erased the site, and people had got used to the new area of shops. Most have never known the bustling old market town as it was, those interesting shops of individual character, or about life as it was over fifty years ago. The memory might have remained with a few for a while and there would be some historical records, but their meaning would fade with the passing generations. And the skilled engineers, who had earned their livelihood with the biggest employer in the town, would soon be forgotten

Looking into a brightly lit window, who could imagine that, in that very spot, a man had gone to sleep standing up at a grimy bench while on night shift during the war in 1942? Or that a man working a large lathe had got his beard caught between two gear wheels and screamed for help, which came just in time from another man, who knocked the drive belt from the pulley. Once, a man lost a thumb, crushed between a chain and a large casting as it was being lifted by the gantry crane. Heavy engineering was never completely free from danger; a momentary lapse of concentration could cause a tragedy.

The pendulum swings, we advance through decades of change, and then suddenly we have reached the end of an era. The painful transformation very soon becomes a new reality that is quite normal, innocently thought of as 'progress'. But the only thing that has been created is a market with a new face, an artificially developed area that is in stark contrast to the region's gradual evolution over centuries. The supermarket has a choice of goods once unheard of; so much money is spent as the trolleys are filled then wheeled to the car.

'Such a humdrum life,' Tom murmured to himself, thinking that the tool room would have been near where he was standing now; where, fifty years before, he had collected a special tool to take back to his machine.

He recalled the wonderment of seeing a large propeller turn slowly, not in a ship but fitted to a gigantic lathe, machining a fourteen-inch propeller boss of shining phosphor bronze on a beautifully cast propeller clamped to a six-foot diameter face plate. Turning so smoothly, it was a magnificent sight, awe-inspiring for a young apprentice. The skilled man who had confidently set up such a large operation bore the responsibility with ease. The blue print of the propeller lay behind him on a large surface plate, just another task, but proudly pursued. He would always be pleased, even eager, to talk about his work, or to give anyone some useful advice and enjoy a good laugh at the same time.

In a large corner of the machine shop, a sixteen-foot marine engine bed plate rolled along a flatbed planer under the cutting tool, a very bulky casting recently transported from the foundry. A huge crank shaft was being machined on a lathe, which, as it turned, looked incongruous because of its shape, with each angle of the crankshaft having to be individually set up and balanced. Those highly skilled operations of heavy engineering might be described as a lost art. Numerous machines for large boring, slotting and milling down to the smaller machines had been continually used for decades.

He thought: 'It's easy to say we know there'll be changes as time goes by; but even when the signs of crumbling started to show, nobody really imagined a complete collapse down to ground level, until the dust had settled and it was too late.'

He tried to remember how the town used to look all those years ago, almost wishing he could turn the clock back. The changes seemed to be mostly for the worst. Money had greater power than the desire to hold on to old traditions. What did beauty matter now, or craftsmanship? The craftsmen were the forgotten ones.

A few boarded-up premises outside the shopping centre had also jolted Tom's memory, among them what had once been the music shop – a sad reminder – and the cycle shop where he'd had many a laugh with the jolly owner. Now all that was left was a sorry little row of run-down shops waiting to be demolished.

The view looked out to some distant hills, where a dominant chimney stack on the edge of the town had once fiercely smoked as the blast furnace churned out fine castings, spreading a fine haze over the area. Tom was moved to dwell upon the greatness of an era that had witnessed such an abundance of creativity. The foundations laid all through the nineteenth century had marked the most exciting period ever of new engineering and technical procedures. In the foundry, metal pieces were first modelled in wood, the patterns from which the castings were reproduced, and on the floor were mounds of black sand where the moulds were bedded. The blower roared as the metal was melted down in the furnace while a strong man wearing a leather apron stood, ready to knock in the clay bung at the base of the furnace. He skilfully pounded the outlet till suddenly the brilliant streak of molten metal shot down a trough into a large ladle. This was slowly moved by a crane to where the metal was poured into the waiting mould, causing sparks to fly.

For many decades, the beautiful things that were made there included ornamental cast railings in a great variety of patterns dating from the previous century. These adorned the whole town. Machines of every description, including agricultural machines and farm steam engines were widely distributed. But there was a menace on the horizon, dismissed by many: the machines of war. People were inevitably drawn into this evil business with no choice.

Tom recalled seeing, at the end of the Second World War, a sad pile of cut-off railings in the foundry yard, taken without permission from private dwellings. They were waiting for the melting pot – the last remnants of a bygone age, misguidedly grabbed for the war effort. The old patterns, so meticulously carved, were mostly lost. Although iron had been urgently required during the war, there was some overreaction locally. Much of the stolen iron was never used anyway, and no compensation was offered to those whose railings were uprooted. As is so common in war, everyone lost something in the end.

Chapter 2
The Apprentice

In 1941 Thomas Hunt left school, and was taken on as an apprentice at Fentons, a marine engineering firm and mainstay of the town. His father had legal documents drawn up and Thomas was signed on for five years, a guarantee that he would gain wide experience in many skills, both in design and in practical engineering work. At that time; an Indentured Apprenticeship was a contract for a legally bound period of training in all the skills of a trade. The pay was low, but the benefits were worth more than money could buy.

He felt proud yet nervous at his interview with the chief designer. Mr Glenn, a short man in a well worn dark suit and sombre tie, held out a firm hand in welcome, his pale, anxious face registering the heavy responsibility of his job. 'So it's Thomas Hunt,' Mr Glenn said with a strong Glaswegian accent. There followed a long lecture, during which he gesticulated wildly and thumped his fist onto his drawing board, as if to emphasise his points. Thomas felt he would never get away. 'You see this drawing,' Glenn demanded as he waved his hand across the board. The drawing looked very complicated. 'There's much to learn.' His voice was serious. 'You must study, study!' He thumped his fist on the board again. 'I want you to put your best foot forward!'

Tom came away weary, contemplating what was in store for him. Back at home, when his father asked how he'd got on, he had honestly replied: 'All right, Dad, I'm looking forward to starting', though he had also confided his feelings of apprehension. Mr Hunt, a stockily built man, was an architect, well known locally as a trustworthy aide to various organisations, and he was also a Freemason. For all his serious interests, he had a great sense of humour and he and Tom were good friends, though when he made light of Tom's fears, it did nothing to encourage the lad.

After some months, Tom had settled into the drawing office routine. He became familiar with how designs were thought out, from which finished drawings were traced onto cloth, and he had learned how to make blue prints from tracings. The craftsmen were all experts at reading the working drawings.

The war continued and consequently there were shortages; but within this oppressive atmosphere, some companies were experiencing a temporary reprieve from the threat of decline that had loomed at the end of the Thirties. The emergency demands of the war meant that, quite suddenly, engineering businesses began to flourish because so much power was needed, including steam engines for ships. Despite the potential threat of invasion, there was little sense – or talk – of fear among civilians. People had grown used to the threat and just got on with what was called 'the war effort'. There were more jokes flying around than at any time before, and people seemed much more friendly to each other – a natural response to prevailing danger.

Two arc lights that moved from side to side on the blue printing machine ate carbon rods at an amazing rate with a brilliant flame. The dazzling, hissing beam of light danced between the vertical carbons that were about an inch apart, and Tom never ceased to be fascinated by this. One of his duties as blue print boy was to maintain as well as use the machine, so he had to clean the glass and replace the carbons. Some days he would find himself making prints for many hours, which was tedious work.

Mr Wills, a plump figure with black hair and horn-rimmed spectacles, always wore a dark blue suit with matching waistcoat and a clean white collar, and often sported his old school tie. Mr Wills was very much Tom's senior and had shown him round on his first day at the firm. It so happened that he had been to the same Grammar School as Tom, though long before Tom's time. The pair got on well, for Mr Wills had introduced Tom to the various foremen in the workshops, who talked about their work, and had encouraged them to pull Tom's leg. But he also taught Tom a few useful routines, and the young boy found the atmosphere there very friendly and enjoyed the good humour.

Frequently, heavy footsteps would come pounding upstairs, and a man would fly into the chief's office, speaking loudly, so that his voice echoed through all the rooms. This was the works manager. 'Oh, Glenn, send me down a new set of prints of the valve gear on job number 2897, would you?' he would bellow, or any other question. Tom thought this very uncouth. 'Maybe force of habit,' he mused. 'He must think he's still in the machine shop!'

One day he mentioned it to Mr Wills. 'Why does that man always shout?'

'Just bad breeding,' Mr Wills answered.

Mr Perry, the dedicated mainstay designer, could always be found sitting on his high stool sucking his pipe, a slender and dapper figure. He was a quiet man in his late thirties, with dark wavy hair above a high forbid, and horn-rimmed glasses. Now he turned and smiled, having heard the conversation. 'That man's the king down in the works!' he said.

There was plenty of laughter at work, and Tom soon felt free to join in. But if Mr Glenn walked in, possibly because he had heard voices raised in mirth, it was invariably Tom he would point his finger at, saying sternly, 'Come into my office, will you'. There poor Tom would suffer another boring lecture; he sometimes felt he was being used as a whipping boy. When Mr Glenn was in one of his 'persecution moods', he would mention voices talking about him. 'Walls have ears,' he would mutter, and warn Tom not to pay any heed to these untrue rumours. Tom hadn't the slightest idea what he was worrying about.

Still, Tom's good fortune was phenomenal in that the opportunity to achieve knowledge combined with practical experience was all there for him to take advantage of. In his case this was instinctive because of his natural talents, though he still found the passage both rough and smooth. For Tom, the going was made less difficult because of his enthusiastic appetite for experience.

Shyness tormented him at times, and he struggled with himself to beat off those youthful feelings of self-consciousness. He was sure his office companions must notice his twitching lips as he spoke. 'Stupid!' he thought, looking into the small mirror in the little washroom. 'I'm not bad looking,' he decided as he raised a left eyebrow while smoothing back his fair wavy hair. Reflected back at him was a face with a ruddy country complexion, the eyes blue and clear.

Day by day, Tom gained confidence and felt more at ease, especially in the machine shop, which he found fascinating. He got on well with the foreman, who was an amiable man, though he found the pattern-maker intimidating – perhaps it was his pale and embittered expression. Tom thought he always looked angry, as if he bore some grudge, but he was nevertheless a highly skilled craftsman who specialised in the first stage of good foundry work.

In those early days, Tom would feel more secure when in the office quietly working on a drawing, though he was prone to daydreaming. When one of the women from downstairs came in to talk to Mrs York, the tracer, Tom's concentration was always diverted. 'There's some lovely women in that office downstairs,' he thought to himself as he looked while pretending to work. And as he watched the young woman, who seemed so much older than him, walking away down the office, he was transfixed.

Fentons' fatherly figure was Mr Methly, he stood before his board in a long brown overall coat, designing layouts for the jungle of pipes in a ship's engine and boiler rooms. He was an expert in his field and his drawings were a fascinating study. His Merchant Navy experience had left him with some good yarns, but there was seldom enough time for stories. If a conversation was not work-related, Mr Methly would utter a brief word of wisdom that would usually end the discussion. On Friday afternoons he, being the senior staff member, would collect a bundle of small brown envelopes – the weekly wage packets – and from where he stood, deal them out like a pack of cards, hurling them through the air to each person with force and a fair amount of accuracy. This was always amusing, especially as it was anticipated.

Old Mr Fenton would shake each of his staff by the hand, wishing them a nice weekend, as was his Saturday custom. This was a nice gesture on the part of the managing director. Tom thought Mr Fenton was kind though somehow a little sad; perhaps he dwelt on the past and could see it all sliding away, like an old oak that is hollow in the centre. He was the head of the firm, with a long family tradition of great creative and ambitious engineering, but his power was now dwindling, evident perhaps from his once firm but now trembling handshake.

It was twelve o'clock and the gentle pounding from the works died to a halt. Mr Perry lit up his pipe. The regular Saturday tour of the silenced workshop, where the machines seemed to creak as they cooled, was of great interest to Tom. With the gentle sound of hissing steam, he and Mr Perry looked at castings, half turned as they were set up on the lathes and new steel parts stacked up. There were engines, some very large, in various stages of construction, but of main interest to Mr Perry was a small marine engine that was almost complete. Tom presumed it was one of his designs, for he stood there gazing at it and puffing his pipe.

'Small, compared with those large engines,' Tom said.

'It's a compound engine.'

'Compound?'

'A two-cylinder expansion engine.'

'Yours?' Tom asked:

'Yes,' he nodded proudly. 'One of a pair.'

Chapter 3
Violin Lessons

It was February and a cold wind was cutting Tom's ears as he struggled to work. He often enjoyed cycling, but not so much on a bitter morning as he tried to warm his ears with one glove, then the other. The frost was beautiful on the trees, and wisps of white fine powdery ice blew across the road in the breeze. Newburne was five miles away along country roads and the only means of travel for Tom was his bicycle, quite usual for many in those days. He pushed hard up punishing hills, then came the cold run down into the town.

It was a relief to walk into a nice warm office, but before he'd had a chance to get himself defrosted, Mr Wills appeared from the shadow behind the printing machine. He lived ten minutes' walk away, and always got down to the Pump Shop early.

'There you are,' he said with a smile, 'you look flustered! Is it cold or something?'

'Gosh, yes!' Tom said, puffing a little. 'Jolly cold for cycling this morning!'

'Never mind,' said Mr Wills, rubbing his hands together. 'You're going to enjoy these Pump Shop prints then.' He pointed to a great roll of tracings on the blueprint machine. 'It'll warm you up!' In this way, he succeeded in making Tom laugh, even though he'd just handed him a boring job.

A long session on that infernal machine, groping with arc lights, messing about with water and drying off prints, was never good news. Someone had to do it, but it was taking up too much of Tom's training time. The boys from the Naval College would spend a month with the firm, including a week in the design office. Although Tom had to show them how to use the printing machine, they were of little help, for they only spent a short time in each department.

'You'll be getting some help soon,' Mr Wills said.

'Another college boy?'

'No, a new apprentice.'

'Good,' Tom said, nodding his head.

'The next office boy,' Mr Wills said with a cheerful smile.

Tom looked down through the spy pane from the print room into the works, and saw Miss West approaching, her golden hair bouncing, her glasses glinting, and a white jumper stretched tightly over well formed breasts. Her red plaid skirt swung over her voluptuous hips as she walked nearer. She had well shaped muscular legs and wore white socks, as stockings were rare then. As she walked, then disappeared under the window to enter the office below, Tom was mesmerised by this petite, almost schoolgirl-like figure, though she was probably about twenty-one.

The cat-calls and whistles from the men in the works riled Tom a little, though it was only their fun. As he waved the hose over a blue print in the shallow tank, he could not stop thinking of Miss West. The waves of hair that surrounded her pale face intrigued him, and he felt a strange and pervading attraction. He really liked individualistic women, and had a penchant for slightly older ones. But in his position as a mere apprentice, he felt too humble and poor for her. Water sparkled in the tank, and she was there in the ripples smiling at him.

He was suddenly jerked out of his fantasy by the sound of Mr Glenn's voice outside the print room door. The prospect of being caught daydreaming by Mr Glenn was enough to keep any apprentice on his toes! Tom quickly hung the last print to dry with the others, near a steam radiator. As he passed by Mr Glenn's open door on his way back to the drawing office, he stopped when his name was called and entered the boss's office with the feeling that he was about to receive a telling off and the usual lecture about how he didn't appreciate this opportunity and was not putting his best foot forward. But this time he was spared the lecture.

'Just take these letters down to the typing office and ask them if they can spare me half a dozen paper clips,' Mr Glenn said.

Walking down the stairs with the letters, Tom's head felt numb and his heart was pounding. He would see Miss West! He wondered how he would get the words out, his throat was so dry. He reached the door and stood there for an excruciatingly long second or so, the noise of the typewriters clattering in his ears.

His excitement was overtaken by apprehension at the thought of seeing Miss West in that rather small room. It was shared by three women: the head typing lady known as Sophie, Miss West and Sally, who usually made the tea. Tom's mixed feelings took him to his own hazy world, from which he was an onlooker trying hard to break out. His emotions were probably closely connected with feelings of sexual guilt, a mystery which governed all his senses and actions. He was puzzled, for only a few youngsters appeared very shy, though they were brought up in the same sexually repressed world as Tom.

He shook himself out of the muzziness and took a deep breath before rapping on the door with his knuckles. The sound was exaggerated like loud cannon fire. At the call to come in, Tom opened the door. The room felt warm and the perfume intoxicating as he glanced at the women sitting at their machines, typing furiously. For an instant, he was spellbound. The typewriters stopped and Miss West turned and smiled at him.

'What brings you down here then?' she asked.

Tom held out the letters. 'From Mr Glenn!' He felt his upper lip twitching and was sure she would notice. 'Oh, and he'd like some paper clips please.'

Sally produced the clips. Some dropped to the floor as he held out his hand for them.

'Aren't you a soppy thing!' Sally remarked. She was a tall, well built young woman and as she stood near Tom, he could feel the warmth radiating from her body, which excited him. He thanked them all and fumbled with the doorknob as he went out, making two attempts to close it. When he heard their laughter, his pride was hurt.

When he had gone, Miss West sat looking at her typewriter. 'You shouldn't make fun of him,' she said.

'I think you're struck on that young man,' Sally giggled.

'Oh, don't be silly! He's too young for me.'

Dark trees swayed in the windy night. Tom was safe in his warm bed, lying on the soft mattress which, in his fantasy, became Miss West. He lay awake as thoughts of love and sexual feelings mingled in one agonising sensation, for at the age of sixteen, sex and love were as one. To him there was only one power, a power that embodied the whole universe, which, it was said, was created by God. Tom was undecided; even in his schooldays, he had regarded various religions as simply man-made with their own sets of rules to suit them, over which brutal but pointless battles had been fought through the ages.

Tom entered the main doors to the works just as Miss West arrived on her bicycle. She was carrying a violin case perched across the bicycle basket.

'Good morning,' she said brightly. Tom smiled and held the door open for her. 'Thank you... what service!' she remarked.

'Good morning,' he replied, looking at her violin. 'That looks like hard work.' It was just something to say.

'Light as a feather!' She gave a burst of laughter.

'Oh!' Tom quickly disappeared up the stairs, wondering why she sometimes brought her violin to work. Maybe she played in an orchestra or gave lessons.

Mr Wills was in already, and greeted Tom with his usual beaming smile. He had just returned from the Pump Shop, where he chose to arrive at the same time as the men began, at eight o'clock. He worked on his own in a little office and would pop back from there at intervals during the day. Any chores he had lined up were given out with his usual humour.

Miss West and Mr Wills would often meet in the little wash room. Tom had to pass through on his way to the print room and they would be standing by the little fireplace, near the wash basin and roller towel. Tom wondered if they were courting, and even began to have odd feelings of guilt about Mr Wills, because of his own secret amorous feelings for Miss West – or was it jealousy? Mr Wills' full figure looked incongruous next to hers, for she was so petite. As the pair stood talking, Mr Wills loudly cleared his nostrils and at the same time, stretched a chamois leather between his hands while she stood there holding letters. Surely she must find that irritating!

When they drank tea together, she would be doing most of the laughing as he joked, but Tom could not help thinking they had little in common, apart from the fact that they both wore glasses. They drank from elegant cups as they held their saucers, but this was certainly not the most elegant of meeting places. The routine rendezvous in the little wash room to the sound of a dripping tap! Tom thought of it as the title for a song, but the setting was not romantic enough.

Her name was Mildred, but to a mere office boy (for that was all he was known as), she was Miss West. He was conscious of his humble position: a young apprentice with no money, still living at home with his parents. Sexual maturity comes too soon in life for most of us to handle, and when it does, it is a drawback because this powerful natural urge is so distracting. In Tom's case, he found studying difficult. Miss West seemed so much older than him, though the difference was only about five years. Tom tried not to dwell on the awful internal struggle. He wished he had money and a little flat somewhere in the town. He could not even afford to live in digs, let alone have a flat; that was in the too far distant future to even contemplate. For now, he would have to make do with his secret daydreams.

Bent over a large drawing board, Tom was mastering the

art of using a ruling pen, whilst listening to snatches of conversation between Sally from the typing office and Mrs York the tracer, whose name was Connie. Sally was a tall jolly girl, aged about nineteen. One morning there was great laughter as Mr Wills chased her around the printing machine. Mrs York was quiet with a calming personality and usually had a pleasant smile for everyone. Tom thought she was very attractive, with her dark hair and fresh complexion. She was probably in her late twenties and her husband was away at the war. Tom got on well with her, for she was kind to him, like an older sister. She and Sally were drinking tea that Sally had made downstairs and brought up on a tray for the office staff. He was never offered a cup of tea; the office was a little private club from which he was excluded. It seemed unfair to him, but perhaps they thought he would not be able to contribute towards the cost of the tea.

Suddenly he heard the names Mildred and Mr Wills mentioned. Sally chuckled, 'He took her to the pictures last night.'

Tom felt jealous, though he tried not to let his thoughts distract him from his work. Despite the young apprentice's keenness, Mr Glenn's most extreme satisfaction in life seemed to be to haul Tom into his office on the slightest pretext. His dread of this did not stop Tom from having his daydreams, which at that time were mostly concerned with his adoration for Miss West. The feeling did not make him particularly happy, but there was nothing he could do about it. He was sure not many people would understand the torment he felt; they would think he was being silly, so it remained locked in his thoughts.

Sometimes, when Tom felt particularly desperate, he would go for long country walks with his sketch book and get lost in a deep wood. He liked to escape to secluded places and sketch away furiously to work off his sexual frustrations, but it didn't always work and he became depressed. In a leafy woodland glade, seized by nature's erotic urge, he would seek relief to stop him from going completely mad. There seemed no other way. His disturbing guilt complex did nothing to bolster his confidence, yet outwardly, he was an extrovert who enjoyed any social activity. He forced himself not to let his self-consciousness isolate him, trying to assure himself that he was simply a victim of prevailing attitudes

One day Tom stopped outside a music shop and looked at the violins in the window. He stood there for some time studying the instruments, thinking of the school orchestra in which his school pal played the violin so well. Letting his mind wander, he imagined himself playing in an orchestra, with Miss West alongside him. The instruments looked expensive and he remained for a while, deep in thought, until suddenly he realised he was going to be late for work.

When Tom got home that evening, he went to talk to his mother, a short and stocky woman with a pale complexion and wavy black hair. She had a very determined character and regarded everyone with suspicion. He told her how he had looked at the violins in the shop window and wished he had learned to play. To his surprise, she agreed to buy him a violin, as she had often encouraged him in his interest in the arts. She was from a large farming family background, but her sisters all played the piano and her father was an artist as well as an engineer.

She insisted on going with Tom to the shop, which he found embarrassing, though he was also gratified. The cheapest reasonable violin cost five pounds, and for another eight shillings, the friendly music shop keeper found him an old black wooden case. Tom invested two and ninepence in a self-tutor book and felt very pleased with himself as he went home with his mother that Saturday.

A friend had given Tom an old folding music stand which, when cleaned and given a coat of gold paint, looked quite smart. He practised in lonely seclusion in a back room at home, so that the excruciating sound he was sure he was making would not annoy anybody. But learning to play just by reading a book was hardly possible and he made little progress, though he was not discouraged and went on trying.

One day he took his violin to work, which took some nerve

on his part, for he was sure there would be sarcastic remarks from some of his colleagues. Tom had the idea that he might have the opportunity to show it to Miss West, and thus reveal a common interest.

He heard voices outside the office door; predominant was the voice of Miss West, which always gave Tom a sensual thrill. Then she walked in with Connie and Sally. The three stood talking, and Mildred West sounded quite upset as the other two tried to pacify her. Tom just pretended to carry on working but could not avoid listening, feeling concerned but unable to say anything. As far as he could gather, Mildred had performed a solo at a local concert the previous evening, and it seemed she was very indignant about how the compere had announced her when she came on. She complained that he'd been very tactless, made silly jokes and had not a glimmer of understanding of what she was about to perform. Apparently he had announced, 'Miss Mildred West will now play to you... well, you know the kind of stuff'. Tom felt he understood her anger; his heartbeats increased as he listened.

The conversation then turned to the firm's dance and when someone asked Mildred if she was going to be there, she walked away, saying, 'I've got something better to do, thank you.' Tom wondered why she sounded so disapproving. Perhaps she wasn't keen on dancing. Or could it be that the dreaded compere with the silly jokes would be the MC at the dance? After all, it would be held at the same Old Corn Exchange Hall. Tom thought he would like to go. There had to be a way of overcoming those stupid fears!

After work that evening, when the others had left for home, Tom took his time packing his things away. Mr Perry, who usually worked overtime, had slipped out for a cup of tea, so Tom was on his own. He put his violin on the table, suddenly wishing he'd left it at home. 'How futile!' he thought; why couldn't I have tried to show it to her at lunchtime? But it was a touchy subject. He turned to pick up the violin case, when suddenly there were quick footsteps, and in walked Miss West. He was startled and a warm glow came over him, but she gave him a quizzical look.

'Everybody else gone?' she said.

'Yes... well, Mr Perry's getting his tea.'

'Oh, I was hoping Mrs York would still be here.'

'She went early.'

'It doesn't matter.' Miss West was smiling as she looked at Tom's violin case on the table. 'That's a good old case. Heavy, I would think!'.

'Yes...' Tom was trying to find words. 'Would you like to look at it?' he said quickly, and opened the case. She lifted the instrument up and slowly turned it over to look at the back.

'Hum... not bad,' she remarked. Tom looked on, not finding words, thinking she would wonder why he'd brought it to work.

'I brought it in to show you!'

'Do you play much?' she said with a smile.

'I've not had it long. I... it wasn't too expensive, I mean for practice. Though I'm not very good, I'm trying to learn with a book.'

'You should have some lessons.' She had surprised Tom, as if she'd read his mind.

'Can you give me lessons?' Tom quickly gushed.

'We must see what we can do,' she said, making for the door.

'Yes...' He was lost for words and smiled broadly.

'Cheerio,' she said with a sing song emphasis to her country town accent.

Tom felt rather pleased with himself, but as days went by, he wondered how he could broach the subject of the lessons. The longer he left it, the more difficult it would be for him to approach her. It was as if his private thoughts were something to feel guilty over, but he knew that was silly and shrugged it off.

Passing the typing office door one day, Tom hesitated as he saw Miss West standing on her own at an open drawer of a filing cabinet. He was thrilled at the sight of her profile, with her clothes fitting snugly to her curves. As if compelled, he stepped into the office. She turned and greeted him cheerfully but politely.

'Hello, Tom, and what are you up to then?'

He could feel his heart pounding. 'I was... wondering about the violin lessons?'

It was not so bad once he had broached the subject and she did most of the talking anyway. In a few words it was arranged that he would have a lesson each Thursday evening after work at her house, which was two miles away at a place called White Heath. As she had not mentioned charges, and Tom was too embarrassed to ask, he dismissed the thought.

'We can cycle up together,' she said.

'Oh, yes...' There was a pause as Tom went silent.

'Yes, we can cycle up together,' she repeated for something to say to cover the silence.

'Thank you very much... yes, OK.' Tom could not believe his luck. He hoped he was not too hesitant in showing his thanks. But he did not recognise that the glittering look Mildred gave him betrayed her fascination for bashful young men.

Another tracing was disappearing into the blue printing machine, but Tom's mind was on other matters, though this was not unusual, for those piles of tracings were becoming very monotonous. He was thinking of the lessons, fantasising again about playing in an orchestra alongside Miss West – a quite impossible dream, in which the conductor was Mr Wills, who turned and looked straight at him. Tom jumped as the man himself walked in through the door behind him.

On the day of his first lesson, before finishing work, Tom lit up a cigarette, something he very rarely did. He took a few deep puffs to steady his nerves. As Miss West came through the door, he was quite calm. Fortunately, he'd just got rid of the cigarette. They left together, Tom carrying his violin case.

As they cycled up White Heath Hill, they talked and Tom spoke of his interest in art, and his painting and sketching.

'They say that music and art go together,' Miss West said. Tom could not help thinking she was suggesting that he and she would go well together because of his art and her music.

'You play at local concerts?' Tom asked.

'Yes, at the Corn Exchange. But it was more of a variety show, the last one. The stupid man introduced me as "Miss Mildred West, who is on the fiddle again tonight".'

'That was very rude.'

'Yes, and he got worse! He said, "She's going to play for you", then he sniggered and added, "Well you know the kind of stuff"!'

'His idea of humour... I expect he thought it was funny.'

'Not for me at the time, the silly man.' Miss West went silent for a moment.

'I overheard you talking about it in the office.'

'Couldn't avoid it, I suppose. The buffoon of a man made me so cross.'

'I think I'd have been pretty mad if it had been me; he obviously didn't appreciate good music.' They were getting on well, and Tom was happy as they cycled up the hill chatting and laughing.

At her house, Miss West showed Tom into the small front room where there was a cool sweet smell. Sheet music was spread out on an old piano that had candle brackets, and there were two music stands, with a book of music on one. 'Put your violin on the sofa,' she said, 'and give me your coat.' She took it away, leaving Tom to survey the room.

As Tom waited, he could feel his heart rate increasing in anticipation of his first lesson. He looked round the room. There was a small polished table in front of the window, and he glanced through the white lace curtains as someone walked by, and down at the polished cold linoleum floor covering and at the pattern on the mat in the centre of the room. A faint 'clink' of tea cups and spoons came from somewhere down the hall – the unseen mystery of the kitchen Tom pictured in his mind. He knew it would be clean and homely.

He was adjusting the bow as Miss West came in with two cups of tea, which she placed on the small table by the window. He was reminded of the tea he didn't get in the office.

'You play the piano I see,' Tom said.

'I'm having tuition, in fact. I have to play with confidence when I'm accompanying the violin during lessons.'

'Ah, yes I see.' And as they talked for a while, Tom gained confidence.

'Well, if you're ready then,' Miss West said as she put down her cup.

'Oh, yes.' Tom quickly drank up and picked up his violin.

'Follow me.' She demonstrated, holding the violin on her left shoulder with her chin. 'There you are, my hands are free.'

'Yes, I see... Oh dear!' He almost let it drop.

'Hold it firmly out over your left shoulder. Watch me.'

'It's tricky!'

'You'll get used to it. Now don't worry about that, just have a look at the strings. Do you know the strings?

'Yes... by learning from a book!'

'So, this is the G string. What are the others?'

'G... D, A and E!'

'That's fine, you must keep the instrument clean, wipe over the sound board with lavender oil. The bridge has to be in the correct position.' She moved it a little. 'Now to make sure it's in tune.' She instructed him in the tuning process and demonstrated how to hold the bow.

Miss West taught him more about reading music in that first lesson than he had ever learnt from a book. She did most of the talking while Tom shakily followed, for uneasiness tended to overwhelm his young mind. He tried hard, determined to master the art, though it was difficult. He struggled with his emotions, but as he tried to ignore nature, he became even more self-conscious. He was sure she noticed. He even wondered if she relished the effect she was having on him!

'You must learn to hold the bow correctly,' Miss West said as she stood close behind him. He could feel the warmth from her body. As he held his violin, she put her left hand on his, and with her right hand she held his bow hand, guiding it slowly forward and backwards across the strings.

'In... out... in... out... in... out,' she said with her soft voice and increasing emphasis. Tom was breathless and just about able to speak. Could she really be unaware of the stimulating effect she was having on his senses?

The Thursday lessons continued and the weeks went by. As Tom cycled home holding his violin, he would cherish and at the same time agonise over his exotic thoughts of Miss West while he ached with frustration. He often tried to understand the way nature worked. It was as if he could not get involved with the world and he was somehow a victim, clutched within nature's grip. Many months had passed since he had first felt a strong attraction for Mildred West and he could never have dreamed that he could get so close to her; yet he had managed to make this happen, and it was an achievement for him. His teacher was a goddess with a violin. He was at an age for believing in romantic love. But it was no good in his case; he was too young and immature, still locked in a time shell like all the people on earth, from which there was no escape.

At times Tom almost hated himself for being such a fool. He felt infuriated and would pedal on his bike so hard that he would arrive home exhausted. His parents did not know why he was so moody; they would never understand anyway. He'd go straight up to his room and fall upon the bed, struggling with his secret passion. Then his mother's voice would break the spell: 'Tom, what are you doing upstairs? Your meal's getting cold.' He didn't much feel like food these days, but he would have to go downstairs and eat.

Sometimes, on his way home from work, he'd stop by the roadside and walk into the depths of a wood where he could hide for a while with his private thoughts in the cool evening air. He wanted to break away from home, but he had to think of his apprenticeship, for he valued this. Having money and freedom was a long way off for Tom, in the land of dreams.

One day, Miss West was sitting at the piano while Tom stood behind her, struggling to make a fair attempt at a simple piece of music. She counted out four beats to the bar: 'One-two-three-four, one-two-three...'

Tom tried to concentrate. He was managing extremely well, for he was battling with his erotic thoughts. He read the music fumblingly; distracted by Miss West's shapely buttocks as she sat on the piano stool. At the end of the lesson he felt almost sick and his throat was dry, so that his voice seemed to him little more than a whisper. Such was the turmoil of youth and immaturity! Miss West told him he was doing well, and before he left the house that evening, she handed him an envelope. 'This is for the first ten lessons.' She hesitated.

'Yes, I see,' Tom whispered, not daring to look at her.

He carried the envelope home, wondering if there might be a letter other than just the bill. How strange, the peculiar imaginations of youth – struggling through the puzzling stages of learning and wanting to appear grown up while still not far beyond puberty.

Tom opened the letter when he got home and in fact a bill was all it did contain. '*For ten lessons, two pounds five shillings*,' he read.

'Two pounds five, that sounds reasonable,' his father said.

One day, Tom was out cycling with some friends – at least he thought they were friends until, to his surprise, one of them made a bad joke about his violin lessons. He wouldn't have minded if it had been left there, but they all joined in and began carping and jeering at him, saying that the lessons were only an excuse for him to get off with Miss West. They were joking but Tom was extremely sensitive and grew irritated because they went on too long. It was almost as if they knew more than he did; it was like an intrusion into his private thoughts.

'Is she charging you for the lessons?' asked one.

'Yes, of course,' Tom said, feeling very irritated.

'I reckon she's jolly mean,' Tom heard another say.

'That's not ruddy true, and it's none of your damned business either!' he shouted as he quickly rode away on his bicycle. He kept up an exhausting speed until he reached home, out of breath and still fuming. He went to the back room where he played the violin with great vigour for an hour or two, before going downstairs.

'You were keen tonight, Tom!' his mother said.

One evening, as Tom's mother was laying the table for tea, she asked him, 'Did you know a boy named Peter West at school?'

Tom immediately thought of a rather fat, jolly boy. 'Yes, but he was in a lower form than me, he was younger.'

'I've just read in the Weekly News that he died last Friday!'

'Oh dear. What was wrong with him?'

'It doesn't say, only that he'd been ill for some time.'

His mother showed him the article in the newspaper where there was a picture of the boy as Tom had remembered him. Must be Miss West's cousin! Tom thought; he lived in the same road as her. Then he remembered that their house had been damaged by fire some years previously. What a sad family!

The next day, Thursday, Tom took his violin to work as usual. During the day he heard Mrs York talking in quiet tones with Mr Perry. 'Did you hear about Mildred's cousin?' he heard her say.

'Yes, very sad,' Mr Perry said. Tom was a sensitive boy; if someone suffered a personal tragedy, he really felt for them. He was thinking about his lesson that night. Would she rather cancel it? Somehow he could not bring himself to go and ask her. He felt it best to say nothing, for surely she would let him know if she wished to call it off. As the time to finish work drew near, Tom began to have uneasy feelings of anxiety.

He had packed up and was picking up his violin with his mind full of questions, when Miss West walked in. 'Ready then?' she said with a big smile, and Tom was puzzled, for she was as cheery as always.

'Yes, I'm ready.' They went off as usual and nothing seemed different. They talked as they always did while cycling up the hill and he stopped worrying. He felt uncomfortable during that lesson, for he was confused.

'Now, shall we play the scales I told you to practise? You have been practising, I hope?'

'Oh yes!' He had repeated those scales many times during the week, but now he was playing them rather badly. Miss West, having got up from the piano, was standing on his right and they played the scales together, getting slower and slower, and she was bearing with him. He caught a glimpse through thc lace curtains of a black car as it drew up outside. He went on with his painful practising, Miss West by his side. Tom made no comment. Someone was let in by the front door, there were footsteps and hushed voices. Something heavy was being carried out through the narrow unseen hall with puffs and groans and faltering footsteps.

'Play that again,' said Miss West. The movement in the hall continued. 'Again!' Tom continued running painfully through the scales. 'Now, surely you can do better than that,' she insisted, taking him out of his strange thoughts. All was quiet outside the room now that the unseen object had gone, and the lesson continued. 'That's better, you're doing well now!'

The following day, Tom found work tedious and he was in a restless mood. During the morning, Miss West and Connie York spent some time together talking in near-whispers. Later, as Tom was trying to work, Mrs York approached him. 'Did you have your violin lesson last night, Tom?'

He was surprised at the question. 'Oh yes... er, but why do you ask?'

There was a pause. 'Oh nothing, I just wondered.' Tom did not wish to talk and Mrs York went back to her tracing. He had a strong urge to walk out of the room.

It was a mystery to Tom why his colleagues seemed evasive. It seemed they did not realise how confused he was, and were unwittingly keeping him in the dark. It was a nightmare because he was pretending to himself that he was letting his imagination run wild. It was only too clear that there was a gossip in the office and he felt threatened. The biggest surprise to him was to hear the newest apprentice (a youngster named Terry that Tom had nothing in common with, for he was more than a bit of a pain in the neck) also seemed to be in the know.

'I couldn't have a violin lesson with that there, no I couldn't,' the nasty boy said while waving his head and making *ts,ts* noises. Tom shrugged his shoulders, feeling he'd like to hit him. But it was best to ignore the remark. He had a strange feeling of detachment and wondered why he should be kept in the dark, even compared with the obnoxious apprentice!

That evening, while Tom was practising, he let his thoughts wander. Suddenly he shuddered. Peter West, Miss West's cousin, the fat boy at school... He thought of the fire. The house was almost gutted. As they lived in the same road, the family would most likely have stayed with their nearest relatives – Miss West's family. The body of the youngster could have been there, laid out upstairs!

Tom dismissed his notion as over-dramatic. It could have just been someone moving heavy furniture; his imagination often played tricks with him. But what about the questions at work? It remained a puzzle. Too late to say anything now; he wouldn't know what to say anyway. He carried on practising, trying to concentrate on the music.

He continued with his lessons and Miss West gave him good encouragement as the weeks went by. Then, one warm Thursday evening, as they were cycling up the hill and chatting, she said, 'This will be the last lesson for the time being. I think we should have a summer break, don't you?'

'Yes, I suppose so.' Tom hoped she was not tired of teaching him.

'Are you going to be good and spend your holiday at home?' This was a reference to wartime propaganda.

'No!' Tom laughed.

'Well, that's naughty! Where are you off to, then?'

'I was thinking of a cycling tour.'

'Oh! That's very nice.' There was a bit of a silence. Tom imagined that Miss West would be with Mr Wills, so he did not dare to ask how she would spend her holiday. 'I'll be staying with a friend for a few days,' she said, breaking the silence.

'Oh... yes.' There was a pause as he thought how nice it would be for Mr Wills.

'She's an old school friend of mine.' Tom immediately came out of his jealous stupor. 'She lives near Eastbrook, not far from Newburne, and she's fond of walking.'

Miss West and Tom entered the house by the front door as usual, but this time he heard her locking the door behind her while he went into the front room.

'I don't know why I've locked the front door,' she said as she came in. 'Perhaps it's because there's nobody else at home.' She grinned and rubbed her hands together.

'Oh, I see...'

'I'll make tea,' she said and quickly went out of the door. Tom was left feeling a little bewildered, a strange mixture of excitement and nervousness. He took a deep breath and tried to feel more confident as he ritually took his violin from the case, then adjusted the music stand. But music was not fully on his mind. He heard Miss West go upstairs.

While the tea was brewing, she looked into her bedroom mirror, patted her hair and powdered her nose. She hardly ever used makeup, or even perfume, so she just put a little cream on her cheeks. 'He's very young,' she was thinking. 'Can't be more than four or five years between us... but he's just an apprentice!'

Tom heard her come downstairs after a few minutes. The rest of the house was an unseen mystery to him, a secret beyond that so familiar front room. With his complete lack of experience, he could not help thinking that there might be more than just a music lesson on offer today. He was fantasising.

Miss West came in with the tea, and they drank in silence. Each time Tom caught her eye, he thought: is her expression amorous? Or was it his imagination? The tea certainly tasted a little sweeter than usual.

The lesson began. 'One-two-three-four, one... Come on, Tom!' Miss West shouted as she sat at the piano. He was blundering on and making the most basic mistakes, trying to concentrate. 'You're not doing very well today, are you?' She stood up. 'Would you like me to play it with you?' She picked up her violin, 'I know it's a bit difficult.' She played the piece through while Tom watched her movements. 'Now, we'll do it together, but slowly.'

'Yes, I'll try,' Tom said, and they went through it twice, with him faltering at first, then improving a little.

'That's better,' she said. Tom smiled and was bracing himself for a further run through when Miss West, to his surprise, sat down on the sofa, still holding her violin. Tom remained standing, wondering if she was going to ask him to sit with her.

'By the way,' she said, 'I thought I would tell you that I intend to devote my life to music. Mr Wills is just a friend, nothing more.'

'I see.' Tom nodded, wondering why she was opening up her private thoughts to him, but also secretly flattered.

'One can't get married and have a musical career at the same time; I don't think the two go together... do you?'

'I'm not sure,' admitted Tom.

'It's just that people talk... get the wrong impression...' She became more hesitant, while Tom just listened respectfully. He was not mature enough to be of help or give advice, though he wished he could.

'But I...' he began, then fell silent.

'What were you going to say, Tom?'

In his mind, the words 'I love you' were forming. But he said, 'I like you very much... the lessons, I mean.' He felt a fool.

'Well, that's good! You're very young, and you have your life ahead of you.' She suddenly stood up with a smile. 'Let's get on with it then!' That didn't make Tom feel any better. If she'd only taken him by the hand and led him upstairs, he would have been gladly initiated into a much needed experience. But that didn't happen, and he would never know whether he was right or wrong not to say, 'I love you.'

When the lesson ended. Tom thanked her, wished her a good holiday and left the house feeling wretched. He even thought of going back but could not think what he would say. He cycled as if he were trying to escape, but from what? Hopelessness grew within him as he thought how inadequate and stupid he must seem to Miss West. The road he was cycling along became, in his thoughts, the road of life stretching before him in one direction, from which there was no turning back. Mistakes that are made en route are, in most cases, not retractable; they go into the memory file that contains so many hidden failures. What Tom was agonising over was probably more in his mind than factual, and he pedalled very hard as he refreshed himself with renewed determination. He was going to look forward to the next lot of lessons.

In another era, and in another place, after many years had wrought great changes, a recently divorced man was clearing rubbish in the garden when he came across a rusted music stand. 'Why?' he sighed. 'Where were the wrong turnings?'

Chapter 4
Old School Friend

A few days into the summer, Tom had cycled over to see his old school pal Henry Hayes, who lived near Newburne. They went walking on the large stretch of heathland not far from Henry's home. Tom always enjoyed listening to his friend, who was very entertaining with his interesting true stories. They would discuss characters they knew from school, and philosophical ideas about life in general. They had been close friends in their grammar school days, but now that they had both left school, it was inevitable that they would see less of each other, for their work was very different. Still, they kept in touch as much as possible.

As they walked, there were few breaks in their conversation. They got onto the subject of music. Henry played the violin rather well, though not near Miss West's standard, and had been a member of the school orchestra. He was intrigued that Tom was having lessons, and couldn't resist a little joke about his teacher. 'Is she a smasher or a little long in the tooth, Tom?'

'No! She's... she's very nice.' Tom went quiet.

'Sounds as if you've fallen for her in a big way. What's her name then?'

'Oh... Miss West. But it's no good though.'

'You don't mean Mildred West do you?'

'Well... yes.' Tom didn't really want to talk about it.

'You're lucky to have her to teach you, she's extremely talented. I've met her at the dancing school a few times.' Tom felt a twinge of jealousy. Henry used to have tap dancing lessons, and Tom remembered going to the dance school with him during their schooldays. 'I only spoke to her once, she was a friend of Frances, the lady who runs the school. I don't go down there any more now. But I've heard your teacher playing at a concert at the old Corn Exchange – she's really good.'

'Yes, I know.'

Lying on the warm grass for a rest, they talked endlessly about their schooldays – days that were not so long ago, yet when he was away from the office, Tom was not a mere office boy, but a young man now. They stopped talking for a moment and Tom looked across the heath to a row of Scots pines. A light breeze gently swayed the grass; it was a moment for silent thoughts.

'What's the work like, Tom? Quite fulfilling?'

'Yes, it's very interesting. I know my stint in the works is due soon. How's it with you?'

'I think you've done better than I have!'

'Why do you say that?'

'I don't think there's much of a future in the photographic business now, with the war on. You're all right, you've got an apprenticeship, you're lucky to have something more concrete to work for.'

'Who knows, could be I suppose... Don't you find your work interesting at all then?'

'Well, it's not as if I'm learning much. All I seem to do is help to store supplies, sweep the floor and be a general dogsbody. I got into terrible trouble the other day.'

'Oh why? What happened then?'

'I spoiled a full box of bromide paper. It was unwrapped, I dropped it, the lid came off and the darkroom door was open.'

'That was a disaster!' Tom exclaimed.

'Mr Blackett was furious when he saw the sheets scattered on the floor. It's a wonder he didn't sack me on the spot! Specially as supplies are short.'

'Well, lucky he didn't. I bet he thought you were a bit clumsy though,' Tom chuckled. 'Has he got over it yet?'

'I'm not sure, I thought he might dock my wages, but he hasn't mentioned it since.'

In Henry's company, Tom had managed to stop thinking of the dilemma that had troubled his mind some days before. He never did discuss those most intimate thoughts, even with his old school friend.

As Tom and Henry walked back to the house, they decided on a holiday together, though it wouldn't have to cost too much.

'How about cycling?' Tom asked. 'That's a good cheap holiday!'

So, a few days later, they set off on a cycling tour, heading in the direction of Wales and hoping that ten pounds each would see them through. By staying at youth hostels it was just about possible. For Tom it was a relief to get away and to enjoy the adventure.

One very hot afternoon, they sat in the garden at a remote tea shop and an attractive young Welsh girl served them.

'Shall I pour the tea?' Tom said.

'If you like,' Henry smiled.

'This is pleasant. Wonderful view!'

'Yes, those bare hills are where the shepherd has to walk many miles to bring in the sheep.'

'I suppose so, there's nothing else here, is there?'

'Forestry of course!' Henry said.

'As long as they don't cover those lovely rolling hills with conifers, and spoil them.'

'Not likely, Tom.'

That holiday was a very happy time for the two friends, and Tom never forgot some of the funny moments they shared. When, months later, they met for the last time, Henry Hayes was in RAF uniform. They wrote to each other a few times, then lost touch when Tom received no more letters from his old school friend. He was puzzled, so he went to Henry's old address, but found the family had moved. Their ways had parted greatly, as happened to many during those war years, and Tom tried not to dwell on the reason for his friend's absence.

As for Tom, he registered for national service, complying with wartime conscription regulations. But then Mr Glenn called him into his office and told him the time had come for him to do two years in the engineering workshops – part of his apprenticeship agreement.

'You'll start in two weeks,' Mr Glenn said. Tom was slightly taken aback at this sudden news, although he had known it would happen eventually. He was partly apprehensive of any change, but at the same time he was looking forward to the experience. He thought about the big difference it would make to his way of life.

The two weeks soon went by and Tom never heard any more about his National Service, which was to him a far more alarming thought than the engineering workshops. When he had registered, he had expressed his preference for Aerial Photography, adding that he would also be prepared to go down the coal mines as a Bevan Boy. He told them that under no circumstances would he be capable of killing anybody.

Chapter 5
The Works

It was a chilly November morning when Tom arrived at the works before eight o'clock. He reported to the little reception-cum-time office, where a girl sat at a desk with an old typewriter, lots of files and various books. She filled in a long card and showed him how to use it in the time clock. He clocked in with the workers in his new blue overalls. On that first morning he felt strangely uneasy, especially as he was known to have come from upstairs – the elite. But he soon found a new companionship and the work interesting and creative.

He was aware of a new disconnection from the office side, as if he was on a lower plane. He felt there was a barrier, and that the people in the design office were no longer interested in him, though this was probably just his imagination. He was there to learn, and was treated as one of the men, though they were highly skilled and he was still a mere apprentice. He soon sensed that there was a 'them and us' syndrome, though it did not seem logical to him. If there was a division, there was certainly something wrong with the system. But he had to fit in, so he strove to become skilled at his work.

Gradually, he became less obsessed by these thoughts. He soon settled in, as the joking and good humour of the men helped him to relax. Their down-to-earth crudeness, which Tom was not used to, was difficult for him to stomach at times, but it was a matter of getting hardened to an entirely different environment. He found the men outspoken and mostly honest, and enjoyed a comradeship that he had not known before.

At first, Tom worked as a fitter's mate with a chap named

Joe, who seemed much older than him, probably in his early twenties.

Bang-bang. Tom was hammering away with a cold chisel at the edge of a large casting. He paused and looked up as Mildred walked by (he had started to think of her by this name now, a sign of his increasing maturity and confidence). As she stepped over a few small fittings on the shop floor, she smiled at Tom and they said hello to each other.

'You're well in there,' Joe said, looking at her as she walked away.

'If you think so!'

'Well, you do a bit of the old fiddling together, don't you? Woe-hoe!' Joe's favourite subject was undoubtedly women and Tom regarded him as greatly experienced in sexual matters. He certainly would not trust Joe with his girlfriend, if he had one!

'I like it when my parents are away,' Joe said dryly.

'Why?'

'Well, I has me woman friend over to sleep with me.'

'Really?' Tom said, showing surprise.

'Having sex does you good.'

'Does it... er, what's it like?'

'Oh, smashing! Don't half make you pant, it's hot stuff!' Tom was increasingly interested. 'I likes it specially with a married woman!' Joe added, his husky voice thick with enthusiasm.

'Why?'

'Can't beat it – specially if it's over at her place! Well, see, it somehow makes you feel... as good as if you're the husband!' Tom was thinking that the husband could be away in the forces, but he would never pry.

'Sounds as if you do all right, Joe.'

'Like a good bit of leg; don't you, Tom?'

'Bare legs?'

'No, it's them silk stockings I like; more sexy!'

Tom always believed Joe was completely truthful about the details of his sexual encounters. Joe was a real rough diamond and Tom enjoyed his company, though he wished he could have some of those experiences himself. But he was always afraid of lurking dangers. In any case, Tom was too romantic, which left him with only his dreams as solace through many long hours. His love life only existed in the realms of fantasy.

As the months passed, Tom became very familiar with engineering practices, though there were digressions. 'National Cocoa', the specified wartime beverage, was given to the workers each day to give them energy, but it was often just a justification for taking an extended break each morning. Tom found himself with a group of men who abused the privilege of this daily break in the old pattern shop. A new pattern shop had been built in the grounds of the foundry in Stanley Road, so the old shop had been made use of as a rest room. There were a few trestle tables, a place to go for the morning break or dinner hour.

Every morning, Tom went with Joe and the rest of the group through a yard, up some steep wooden steps and into a long room over the old pattern stores. A woman wearing a scarf round her head and a wraparound empire-style apron dished out the mugs of steaming chocolate from an urn in the small kitchen that had once been the pattern maker's office. This was no doubt the highlight of the morning and the jokes were abundant.

'You look miserable this morning, Maggie,' Joe said.

'Go on with you, Joe, you always say that. Don't know how I put up with you lot!'

'Smile then, Maggie.'

'Don't be stupid, I *am* smiling!' She tried to suppress it as she spoke.

'If that's a smile, Maggie, how do you look when you're miserable?'

'Pack it up, Joe, and get the cards out,' one man said.

'That's right, you tell him,' the woman said as she disappeared into the kitchen.

Tom was there because he was Joe's mate but unfortunately

for him, cards and money were always on the table. Every day the breaks got a little bit longer. It began to worry Tom, but he said nothing.

Then, one morning, with a great bang, Mr Wakely, the works manager, burst in. 'So this is what you get up to!' he shouted. 'Cards! Money on the table! In working time!' The men quickly put money in their pockets and the cards disappeared. 'All of you will be closely watched by me personally.' He was looking straight at Tom now: 'Yes, and especially you! You should know better. Now get back to work, layabouts the lot of you!'

Tom could only shake his head. It did not matter what he thought; he had to side with the men even though he disapproved of the gambling.

Mr Robinson, a big man from Newcastle with a powerful rolling voice, was the foreman of the fitting shop. Tom was given work there at times. He had been drilling holes in a flange on a very large casting, using an air-driven engine drill which Joe had helped him to set up. The contraption had to be clamped in position for each hole.

When he had finished the work, he said to the the foreman, 'I've finished that drilling. Have you some more work for me?'

Mr Robinson turned to Tom, whom he towered above.'I'll see about it, just hang on will you.'

'Thank you.' Tom watched Mr Robinson walking away. He reminded Tom of a steam engine: huge but steadily chugging along. Slow to make a decision. He didn't come back, so Tom wandered into the blacksmith's shop.

Some of the workers were playing a game, like the old game of 'throwing the horseshoes', but with very large washers instead. Tom spotted Joe with them. They threw the washers and scored shots over a steel rod that had been hammered into the blackened earth floor. A man was working at a forge, the orange flames from the fire lighting up his face under a black cap. Jack Bracegirdle, the blacksmith, seemed oblivious to the players. Nothing stirred him from his craft. He put his arm up and grabbed the bellows operating handle, pulling it down several times. The fire roared and an iron rod glistened brightly. Another man helped as they carried it from the fire with tongs. Then, as quick as lightning, the two men carried it straight towards a young workman sitting on a tool box, who shouted,'No, no, help!' as they drove the glowing rod at him and he had to open his legs wide, pushing himself back against the immovable brick wall as his vitals were threatened. A great cheer went up and there was a lot of laughter. The rod was quickly taken back to the anvil where hammering began.

Back in the fitting shop, Mr Robinson was in discussion with Mr Wakely, who was gesticulating, pointing at a print he was holding and doing most of the talking. Tom hid till he saw Mr Wakely fold the print and strut off, still muttering. Mr Robinson looked steamed up, but he walked slowly over to an engine under construction. Tom hesitated for a while, then he went up to him.

'Mr Robinson!' he shouted, for there was very loud hammering as someone worked at a large condenser. The noise was piercing his ears, Mr Robinson turned and looked at Tom as if he'd never seen him before. 'You had some work for me...?'

Mr Robinson scratched his dark brow. 'Yes,' he hesitated. 'Look, I must see someone, hang on.' He slowly walked off, leaving Tom feeling frustrated again.

After waiting a while, Tom decided to go out into the yard. There he caught a glimpse of Joe going into the welding shop. The showers of blue sparks bounced onto the floor as Steve cut a large hole in a half inch thick sheet of steel plate. Susie was helping; she was gripping one edge with large tongs using both hands as she held it with her strong arms while they moved the plate round. Then, with a bang, the cut out piece fell onto the concrete floor. The Oxyacetylene flame spluttered and popped as Steve turned it off and he put down his welder's mask. Steve, the welder, was plump, quite short and had straight carroty hair. Susie, his mate, was a tall, well built girl with black curly hair. Her dark eyes sparkled as she joked with the men. She was attractive, but they all knew she was tough.

Joe walked in. 'Here he is again, Susie!' said Steve with a fair amount of tolerance.

'Come to see my lovely,' Joe said. 'What about a cuddle, darling?'

'I'm not your darling. Haven't you got any work to do Joe?'

Steve was squinting through the grubby window, moving his head as if to get a good view. 'Hey, watch it!' he said with emphasis. 'Here comes Wakely!'

There was laughter as Tom came in.

'Gave me a scare then, Steve,' Joe said.

'Silly bugger!' Steve laughed. 'How do you know he's not just coming in now after Tom?'

'I'm not bloody stupid you know. Whatcha, Tom! Is Wakely coming in behind you?'

Susie was trying not to laugh.

'What's going on?' Tom said, glancing quickly back at the door.

'Just the usual, Tom,' Steve said and he turned to Joe. 'Didn't think you were afraid of Wakely, Joe!'

'Daft idiot, don't want any trouble, that's all.'

'You another one without any work to do then, Tom?' Steve said.

'Huh! It just so happens that I haven't at the moment, so thought I'd wander over. Hope you don't mind?'

'No, of course not.'

'Come on, let's have yer!' Joe said, and he suddenly grabbed Susie by the waist. 'She's lovely, isn't she, Tom?'

'Yes, of course,' Tom said. He was thinking what a fine figure she cut, so tall and shapely in her light blue overalls.

'She'd make a man of you I reckon, our Susie,' Joe said with his husky voice.

'Hey! You'll give 'im ideas,' Susie said. Tom laughed with embarrassed excitement.

'Good ideas too, eh Tom!' Joe said.

'I've got some work to do and so's Susie,' Steve intervened.

'Come on, Tom,' Joe said patting him on the back. 'We know when we're not wanted.' They walked back across the yard together.

Mr Robinson saw Joe and Tom as they came into the fitting shop through the large doors. Joe was holding forth while Tom listened.'You two,' the words rolled off Mr Robinson's tongue, 'Jack wants some help in the Smiths,' he pointed in the direction of the blacksmith's shop.

'OK, come on, Tom.'

Jack Bracegirdle pulled a red hot length of flat metal from the brightly glowing fire with tongs and laid it on the anvil. A man hammered a punch as Jack held it in position. They made four holes, cut it to length with a flat chisel, bent it half way to form a right angle and plunged it with a steaming hiss into water. Two rough brackets were made in this way.

A ladder leaned against a darkened wall where Tom was fixing the brackets, and Joe stood with one foot on the bottom rung.

'Busy again I see, Joe, holding up your man,' said a tall, lanky chap with alopecia who had just walked into the blacksmiths shop. They called him Eggo. Tom thought that was unkind but the man didn't seem to mind as he was good humoured, always laughing and showing his protruding upper teeth. His pale face and bald head did remind one of an egg. He was a machine operator and Tom liked to chat with him at times.

'Always busy, Eggo,' Joe said.

'Huh, look's like it!' Eggo said, glancing up the ladder.

'Cheek! You all right then?' Joe asked, looking at Eggo while still holding the ladder.

'Hey, stop wobbling the ladder, Joe,' Tom said, giving Eggo a wave.

'You watch you don't fall, mate. What y'doing up there anyway, Tom?' Eggo called.

'Playing silly buggers, of course,' Tom laughed. 'I'm trying to fix this flipping bracket up here, a bit of a struggle actually.'

'Making heavy weather of it, are you?'

'Can't find the hole,' Tom grinned as he struggled.

'What's he smiling at now?' Eggo said, his own grin wide.

'Something bloody crude, I shouldn't wonder,' Joe said.

There was an air raid warning that afternoon, just before knocking off time, and the terrifying sound of bombs dropping quite near. Then suddenly, the men in the fitting shop, including Tom, saw a bomb bounce from a wall and land spinning in the yard. They instinctively ducked and fortunately it did not go off, but there was a row of very pale faces. It was rumoured that bombs were sometimes sabotaged by forced labour in Germany and, luckily for the men, this looked like one of them.

After about a year, the time had come for Tom's transfer to the machine shop. There were machines of every description and size within a forest of pulley belts. This vital experience was greatly valued. He was put in charge of a large old Whitworth lathe that had part of a main gear wheel tooth missing. An even *clonk, clonk* noise could be heard in that part of the shop; this persistent sound would, after a while, become so familiar to its operator that it would be almost like an old if nagging friend. Tom felt proud to have been given such a machine to work with and to make metal parts of great importance, up to six feet long. That lathe had rolled away so many years of toil. Were the ghosts of long gone operators looking on? he wondered.

It was a cold day and Tom walked over to the grinder with a machine tool in his pocket. He stood at the grinding machine, his mind momentarily diverted with affairs of the heart as he looked at the two grinding wheels, then gazed up at the switch. As he was taking the tool out of his pocket, he was startled by the sharp voice of Mr Wakely, which scared the wits out of him.

'Why aren't you at your machine?'

'I'm just going to grind this tool,' retorted Tom.

'Never mind about grinding, get back to your job!' Wakely yelled bad temperedly, pointing towards Tom's machine.

'Yes... but...' Tom tried to say something.

'Don't you argue with me,' Wakely snapped, before stalking off.

'The bloody fool,' Tom said under his breath as he walked back to the lathe. He waited till he was sure Mr Wakely was well out of the way before returning to the grinder.

Mr Wakely was hated by all, not least by Tom, though hatred was not in Tom's nature. The manager seemed to pick on him for trivial reasons, or for no reason at all. He wore a permanent scowl, was never seen to smile. He was lanky and would stride menacingly through the works, bolt upright with his shoulders back and his arms pressed tightly behind his back, hands clasped as he screwed them together. His suit was always dark blue, which camouflaged him as he looked down from a lofty height, eyeing everybody grimly and ready to explode at any time.

Mr Harris, the foreman of the machine shop, was more like a friendly uncle in his brown work coat and greasy cap. With his guidance, Tom was quickly learning machining skills. One day the foreman gave him a blue print of a special stud and nut. 'Here's a nice job for you,' he said, 'should keep you quiet for a while – there's forty of them. I'll show you where the nut forgings are.' He led Tom to a rather large and dismal looking stack of rust-coloured, nut-shaped lumps. 'You'll need a trolley. Cut the bars for the studs to length outside on the hacksaw.'

Tom was left holding the blueprint, pondering on how long it would take him to make forty huge studs and nuts. Back at his lathe, he had a good look at the print. The studs were pretty big, about four foot long and more than four inches in diameter. He had to set up the threads on the gear train then cut them, forty studs and forty nuts, twenty for each engine. They were holding down bolts to secure the engines of a twin screwed Corvette through the bed plates, down to the ship's frames. He felt proud that he'd been given such a responsible task, even though it was quite daunting.

Tom crossed the yard to the metal store. The very large mild steel bars were on heavy racks made from girder sections. It was so cold out there and the metal, which was brown with rust, had to be levered up to attach the huge bars by chains to a pulley crane. This was so that they could be pulled out and manoeuvred onto a mechanical hacksaw. Fortunately, one of the labourers helped him, so it was not too difficult. But with so many lengths to cut, it was cold standing in that open place wearing only overalls, so Tom jumped up and down with his hands in his pockets, while the hacksaw seemed to take forever to cut through each length. His old work mate, Joe, walked by up the yard, loudly singing a rude song he'd made up about the lavatories being pulled down, which was inspired by a joke going round the works. Tom had never bothered to ask what it was all about, as it was so vulgar.

He wheeled the heavy lengths of metal on a trolley, a few at a time, into the machine shop and piled them up near the lathe. The primitive wash room had a long wide metal trough along one wall, filled with hot water. Lumps of coarse soap were on a board at the back. On the other side of the room, behind the men as they stood at the sink, there were a few roller towels, fortunately changed daily, for they soon became grubby. One of the men, who they called Chas, was always questioning Tom and chiding him about his musical interests as though he was trying to test him and catch him out, so Tom always tried to avoid him.

However, one day at the end of a shift, Chas came and stood next to Tom while they were washing off the grime. 'What do you play?' Chas said.

'Oh, mainly practising,' Tom replied.

'D'you know how many bits a' music Eric Coates wrote?'

'No, I have no idea,' Tom said with irritation.

'Name something by 'im then?'

'I can't think of any at the moment!' He wished Chas would go away.

'Go on! I don't think y'know anything about it!' Chas said as he dried his arms and hands, then went off, looking back at Tom with a jeering expression.

'Blast him,' Tom thought.

The next day, Tom was standing at his lathe waiting while the tool slowly travelled along a cut that would take several minutes. At the end, he would release the tool and wind it back the full length, ready for the next cut, having taken the tool in a few more thou' – an arduous process. At the beginning of a cut, he picked up his engineering mathematics book to have a brief glance at the chapter on gear trains, rather than just standing there doing nothing, but at the same time he was keeping a keen eye on the machining.

'Just what do you think you're doing?' bellowed the unmistakable voice of Mr Wakely.

'Oh... this is mathematics. I... I...' Tom stammered.

'Reading on the job!' Mr Wakely rapped.

'But...'

'Never mind about that.'

'But it takes quite a time for each cut and...'

'You insolent blighter, answering me back!' Wakely looked down at Tom, as if from a great height.

'But, I'm studying...'

'The tool could dig in while you're not attending. You're more trouble than you're worth,' Wakely said angrily. Tom threw the book down onto his tool box. 'Attend to the job,' Mr Wakely said, as he slowly walked away, screwing his hands behind his back. The man on the next machine looked at Tom and mumbled something threatening under his breath, nodding in the direction of the works manager, but with the trace of a smile for Tom.

A few minutes later, Mr Wakely came back and Tom stood bolt upright with his hands tightly behind him as he stood facing the cutting tool. He just stood still, looking down at the shining swarf peeling from the moving tool. He was shaking a little, partly from nerves, as he was keenly aware of being watched.

Mr Wakely came straight over to him, shouted, 'And don't mimic me!' then he continued back to his office.

'What did he say?' asked the man on the next machine.

'Don't mimic me!' Tom said. It caused great amusement, and went round the machine shops as the joke of the day.

Why should there be such a clash of personalities? Tom could see no reason why he was so often the target for Mr Wakely's aggressiveness, which was beginning to undermine his confidence. He knew there was nothing wrong with the way he worked, nor with his interest and enthusiasm. He decided that he was probably the victim of a man who liked to pick on a person, upon whom he could vent his sadistic fervour. Tom, being out of his usual environment, was Wakely's ideal target.

Tom's mates were good to him and treated it as a joke, telling him to forget old Wakely and enjoy life. In his dream world, Tom expected life to be too perfect, just like his fantasies.

'Haven't you got a steady girl friend?' one of the men asked him one day.

'Not at the moment,' Tom answered, feeling inadequate. He was thinking about how sexual desire matured before one was able to do much about it. He never knew how to take advantage of his opportunities when they came his way. If at any time his feelings seemed to be getting the upper hand, he simply pushed them aside. The tension was concealed under a safety valve, but it was always ready to blow.

One morning, when Mildred walked by, she stopped for a moment. 'Hello, how are you getting on?' she called to him.

'Oh, fine thanks,' he shouted, competing with the machinery.

'It looks as if you're doing well.' She was looking at the turning on the lathe, where Tom was anxiously glancing.

'Yes!' Tom quickly turned to the handle as it was getting towards the end of a cut.

'I mustn't disrupt your work.'

'Oh, that's all right,' Tom said, winding the tool back.

'Cheerio then,' Mildred shouted. Tom smiled and raised his hand in a gesture. As she smiled back and walked away, Tom was conscious of the men looking on. He watched her till she disappeared behind the jungle of machines, then he drifted into a dream for a few seconds.

'What are you doing?' Mr Wakely had shouted so quickly that it sounded like some foreign language. Tom jumped and turned round rapidly. 'Why aren't you attending to your work?'

'Well...' Tom tried to speak, but Wakely cut him dead.

'Watch what you're doing,' he shouted and strutted off with a nasty scowl on his face, an expression of deadly judgement.

Tom was trembling, enraged by the dark blue figure receding across the shop floor away towards his office. Suddenly, he struck a blow to a box of nuts and bolts and sent them scattering along the floor after him.

After this, it was inevitable that Tom would find himself in Wakely's office, which was high up over the time clock, and approached from the works floor by a flight of steep wooden steps. The office had glass all round, which commanded a good view of the works and those who laboured there.

'What are we going to do with you?' snapped Wakely.

'What... do you mean, Mr Wakely?'

'You know very well what I mean.'

'I don't actually,' murmured Tom. 'I do my best!'

'Your best doesn't make up for the trouble you are to us.'

'Trouble?' Tom hesitated, mystified as to who Wakely meant by 'us'. Had there been a discussion about him with the management? Or was this a figment of Mr Wakely's troubled mind?

'Yes! This can't go on, you know.'

'I want to return to the drawing office,' demanded Tom, feeling braver all of a sudden.

'Don't dictate to me what you're going to do. We'll see about that!'

'But my apprenticeship agreement...'

'You can get back to the shop now. I've got to decide what to do with you. We might talk about it later, so pull your socks up.' Tom thought for a moment, puzzled as to what he was supposed to have done wrong, when Wakely said sharply, 'You'll never get anywhere, you know. You'll most likely end up selling boxes of matches in the street.' Tom was completely startled by such a statement, and felt depressed by it. He turned away, his confidence shaken, and nearly fell down the steep wooden steps.

He was in no hurry as he walked back to his machine. 'Bloody bugger,' Tom said to himself, 'I'm not going to let him get me down.' He could not think that he had done anything particularly bad during his time in the works. He was always diligent and enthusiastic, no matter what he was asked to do, and he was hardly ever late. A strict time keeping rule in the works had to be heeded. Any worker more than ten minutes late lost that shift and the pay that went with it. Tom had been late one afternoon and was told to go home, but he stubbornly refused and worked the shift for nothing. The men had chided him and sung 'I love my work' to the tune of 'O Sole Mio'. Mr Harris, the machine shop foreman, came up to him that afternoon and said it was up to Tom if he wanted to stay, reminding him that he would not be paid. The incident was never officially mentioned again, even by the works manager.

Tom had accepted the fact that he was a victim of a man with a grudge, though he even wondered if the man was mad. His contretemps with Wakely went quickly round the shop floor and were joked about, so he had a good laugh with the men, and that made him feel less disturbed. He wondered how much longer he would be kept in the works, as the agreed two year period was now completed. But he had a feeling of apprehension about the impending move upstairs, for he felt quite attached to the lower camp in spite of having to put up with the disagreeable works manager. It was where all the action took place. The time that Tom spent in the factory with the workers, most of them skilled craftsmen, was of great importance to him, for he had learnt a range of engineering methods, the advantage of which he came to realise more as time went by. But there was still no word as to how much longer he was to remain there.

Alf was a rough character with ginger hair and Tom always tried to keep out of his way. His jokes were of the crudest brand which Tom never found in the slightest bit funny. One morning, Tom was having his leg pulled by some of the men, which didn't usually bother him; but there were limits.

'You look rough this morning, Tom,' said one.

'Looks as if he's been having it off all night,' said another with a dirty laugh.

'Been having it off with Mildred West, has he?' said Alf, who had just walked up.

'He's all right there, mate,' said another. Tom forced a laugh but felt he was not hiding his embarrassment and his increasing annoyance.

Alf's sneering voice rasped in Tom's ears. 'He found his prick was all crumpled up this morning, when he went to fuck Mildred, it wouldn't go in because she had her knickers on—' there was laughter '—and it went crunch like a concertina.' Alf's leering expression became more and more repulsive to Tom as the laughter jarred in his ears. Alf's face was almost a blur as the awful joking went on, and suddenly Tom's fist met Alf's bristly chin, which made him stagger back with a gasp of surprise. Tom waited for the return blow, but they were both held back by the other men.

'What the bloody hell?' Alf said angrily.

'You did go a bit too far there, Alf,' said someone.

'Well, I was bloody joking, wasn't I,' he muttered as he struggled free and went off quickly.

Later that morning, Alf came and told Tom he was sorry, offering him a handshake. But Tom was still too disturbed, and he turned away from the outstretched hand. For his immature mind, it was too soon for apologies. When Alf had gone, Tom began to worry over this but still could not bring himself to go to Alf. As time went by, it became more difficult. Tom wished desperately that he had taken Alf's hand, or even just called him back. If he could have just said, 'Let's forget it', it would have made things better. But it was too late, and they never spoke to each other again.

The machine shop foreman entered the manager's office. 'You wanted to see me, Mr Wakely.'

'Oh, good morning, Harris, I just want a word with you about Tom Hunt. Is he giving you any trouble these days?'

'Not at all, Mr Wakely, I would say he's pretty keen.'

'Oh, is he...? So you find him useful then, do you?'

'Yes. No problems, are there?'

'Well, you'll be losing him now, I'm sending him back to the drawing office where he can make a nuisance of himself.'

'Never given me any trouble, Mr Wakely.'

'Glad to hear it, Harris. Anyway, I've had a word with Glenn so he's expecting him next Monday. That's all. Oh,' he added, 'and inform Hunt, will you.'

So the time had come for Tom to return to the office, back to where he had begun after more than two years in the workshops. Although he knew that was his legitimate place, there were regrets and an unavoidable feeling of sentimentality. Life in the workshops was so different, almost another world; he had come to realise how great the contrast was, but he had loved it. He had changed from one set of workmates to another, but it was more than that. Tom was not quite the same person any more. He felt that in no way could he ever be a member of one camp only, though his mates would probably think differently. It was all part of the class system, he thought, and not easy to come to terms with. Tom had always been unconventional in his thinking anyway, and often felt he was an outsider.

But although he had matured and changed in some ways, he was still the same fundamentally. The gnawing timidity persisted, though he tried to throw it off, and at times he put on a very good act. It was as if the shell was still there that he was enclosed within but the walls were cracked and he was trying to break his way out.

One day, some time later, Tom saw Alf approaching in the street with quite a smart little woman who was probably his wife. The small conflict of the past loomed up in Tom's mind. 'I forgave him,' thought Tom, 'it's in the past.' He hoped that

Alf would have forgotten the small skirmish of so many months earlier. So, as they passed in the street, Tom struggled against his nerves, looked at Alf, forcing a slight smile, and was about to speak, when Alf turned his head away in an obvious snub. Tom's pride was hurt and the incident niggled for a long time. He wished again that he'd taken that outstretched hand. It was as if he had walked into a different world, and he had to fit.

Chapter 6
Connie

It was late September 1945. The war in Europe had been over for more than four months and Tom was into the fifth year of his apprenticeship.

At first, on returning to the design office routine, working again alongside those who diligently pored over complicated drawings, he felt out of place. After over two years in the works, he had to readjust himself to the change. He had to endure a long lecture from the chief designer, with those old words of advice, as if he was the new boy all over again. As he stood waiting patiently for the drawn-out talk to end, he wondered which was worse: this or Wakely? The path was laid, and he had to get back through the barrier, like coming out of a dream. He felt less important; it had something to do with missing the feel of metal with oily hands and the smell of the workshops. He had lost the power he had felt while working with machinery.

He got on well with his old office colleagues, but now there seemed to be a different atmosphere. Or was it all in his mind? He imagined that they had changed, but of course, it was he who had changed.

Still, there was plenty of fun at times with his colleagues, and the feeling that he did not fit in gradually began to wear off. He often wished for change, but when it happened there would be something missed and longed for. Life was full of experiences gained and lost, it seemed, which in turn made their contribution to life's know-how.

Tom's wages remained at three pounds fifteen shillings a week and his requests for an increase were in vain. He pondered over his position and could not help thinking that he must have had a poor report from Wakely, the works manager whom he thought had it in for him, and he puzzled as to why this should be. Then one of his colleagues convinced him that this was unlikely and that the money was not too bad compared with many at the time. His five-year apprenticeship period was now well over and he thought a rise was due, but he stopped complaining.

Tom liked to chat with Connie York, whom he was now able to call her by her Christian name. He admired her very neat work and had always felt a warm, close feeling towards her, especially as she had given him so much advice on the use of tracing cloth, ink ruling and hand lettering when he was a raw beginner. Now he was even able to talk to her quite freely about his personal worries as she was a sympathetic ear, and seemed very understanding.

'Come to the dance at the Corn Exchange on Saturday,' Connie said one day.

'Oh... I can't dance,' Tom said, feeling a tingling sensation in his spine.

'That doesn't matter, there's a few of us going.'

Tom was thrilled at the thought. He had a nice feeling with her as he was attracted to older women. He was less shy with a mature married woman.

The next day he was surprised when she gave him a ticket, though also excited. Why the favour? he wondered.

'Thank you, but what do I owe you?'

'Nothing. It's a kind of complimentary,' she smiled.

'Oh but...'

'No buts, just make sure you use it.' And with both hands Connie gripped Tom's hand that held the ticket. He went back to his work and drifted for a moment into a dream, thinking first of Connie, then of Mildred. He wondered if the girls were up to something between them and his nervous excitement grew. Yet he was sure Mildred would not be at the dance and he was certain that she would have nothing to do with any intrigue – if it wasn't just all in his imagination anyway!

Tom, in a state of elation all that day, was more jovial than usual. He went down into the works and had a laugh with some of his old chums, and they joked about him being 'back with them upstairs'.

'I suppose we should have to pay to speak to you now!' shouted a man from his machine.

'Don't be daft,' Tom laughed. But he was careful to keep clear of Wakely as he wandered through the workshops.

At the end of the dinner break, Tom had been having a serious chat with Mr Perry. 'It's just on two,' Tom said suddenly, looking at the clock.

'That's all right; what's the rush?' Mr Perry said.

'I've got to get those prints to take to the pump shop,' Tom said and hurried to the office door. Connie had just come up the stairs and as Tom went through the door, he stopped short as he almost bumped into her. 'Oh!' he exclaimed.

'You're in a hurry,' she said.

'Sorry... er'. She stood, blocking his way through the door, with her legs slightly parted, laughing. Tom became inarticulate and merely laughed as he experienced a tingling thrill. She was facing him so closely with her hands in the pockets of a grey pin-striped skirt, so that the front stretched tightly across her hips, as if to test the strength of the stitching.

'Steady down, Tom; is it that important? You shouldn't rush like that.' But as she spoke, Tom was barely listening, for she was having an erotic effect on him.

'Excuse me,' he mumbled, in a kind of cold sweat as he squeezed by her and walked up to the print room. He was thinking that she might not be aware of the effect she had on him. He felt sure that sometimes a woman could be deliberately provocative; but sometimes only subconsciously so. It was agonising for Tom, who was very much aware of his own emotions. He rushed over to the pump shop and dumped the prints on Mr Jackson's desk, forgetting to trim them, for which he later received a reprimand from the man, who stormed at him in a rage, 'You can trim these prints, Sonny Jim!'

On the Saturday afternoon of the dance, Tom smeared Brylcream on his hair and put on his best sports jacket. He took a late afternoon bus into Newburne, then made his way to his favourite music shop. There were piles of sheet music, both new and second hand, as well as lots of second hand instruments at reasonable prices, though the new instruments were quite pricey. He chatted with the good humoured music shop owner until the shop closed up for the weekend. Tom remained outside, gazing for some time at the expensive violins in the window and thinking of Mildred. A vision of the past, with those old feelings, drifted back to him. Since time had rolled on, he could not get away from feeling that his world had irreversibly changed.

For an instant Tom remembered VE Day, the end of the war in Europe – a day that was full of mad passion, laughing and dancing in the streets. He recalled the high-spirited but foolish setting alight of a piece of common land that had become overgrown with gorse bushes, where the surrounding houses were dangerously near the flames. A woman had come out of one of the houses in a bit of a state, though her house was not in danger. 'This isn't necessary you know! Victory is one thing, but even Hitler didn't set fire to our common!' Tom thought of her view from the house, suddenly turned to blackness. He thought of all the pointless death and destruction of the past five long years.

When the war came to an end, many people's lives changed from what they had grown used to over the war years. For a minority, strangely enough, it was not necessarily for the better. Tom knew there would be changes and he was slightly frightened by the thought, knowing he would have to move on and the future was in the balance. He shrugged his shoulders, then turned away.

As he walked away from the music shop, waves of thought

surged through his mind of all that had happened during the past five years and more. He cursed himself for not having a more determined mind, for letting some people ride roughshod over him. 'To hell with it!' he thought, took a deep breath and walked on into the town.

He'd always had a healthy appetite and was soon in his usual fish and chip bar, a long narrow place where you sat at a counter facing the man and woman busy at the fryers. He watched the lids being rapidly opened and closed at intervals, to fry and remove the scrumptious looking pieces of battered fish and great quantities of chips.

'Yes?' said the woman.

'Cod and chips please,' Tom said.

'Cod and chips once!' shouted the woman.

As he waited, Tom sat gazing at the painted tiles above the fryers showing fish and mermaids with long golden hair intertwined with seaweed. His tasty meal cost him one and sixpence.

There was still over an hour and a half to kill before the dance was due to start. He took his time sipping a cup of tea, while dwelling with slight apprehension on how he would make out that evening. He was getting his usual jitters that always preceded any kind of social gathering, especially when there would be girls there. He had always liked girls and would play with them rather than the boys when he was very young. But a dance was different. He had only been to a dance once before, and that was with his parents when there was a social evening at his father's firm and all the families went. The mixture of Tom's excitement and his strange nervousness seemed to heighten his natural sexual sensitivity.

He climbed off the stool, found his raincoat under a bundle of other coats on the hooks in the corner, and wandered out into a cool October evening. At least there was some lighting now that those 'blackout' days were almost forgotten. He strolled by the shops, pausing to look into some of the windows, and lingered for a while at a second hand shop where he spotted a

Meccano set. Those metal rods, gears and plates always fascinated him, and he had a large set of his own, collected during boyhood days and still treasured. He brooded for a while, thinking of the boy who had contemplated adulthood as too far away to imagine. Did time become compressed as one grew older? He dismissed such philosophical thoughts and walked on.

He stood on the old stone bridge and looked down at the dark, swirling water as seen by the light of a path lamp and light from a window in shimmering reflection. A shiver went through him as he thought of eternal time. He quickly shrugged off the thought; he would rather think of time as something that did not exist and had no meaning.

'Hello, Tom.' It was the voice of David, one of Tom's colleagues. Though he did not work with Tom, David was helping Mr Wills in the pump shop at Fenton's.

Tom turned to look at the smiling face. 'Oh, hello, David.'

'Not contemplating diving over, I hope?' David said jokingly.

'I don't think I'm likely to do that!' Tom was laughing now, having been taken out of his malaise.

'You thirsty?' David said. He was wearing a smart grey suit and a brightly coloured wide tie but no overcoat:

'I've had a cup of tea.'

'I'm going for a beer,' David said as he stood shivering, his hands in his pockets.

'You look cold.'

'Only live down the road. Coming across to the Dolphin?' And David nodded in the direction of the pub across the road.

'Oh... Yes, OK.' Tom hesitated as he was not used to pubs.

As they crossed the road, there was a gust of cold wind and a few spots of rain.

'Brrr!' David rubbed his hands together.

'You really should have brought a coat!'

'Soon be in the warm, Tom. Are you coming to this hop tonight?'

'At the Corn Exchange?'

'Yes, course! Should be a good night. Good band too.'

'Yes, I've got a ticket.' They pushed through the pub doorway. Tom felt a little awkward, not wanting David to find out who gave him the ticket.

'That's good.' Although they were about the same age, David was more mature and seemed older. 'There should be some nice chicks there.'

'Yes!' Tom laughed rather foolishly.

'Pint of bitter or mild and bitter is it then, Tom?'

'Oh, better just have a half of bitter.'

'OK, just a half then,' David said. They stood there at the bar, David with a pint of mixed and Tom with his half pint. 'Old Mr Fenton's ill. I suppose you've heard?'

'No, I hadn't heard, though I wondered why I'd not seen him lately.'

'On his last legs, I think.' David sipped his beer.

'I'm sorry,' Tom said. 'I liked the old boy.'

'Yes, but we can't tell what he was like before he got doddery.' David gave a wry smile. 'I don't think we'll see him again.'

'Well, it seems a sad thing to me.'

'Yes, and there's not much future at Fenton's now you know, Tom.'

'Oh! In what way?' Tom thought David's statement seemed strangely astute.

'The Pump Shop have orders, the small casting machines aren't much. But what orders are there on the books for steam now?' David laughed dryly. 'No future there, and that's the best part of the firm. You mark my words, Tom, they're going down. Men are leaving and there's no new work force being taken on, you know: What's the point?'

'I see,' Tom said. 'Bad as that, is it?'

'You won't be staying much longer, will you?'

'Don't suppose so,' Tom said. They drank silently for a while as he didn't want to talk about work. His apprenticeship days were long gone and he would rather not wait to become a victim of staff cutting. But he hadn't given much thought about his future.

'Good place this!' he said finally.

'Where I usually come.'

'Oh, better buy you another drink.' Tom was looking at David's empty glass. He got the same again. They sat at a round marble-topped table with a cast iron frame and continued chatting. While David's topic of conversation was mostly about what girls might be at the dance, Tom was worrying how he would cope with his shyness. The pleasant meeting with David was quite cheering for Tom, but the beer went to his head a little. 'Mustn't have too much of that,' he thought to himself.

At the Corn Exchange, Tom stood in the dance hall and suddenly felt lonely, surrounded by strangers, for David had disappeared somewhere. The atmosphere was strangely exotic. He felt gripped by a kind of magnetism, spellbound by the sight of so many lovely girls.

Then he spotted some familiar faces, a group sitting in the corner who were from Fenton's. Connie was with them and, with a captivating smile for Tom, she beckoned him over. As he joined the group, which consisted mostly of some of the girls from the firm and their friends, Tom began to feel more confident than usual, slightly boosted by the beer.

When the band started, their shining instruments loudly reverberating through the hall, the drumbeats greatly excited Tom's primitive urges. 'Time stops here,' he thought. It was magical.

David appeared with drinks on a tray. He seemed to have things well organised. 'We've got a kitty. We're putting in a half crown each, just the chaps, that is. All right with you, Tom?' he said as he handed him a pint of beer.

'Yes, of course, David.' Tom could only agree, being with the party from work. As he chipped in his half crown, he wondered how he was going to get through such a large drink. David was doing a lot of dancing while Tom held his beer, taking a few sips at a time. Standing near the chairs where the girls from work were sitting, he set his beer down on the table.

'Haven't seen you dance yet,' said Sally, looking at Tom as David grabbed her and swept her onto the dance floor.

'Come on, Tom,' Connie said, getting up. Tom was overwhelmed by her beauty. She was wearing a floral dress that flared out over her hips, a little gold brooch, and her soft light brown hair shone in the light as she looked at him with sparkling eyes. It was such a contrast from her working image.

'Oh...' He hesitated, suddenly overcome by bashfulness again. 'I don't know if I can.'

'I'll show you, come on,' she insisted.

Tom was in a strange world, clasped against Connie as she tried to teach him a few basic steps, while he made clumsy movements around the floor. He was enraptured, painfully conscious of her trembling, like an electrical current that passed between them, making him ever more aware of his erotic desires. He wished he could dance better, but he could not imagine how he would ever learn, so distracted was he by the enchantment of the evening and the lovely woman in his arms.

As the night wore on, Tom became increasingly dazzled by the stimulating atmosphere. The MC was making some poor jokes, and it crossed Tom's mind that it could be the same man Mildred had complained of years ago. He watched the dancing, the sound of the band seeming to engulf everything.

'I think they're a very good band,' Tom slurred as David handed him another pint. He'd stopped counting the drinks now and was in a haze. He found himself sitting next to Connie and it all seemed unreal, like an illusion as he became more and more inebriated. 'I've got to go and cash a buzz.'

'What bus is that at this time, Tom?'

'Oh, s'ten o'clock,' he said in a befuddled state.

'You've missed that, it's almost eleven!'

'Oh, thaz-vunny,' he said, past caring. 'Is, ish-it that late?' he said as he tried to look at his watch, swayed and almost fell off the chair. He wanted to have the last dance with Connie but instead only made a fool of himself.

Things went pretty vague after that and among the mixed

voices, he could just pick out Connie's saying, 'I can put him up.' Poor dazed Tom dimly remembered being led through the cold night streets, gripped by waves of nausea and constantly stopping to take deep breaths. In his stupor, muddled thoughts of glamorous expectation came and went. He was embarrassed at having made a fool of himself, so it was fortunate that he was with friends.

The others had now turned off up another road, leaving him with Connie. Together they turned into a gate and she put her key into the front door. He felt he'd really messed things up and kept on saying how sorry he was. 'Don't be silly. No need to apologise,' she said with a smile.

He found himself in a nice comfortable bed in a strange room, and dimly recollected his jacket and shoes being removed. Then he was alone. As he lay there in the darkness, the room seemed to rotate over and over as if it was a car on a large fast moving Ferris Wheel, but with the room going in the opposite direction. He eventually dropped off to sleep. He dreamed he was standing in the middle of a hall, where Mildred was on stage playing the violin. There was no audience apart from himself, and as she played, Mildred had tears in her eyes, for standing next to her on the stage was that same MC, puffing away at a cigarette and blowing the smoke in her face. Then Connie came onto the stage from behind the wings, told the man off and they went away arguing while Mildred went on playing. The dream disappeared as he woke and it was morning.

'I've brought you a cup of tea Tom, and how do you feel this morning?' Tom opened his eyes and there was Connie smiling at him.

'OK, thank you. Oh dear, I was such a fool last night! Thank you for...' His voice trailed off.

'Now that's all right. Come down and have some breakfast when you're ready.'

Staying at Connie's home, with her bringing him a cup of tea on a Sunday morning, was a situation Tom could never have envisaged. The dance had been quite an experience, and had to some extent boosted his self-confidence, despite making a bit of a fool of himself. Perhaps he had grown up a little.

But what had he let himself in for? Was Connie alone in the house? After all, she was a married woman, though she had come to the dance unescorted. He thought about the previous evening, before he'd made a fool of himself. There was no denying the thought that the time had come for some kind of initiation into love, sex. He just didn't know what to expect; he seemed to have an inexplicable fear; but of what?

He'd had too much to drink, like a callow youth. Now he had to face reality. Incredibly, his recovery from the previous night's excesses was, apart from a slight headache, surprisingly speedy.

'In the kitchen, Tom!' Connie called as he went downstairs.

As he entered the kitchen, she was reaching up to get some cups from a cupboard, wearing a well fitting grey skirt which accentuated her figure. Connie turned and put three cups and saucers on the table.

'Would you like an egg, Tom?'

'Yes please. Oh, but your ration,' he said, his voice croaky.

'I've a supplier, don't worry about that,' she smiled. Tom looked at the table, wondering what to say, as she'd laid three places.

'We keep chickens at home,' he told her. 'We can always let you have some eggs.' He was anxious to repay her kindness in some way.

'We're all right for eggs, really, Tom, but thank you for offering.'

Tom decided to ask what was on his mind. 'You... not on your own...?' he ventured.

There was a noise in the hallway behind and he looked round to see a man in the doorway, supported by crutches. It gave him a bit of a shock, which he tried not to show.

'Good morning,' Tom said awkwardly.

'Ah, Frank, this is Tom.' Connie seemed to chuckle a little as she spoke, which somehow bothered Tom. 'Tom, my husband Frank.'

'You had quite a night of it young fellow! Sorry, can't shake hands properly.'

'I'm sorry... er... I...'

'No need to be embarrassed. I'm lucky to be alive.'

'Yes,' Tom said slowly. 'Well, I suppose you've heard all about last night.'

'Connie told me,' he said with a smile, getting to a chair at the table.

'Can I help you?' Tom offered.

'He can manage. You sit down, Tom,' Connie said, but Tom pushed the chair in and took Frank's crutches.

'Thank you,' smiled Frank. 'Just put them on the floor.'

'Frank was wounded three years ago,' Connie said lightly. 'He was in the Tank Corps.'

'Yes, I'm sorry...' Tom was lost for words for a moment. He thought Connie seemed a little casual about it. But then Tom supposed she'd had a lot to put up with.

'It's all part of this whole bloody messy game. Nothing to be proud of in being caught out. Nothing to concern you, Tom.' Frank spoke very thoughtfully but still kept a slight smile. 'No fun for Connie though,' he said gravely.

'I suppose I'm one of the lucky ones,' Tom said, almost wanting to eat his words.

'Here's your egg, Tom. Now I hope you've not lost your appetite.' Connie said it with a smile. Tom was feeling guilty as usual, as he was thinking of Frank having served in the Tank Corps. It seemed to him such a sad thing to have happened to their lives.

'I don't mind Connie going out and enjoying herself at times. It would be selfish of me to think of trying to stop her.' Frank was remarkably cheerful.

'Well it must...'

'There's no need to get all worried, Tom,' Connie interrupted him.

'I'm sorry to be such a nuisance,' Tom said.

'Nonsense,' Frank said.

'He's not used to drinking,' Connie smiled. 'You know what that David's like!'

'Huh, we've all been through it sometime.' Frank said and laughed.

'You've been terribly kind,' Tom said.

Tom knew he had to forget about making a fool of himself, for he was left feeling troubled and frustrated, having let himself down rather badly. The alcohol had also left him depressed. When he phoned home to explain to his parents about not getting back the previous night, his mother seemed unnecessarily worried. After all, there were many young men the same age as Tom who had already served in the armed forces for over a year. So although Tom felt contrite, he was also annoyed because he felt over pampered. Tom's father, who had left home young himseld to fight in the Great War of 1914, was quite amused by the whole thing. It was his mother who made all the fuss.

'She'll get over it,' his father said. 'I'll come and get you in the car.'

Tom had thought he would have to take to the road for the five-mile walk home. As it looked as if it was about to rain, he was very glad of his father's offer to pick him up. Having said his goodbyes to Connie and Frank, he left the house and soon saw his father's car approaching. Tom still felt humiliated but his father was soon having a laugh with him about his plight. They got onto a more serious note when he told him about the awful predicament of the Yorks.

Tom had made up his mind that he would like to get away from home, for he had a natural desire to be independent. The war in Europe was over and he thought he was not likely to have to do national service now. He wanted to get right away from Newburne, and it had occurred to him that if it was difficult to get a job, he could always join the RAF as a photographer or something useful – if they'd have him.

Chapter 7
Monday

Waking on Monday mornings was something Tom always loathed. Rain was beating against the window panes, and he shuddered. His father opened his bedroom door. 'Are you awake, my boy?'

'Just about!' Tom yawned. 'Oh, what a morning!'

'It'll clear up by eleven. Don't be long, I'll be quick in the scullery this morning.'

'OK, I'll be down before you've finished shaving, Dad.'

'I wouldn't like to bet on that!'

'Too early for betting,' Tom said with a yawn and slowly climbed out of bed.

'I'll hurry up anyway!' Tom's father said as he rushed down the stairs, 'we're a bit late I think.' They all washed in the scullery, his mother always first, before she cooked breakfast. An electric water heater was a luxury. They had to take turns in pumping water up from the well to a tank in an upper room.

His father, newly appointed to a Newburne Civil Service department, was allowed a ration of petrol and the car was off its blocks, from where it had been standing in the old wagon shed. Tom had now got a provisional licence, which at that time gave cover for one year, and they took turns with the driving. At least it meant a dry journey: no more yellow cape and leggings flapping in the wind.

The car was a 1934 Rover and Tom had to learn to drive with his father's help. He'd mastered the gears on a few practice runs at weekends, but the most difficult part was changing down as they ascended a hill, and there were many on the narrow country roads, some very steep. Learning to double declutch and rev up at the same time was the most tricky part, but he soon mastered it.

After leaving the car, Tom walked quickly along a rough unmade road, his short cut to work from the main road. It was full of water-filled potholes and large puddles where the drops of rain made a mass of overlapping circles. There were sudden strong gusts of wind and a lady's umbrella turned inside out. Tom helped her and she laughed cheerfully as they both got soaked. He went on his way, his hands in his raincoat pockets, but there was no dodging that heavy rain.

As he beat his way through the windy deluge, it reminded of that Saturday night and Sunday morning. He felt that his life as he had known it was bound for some kind of transformation. His thoughts of change merged with every puddle he splashed through.

In the print room, wet coats and open umbrellas steamed. Tom left his coat to dry and heard Connie coming up the steps.

'Phew,' she said as she held a very wet, half-folded umbrella.

'What a morning, eh?' agreed Tom. 'Let me help you with that, Connie.'

'Thanks, Tom' He took the umbrella from her, opened it and laid it down. He then helped her remove her wet coat and draped it carefully over a rail near a radiator.

'I was very grateful for your help on Saturday night. I hope you enjoyed the dance... I'm sorry I was such a fool,' Tom spluttered.

Connie looked amused. 'For goodness' sake, stop muttering, Tom,' she teased, making him feel a little foolish.'Don't worry about it!'

'Oh!' He felt unable to say more and they just smiled at each other. As she walked to the door, he was obsessed with desire for forbidden fruit. The very thought of it made him feel guilty, but that didn't make the feelings go away, for the more he tried not to dwell on those thoughts, the more intense was his burning craving.

But he was thinking about the plight of her wounded husband. Could Tom ever talk to her about the pain and suffering they had endured? He wondered how they managed and was surprised how cheerful Connie always seemed. She must surely be thankful Frank had not been killed, but would also wish to God it had never happened at all. Those thoughts remained with him, but the delicate subject was never discussed.

These days, Tom veered between contentment and restlessness, and wondered if that would ever change. He knew it must eventually, but how and when he could not guess at the time. When the feeling of not fitting in came over him, he yearned to get away.

Walking through the works, Tom could see the changes taking place, and he felt it like a cold breeze. There were too many machines standing idle; notably, most of those great giants were motionless, as if dead. Fewer men could be seen plying their skills; most of the older ones had gone, but as he walked through those unforgettable areas, Tom recognised, with a nod and a smile, some familiar old faces. For now that he was no longer a part of the works where great engineering was once created, he had warmed to it and feared its demise. But they were all helpless in the face of progress, and Tom knew he would probably have to leave soon. A feeling of sadness came over him briefly. 'Silly sentimentality!' he murmured to himself. There was nothing to regret, especially when he thought of that works manager...

Tom spotted Joe with a young fellow, and thought of the days when he was Joe's mate. They were working on a small repair job.

'Hello, Joe!' Tom shouted as he walked towards him. Joe looked up from what he was doing, but with hardly a glimmer of a smile.

'Oh, how's it going, Tom? All right with you, I suppose?'

'OK, Joe. How about you?' Tom put out his hand.

'This and that; better not shake hands, make y'hands grubby.' Joe held his black oily hands apart with a slight smile.

'What do you mean, Joe, by "this and that"?'

'Can't see much future here now; can you?'

'Seem's a bit slack, Joe.'

'You can say that again, and problems you wouldn't want to know about.' Joe seemed changed. Tom had never seen him look so downcast or serious.

'You seem worried, I don't know how things...'

'I'm married now, see,' Joe interrupted him. 'Got responsibilities, and all that!'

'Didn't know you'd got married, Joe. Well, is congratulations the right word?'

'Well, I suppose so. Had to get married, see, got a kid and that. Thing is, she's a real good wife to me anyhow.'

'That's good... But the future at Fenton's – gloomy, you think?'

'Don't know, Tom.'

'We just have to keep our fingers crossed. See you then, Joe.'

As Tom went on his way, Joe called out to him, 'Watch those girls!' Tom glanced back with a little wave. Joe was standing with a vacant expression which he held rigidly while he watched Tom walking away between the machines and a few slightly rusty looking castings. They looked as if they had been put there ready for machining and just forgotten. As Tom returned by a different route, to avoid the awkwardness of bumping into Joe again, he glanced at the once busy but now quiet corners and remembered how it used to be while he was there, not so long ago. He went back to the design office, thinking of a large dying animal taking its last few breaths.

One Monday morning, while Tom was driving with his father on their journey to work, it was sunny and spring-like, making even the dreaded Monday a pleasure. As they were just entering town, Tom was surprised to spot old Mr Fenton on the other side of the road, slowly making his way with a stick.

'There's Mr Fenton, Dad.' He was surprised to see him, knowing he'd been ill. 'Better offer him a lift.' Tom pulled in and called out, 'Good morning, Mr Fenton!'

'What's that?' Mr Fenton turned but did not recognise Tom.

'Would you like a lift, Mr Fenton? I presume you're going to the office.'

'Oh, that's most kind of you, most kind indeed.' Tom quickly got out of the car and helped him into the back. They were on the wrong side of the road, but there was so little traffic about, as petrol was still rationed. The old man looked pale and seemed very frail. Tom thought he should be resting at home, but perhaps he could not let go.

'How are you now, Mr Fenton?' Tom enquired as he drove off.

'What was that, I'm sorry....?' Tom's father turned round and spoke to him very loudly as Mr Fenton leaned forward with his hand held to his left ear.

'Tom was asking how you are, sir?'

'Very much better, thank you. I've been quite unwell you know, it's so good of you to ask.' He sounded sad, as if he was thinking of bygone days. 'You're so kind; could you tell me your name please?'

'Thomas Hunt,' Tom said loudly as he pulled up.

'Hunt, oh yes, Hunt... This is such a help for me, thank you very much, I'm very grateful to you,' Mr Fenton kept repeating as Tom helped him out of the car.

He watched Mr Fenton slowly walking through the passage, which was Tom's usual route. He waited while his father moved over to the driving seat, not wishing to accompany the old man on his slow progress.

'I was surprised to see old Mr Fenton, Dad. I'd heard he was very ill.'

'He seems to have recovered then.'

'Well, I don't think he'd ever retire. Anyway, cheerio, Dad, see you tonight.' Tom walked quickly through the passage and soon passed old Mr Fenton making his way with his stick along the pot-holed road that led to the other street.

'Good morning,' Tom said turning as he passed him.

'Yes... thank you so much.'

'Very welcome, Mr Fenton.' And Tom waved as he continued on his way, feeling a little embarrassed.

Some days later they spotted the old man again, making his weary way on one of his by now infrequent visits to the firm. He would arrive in good time on those mornings, as if to prove that he was still in charge, whatever his state of health. He was one of the remaining gentlemen of a lost era. Grateful when he was offered a lift, he always thanked Tom and his father most profusely. They picked him up on three mornings, and each time he asked Tom his name. On the last occasion, as Tom passed the old chap in the passage that led to the potholed road, he saw that Mr Fenton was holding a small scrap of paper to the wall and making a note – no doubt writing down Tom's surname. That was the last time Tom ever saw him.

Charles Fenton was very slow since his last illness. But in spite of that and arthritis troubling him, his old drive still lingered. He walked out most days; his visits to the firm were habitual if more occasional now, for he was still the managing director, although there was little for Mr Fenton to handle since his co-director, Mr Meddows, had taken over the main decision-making in the diminishing firm. He would be asked to sign a document at times, and would study the contents. On the few days that the old master was found to be in his office, he would always have made an early start, in spite of his eighty-seven years.

Now he gazed after the young man walking away so briskly. 'I know that young man,' he was thinking, 'It was kind of him to give me a lift in his car.' He thought for a moment of his own son, long gone now. 'He loved his cars!'

His memory was letting him down, especially names, yet the faraway past was so clear that he lived on old recollections. The waves of memory floated through his mind. He drifted back to when he was himself like the youngster walking off into the distance.

Chapter 8
Charles and Emily

It was the summer of 1878. Charles Fenton was a very agile young man, just twenty-one, and he had a compulsive interest in all kinds of engineering, and especially in ships. Although that was his great love, his very amorous feelings for Emily Parson, the daughter of a country doctor and long-standing friend of the family, grew stronger and he was often drawn away from his engines to be with her.

He drove his horse and trap fast on his way back from Eastbrook after leaving Emily on that sunny afternoon when life was so different. The road was rough in places and as his horse splashed through the ford, the water glinted and the wheels crunched as he drove quickly through the gravelly brook. In the woods, the road was narrow with dangerous bends. He had left too late, and was already due back in Newburne where his father and uncle waited with a small crowd of onlookers at the wharf.

The two men stood at the riverside wearing their top hats; for the launching of a new boat of any size was an occasion to celebrate. George Fenton, a short plumpish man with a strong featured rugged face under a bushy moustache and large forked beard, looked towards his brother Edward. He was less plump, clean-shaven and though he showed the same strong features, he had a yellowish look. His expression was morose, not a man one would expect to see smile.

'I somehow feel we're not going to see my son this time,' George said.

'That wouldn't come as a surprise. Can you not persuade him to take more interest?'

'There's no lack of interest. I know for certain that he has outside distractions.' George looked at his gold watch. 'We'll give him a few more minutes.' And he forced a smile.

It was a very warm June afternoon in the garden at the house near Eastbrook where Emily lived. In a meditative mood, she walked slowly round the well kept lawn surrounded by rose beds. She looked very graceful in a white lacy dress, her slender waist enhanced by a pink satin belt and a matching band round her hat, with fair curls showing under the rim. A lace fichu was pinned with a small oval cameo and her complexion matched the freshness of the pure country air. She lowered her head to sniff a pink rose.

Emily ducked as she walked through a rustic arch where the roses hung thickly, then heard the sound of a horse and trap. It was her father, the country doctor, returning home from his rounds. A blackbird sounded a loud cheeping as Mr Duckworth went to take the horse.

Dr Parson came through the gate carrying his bag, took off his brown Derby to show thinning grey hair, and wiped his brow. His round face with genteel features was quite red.

'Papa, you look so hot!'

'Hello, my dear. Yes, and you look nice and cool.' She smiled as her father approached her. 'Has Mrs Duckworth returned from the village?'

'Yes Papa, she was here some twenty minutes ago, and said she would bring the tea out to the veranda.'

'Good.' They walked up the pathway to the house. 'Did that Fenton fellow come here again?'

'Why, yes! Do you not approve?'

'It's not really a matter of whether I approve, my dear. After all, I'm hardly acquainted with him. Though I know he's a handsome young fellow, and probably very keen. I just wondered if perhaps you might be getting too serious with him. I wouldn't like you to get hurt, Emily.'

'He's almost four years older than me, Papa, and very responsible about his work.'

'Certainly, his father is the owner of the Fenton works, but he's a bit of a daredevil from what I've heard!'

'Please, Papa, I know you're concerned, but I can look after myself.' Emily was slightly irritated.

'Yes, of course my dear, of course.'

'He really is most interested in his work, so much so that I think at times he would rather have a steam engine for company than me!'

'I find that hard to believe.' The doctor smiled.

They walked along the veranda to where Mrs Duckworth, the housekeeper, a wholesome country woman, came out with tea and freshly made cakes on a large tray.

'Good afternoon, Doctor,' she said.

'Hello, Nora. My goodness, that was well timed!'

As they sat at the table on the veranda there was a gentle breeze blowing. 'You know I'm only concerned for your welfare, Emily,' Dr Parson began again.

'Papa!' Emily frowned, then her eyes lit up as she smiled. 'Of course.'

Emily was thinking of Charles Fenton, a handsome young man with dark hair and a full moustache. She worried that he had left with too little time to get to the wharf at Newburne, four miles along a rough country road before reaching the main road over White Heath. She had visions of him driving the trap too fast round the bends with that strong black horse of his, leaving trap and driver on its side in some ditch.

'What are you thinking about, Emily?'

'Nothing, Papa, nothing at all. Let me pour you some more tea.'

Charles drove his horse at such a gallop that the trap was in danger of losing a wheel along the twisting way. But all was well and he was soon on a straight route across the common to where he joined the main road, then took a sharp left there by the Bell Tavern. Then it was down White Heath Hill to the small market town of Newburne. He was expected at the wharf for the launch of a new boat built by the family firm. His thoughts turned to Emily for an instant, her smile and sparkling eyes pictured in his mind. But then he quickly shrugged aside his romantic thoughts, for he was ambitious and anxious to play his part in his father's business.

The road down the hill was wide with a hard Macadam surface, for it had been a main coach road that was now much quieter since the railway had been completed. On either side of the road there were large new houses of individual design. Near the bottom of the hill, Charles's father had purchased about an acre of land where he was having a new and larger house built well away from the works. The architect had followed this concept, which included a spacious conservatory at the rear. The family would be moving into the new house the following year; in the summer of 1879.

Charles crossed over the main railway bridge that his father had helped design. Some of the construction work had been undertaken by the firm almost thirty years before, and the bridge had been recently painted. Charles turned into Market Street which ran past the firm where the family lived in a house at the front. An entrance at the side where the wagons entered the works had a curved fascia board over it with gold letters on a green background: 'FENTON AND SONS, EAGLE IRON WORKS'.

As Charles drove down the narrow street leading to the wharf, endangering people who quickly stood aside, he was soon in sight of the quay. There were many barges there, and he heard a cheer on the other side of the wharf as he drove round, having just missed the launch. A few onlookers stood there, to see another boat slip down into the river.

George Fenton stood with his brother in the midst of the crowd. As Charles arrived, his father looked at him angrily. 'Where on earth have you been, son? We waited as long as possible.' Then, suddenly realising he was surrounded by a crowd of local people, he calmed down and forced a smile. 'Well, there we are, another success!'

'Sorry, Father.' Charles was also conscious of the watching crowd. Uncle Edward just kept quiet, his expression stern.

'Nice lines,' George said, rubbing his hands together.

'Yes, she should give good service on the river once the superstructure is completed.'

The boat had drifted round to reveal her long sleek lines seen from the side with the boiler and engine in place. The men were pulling her into the moorings.

Charles Fenton walked across the yard from the stables and wagon sheds at the back of the works. He approached the engine house, passing a row of coal bunkers for different sizes, from very large lumps of coal down to a bunker at the end where a young labourer was shovelling small coals into a barrow. The man looked up as Charles approached. Giving him a smile and a nod, he mouthed 'Morning, Sir' then got on with his work.

The engine house with its square chimney had double doors, which were open. The boiler fire near these doors was kept stoked up to run the large engine that was beyond the boiler on the works side. It was twin-cylindered and horizontally built with a governor turning on top to keep it running at a constant speed. There was a large flywheel with a belt running up to a pulley on the end of a shaft. That shaft ran through a hole in the high brick wall into the workshop with pulley wheels driving a surprising number of machines. Charles liked to stand watching the engine and smell the oily hot steam. Wally White was in charge of the engine and kept it in excellent running order.

'Good morning, Wally!' Charles shouted.

The man, who had not seen Charles enter, was busy with an oil can and he turned round quickly with a beaming expression. 'Morning, Master Charles, I hear she floated fine yesterday.'

'Yes, the new Princess Class. Father was most pleased, though he wasn't so happily disposed towards me when I turned up late!'

'Oh dear, you were in trouble then, Master?'

'Couldn't be helped,' Charles said quickly. 'It went very well anyway.'

'You can always be sure of that, huh! Never known one to roll over yet!'

Wally always made Charles want to laugh; he'd known the man since he was a boy. 'That would be a sore sight with all those people standing there!'

'Standing there,' Wally said at the same time and they both had a laugh.

'Unthinkable, Wally,' Charles said as he went through the small door leading into the machine shop.

'Unsinkable!' he heard Wally shout.

A new screw-cutting lathe from the recently formed Whitworth Company at Openshaw was being installed. It was brought in on a wagon from the station a few days ago. Charles stood there gazing with enthusiasm at the gleaming new machine now in position, but with the main drive belt not yet fitted. Always excited by newly designed machinery, he was eager to see the performance. What he liked best of all was if he could try out the machine himself; he knew the power it made one feel, the power that is given to a craftsman as he masters the controls. The gear train wheels stood in a neat pyramid on the floor. Charles placed his hand on the very large and robust face plate and looked along the bed towards the tail stock, more than five feet centres. This machine would give long service. He dwelt upon that thought. He could never have imagined that it would still be in use more than sixty years later.

In the summer of 1879, the family had just moved into the new house in Whiteheath Road. It was so peaceful, away from the rush and bustle of the town and the noise from the works. All except Charles were greatly excited and went round the spacious house going from room to room. Extra staff had been taken on and were busy helping to get the household looking orderly for a family gathering. No one was surprised that Charles showed less enthusiasm. He had expressed often enough that he preferred to live at the works where he could remain in close contact with the engineering pursuits to which he was totally devoted. But the family and others were also aware that he was otherwise diverted lately. Now he was nowhere to be seen, either in the house or in the garden that was in the process of being laid out by expert gardeners and handymen.

Charles, like the rest of them, had taken the afternoon off, but his instinct had pulled him away from the new house on such a glorious afternoon. The flashes of sunlight glinted through the trees onto the smoothly brushed shining black coat of his horse and slender shafts of the trap, on that so familiar wooded road to Eastbrook. He smiled happily as he drove, thinking of Emily, for now she was teaching at the village school, and as if carried by some secret wave, Charles had not hesitated for a moment. He would meet her at the school that afternoon, while the rest of the family were absorbed by the new house.

Emily would walk from her home to the school, then back home in the late afternoon each day, a distance of about a mile. Charles got there in time to see the children leaving; then waited, keeping his horse steady as a few children ran by, in the speckled shade of some large oaks. After what seemed a long time, Emily came out of the school gate. Charles drove up by her, she stopped and turned as he steadied his horse.

'Oh... Charles!' She was surprised to see him and her eyes sparkled as she smiled up at him.

'I'm sure you'd like a ride Emily.'

She nodded shyly as Charles helped her up. 'This is a pleasant surprise! Should you not be working?'

'I was busy this morning from seven; you know that father doesn't insist I work every hour God sends.' He said it with a smile as he shook the reins and they drove off. The seat and dash panel of the trap were of black leather and well polished, though a little worn. Emily remained silent for a while as she gazed at the fine black horse, his long mane shaking as he trotted.

They chatted for a while, and the conversation naturally moved to the house move.

'How do you like the new family residence?' Emily asked.

'It's a fine house, Emily, much more room of course and the new garden is being laid out... Well...' He hesitated. 'That includes a tennis court.'

'I don't think I would be very good at the game.'

'I can't believe that! Come and try?'

'Yes.' She gave a laugh. 'I think I'd like that, Charles.'

'You'd probably do better than I, it wouldn't surprise me.'

'How can you say that Charles; I don't even play!'

'Nor do I!' He laughed. They reached Emily's house and stopped. 'Here we are Emily; this is my favourite house!'

'More than the new family mansion?'

'Well, that's another story.' There was a pause while they looked at each other in silence, except for the sound of birds.

'I think Papa is out on his rounds still. Would you like some tea, Charles?' She hesitated. 'Mrs Duckworth will be in.'

'Splendid, I certainly would.' He paused with a beaming smile, then jumped out to help Emily get down and she went to the gate.

'I'll tell Mrs Duckworth you're here,' Emily said. 'Would you wait on the veranda? I'll not be long.' She turned and walked quickly up the path.

'Afternoon, Mr Fenton.' Mr Duckworth, who seemed to appear from nowhere, took hold of the horse.

'Thank you, Duckworth.' Charles walked through the gate.

It was a perfect afternoon with the gentle sound of rustling leaves, and chickens could be heard behind a hedge nearby where Mrs Duckworth collected a few eggs each day.

As they drank their tea, Charles felt deeply content. 'This is most pleasant, relaxing.' He took a deep breath.

'At least your family will have more peace now, away from the works!' said Emily.

'I preferred the old house, engineering is my life. But I don't want to bore you with that, Emily.'

But Emily was interested, and wanted to know what would happen to the old house now.

'It will be turned into offices; but please, don't let's talk about that now.' He placed his hand gently on Emily's, and they sat there in silence for a while. In the distance there was the sound of a farm cart rolling along a gravelled road. For Emily, it was a memory to cherish. Charles was deep in thought, searching for words that he could not quite find – though words could not express the love he felt, and words were not necessary, for the feeling was mutual. He knew he would always remember that day as a magical moment.

The following Sunday at the new house, the Fenton family were sitting in the drawing room with the French windows open to the terrace. It was just before a midday dinner party. George Fenton and Mable had invited Edward, along with his wife and daughter Jane, to join them for their first Sunday there. Charles's sister Edith was also present but they were waiting for Charles to arrive with Emily. Jane and Edith were good friends and sat together talking all the time.

'Is Charles going to marry Emily?' Jane asked.

'Do you know, I can't imagine that!' Edith mused.

'Why? He seems so devoted to her and I don't see your brother as the bachelor type.'

'Well, I can almost see him being married to a steam engine,' Edith said with a laugh.

'Will Doctor Parson be coming to dine with us today?' Jane asked.

'Good gracious, no! Can you picture Charles bringing Emily and her father? A most unlikely idea! Anyway, Emily's father seldom socialises, he's terribly busy; doctors have to be very dedicated you know, Jane.'

'Yes of course...' Jane realised that Charles's father was listening nearby. He turned towards them.

'You two seem to have affairs well formed in your pretty little minds,' George Fenton said with amusement.

'Not really, Father,' Edith said.

'We were talking about doctors not having time to socialise, Uncle George,' Jane said.

'That's probably true,' said Aunt Amble. The two girls glanced at each other. 'And of course Doctor Parson is so dedicated and equally devoted to all his patients.'

'You're absolutely right,' said Uncle George.

Jane's parents hardly ever joined into a conversation, especially Edward, who always looked very serious and grim to Edith. He nodded in agreement and remained tight-lipped. But since Jane had told Edith that her father was not in good health, she felt quite sympathetic towards him in her way.

The sun on the terrace cast patches of light on the newly laid tiles, and most of those inside looked outwards, while the clamour of informal family conversation continued.

'Why don't we go out onto the terrace?' Edith said to Jane, who nodded in agreement.

'Do you mind, Father?' Jane said.

'Do go, you might catch sight of Charles and Emily. They've probably arrived already, and are wandering in the garden somewhere, forgetting all about the rest of the family, I shouldn't wonder!'

And indeed, Charles and Emily were walking down a path from where there was a good view of Newburne and they could see the new house half hidden by the trees. They were blissfully happy, but only they knew then; soon the world would know how they had sealed their future. On Emily's left hand, a diamond ring glinted in the sun on that beautiful day. When they reached a field at the bottom of the hill, Charles embraced Emily and she trembled in his arms as they kissed.

They were spellbound for a while, then Emily realised that Charles was staring at the field. 'Look at that!' he said.

'What is it?'

'That old plough in the long grass, I do believe...' Charles took a close look, pushing the grass away with his feet. 'Yes! See the name?'

'It's very rusty,' Emily said.

'There you are, Fenton and Son, patent plough!' Charles was excited.

'I would say it's been lying there for years and forgotten.'

'Yes! I must see if I can find the farmer sometime, I'm sure Father would be interested, could be seventy or more years old.' Charles was deep in thought now. 'My grandfather would have designed that.' He took Emily's hand. 'Come on, we'll be late!'

They walked hurriedly, hand in hand, through a small gate leading to the garden. The work of preparing the lawns and especially the tennis court, where they paused for an instant, had been started long before the house was finished. It was looking reasonably orderly but the gardeners would still have much work to complete. All was quiet now on Sunday as they carefully kept to a dry path that continued from the gate.

Charles and Emily came from the garden up onto the terrace, where the family had gathered.

'Ha, there you two are!' George Fenton said with a smile.

'I've been showing Emily the new tennis court, Father.'

'Ah! I thought you might have got distracted! Nice to see you, Emily, you're looking as lovely as ever.' She smiled shyly.

'Sorry to have kept you waiting!' Charles said as he stood there in the doorway with Emily. 'Before we have dinner, I have something special to say to you all.' He paused. 'Emily and I are going to be married!'

The old man shuffled along with his stick. As he turned into the main works entrance, he was still deep in thought about those far-off happy days. Suddenly he was aroused by the harsh voice of the works manager.

'Good morning, Mr Fenton.'

'You're very kind, my boy, very kind.'

Chapter 9
Moving Out and On

On the train bound for London, with the rhythmic rumble and gentle jogging as the wheels rolled along the line, Tom's thoughts drifted. He had worked at Fentons for over six years. It seemed a long time, and so much had happened in an epoch that was engraved into his mind. He had acquired skills, the benefit of which balanced the low pay. There were people he would rather forget, but it was the friends left behind that he would miss. His expectations for his future in that company had dwindled once he had stopped being a humble apprentice. During that five-year period, he was adopted under a signed agreement, but the last year had not been at all encouraging and he was convinced there was no future at Fentons. Thinking of those he had left behind, a little sadness entered his mind. A big part of his life was floating away with those whose outlook seemed uncertain. There was the inevitable wind-down at the end of the war, when new orders failed to come along. Tom did not want to see the decline and inevitable end to a company that had gradually expanded for more than seven decades.

A drawing instrument hit the wall as Tom had an outburst of frustration. He was suffering a creative block, and as he gazed at the drawing in front of him, the lines on the paper became an increasingly jumbled blur. Nobody took any notice, but Tom was angry with himself, for he had allowed himself to overreact.

Tom quickly filled his pipe and puffed away to soothe the inner turmoil he felt as he thought of his position with the firm. A move away from Fentons now seemed inevitable, though the thought of change and losing contact with friends he had made perturbed him. He went out of the office to get away from the offending drawing and walked up the steps to talk to Connie. She was now working in the room above the front entrance to the works where the large window overlooked the road. She would always listen to Tom when he needed to talk.

'Thanks for listening to me Connie,' he said after he had poured out his troubles. 'Sometimes I just don't think I count at all in this place!'

'Don't make me laugh, Tom! I know that's not true. But perhaps you should look for work away from here. You need a change!'

'I don't know. It's not easy, is it?'

'You could write to some firms and get an interview. I think that's what I would do, Tom.' She paused. 'Not that we want to see you go of course!'

'I think some people would like to be rid of me!'

'You don't believe that, I know!'

'I suppose not... it's just that I don't feel I'm getting anywhere, at least not here. So how would I get on elsewhere?'

'You do talk nonsense, Tom, you're going to do well.' She patted his hand to reassure him.

'Yes... silly to worry I suppose.'

'I'm sure you'd get an interview. Take a day off, make some excuse!'

'Yes, perhaps I could. Wonder what they'd be looking for?'

'Someone like you, I expect,' she said with a smile. 'You can only try. Have confidence in yourself!'

'Yes, you're right! I think that would be the best way – to write a few letters and get some time off somehow. Could be interesting, that's if I'm lucky enough to get an interview anyway.' Tom hesitated. 'You won't mention it to anyone, will you?'

'Don't be silly, as if I would,' she smiled. 'You are a worry guts you know.!

There was a noise behind and Mildred West came into the room. 'Hello,' she said, 'and what are you two nattering about?'

'Just chatting,' Connie said. 'Oh, I'm sorry, it's tea time!' She looked at her watch.

'It's gone half past three,' Mildred said. 'I don't know! Too busy talking!' Mildred was rocking from one foot to the other as she spoke. 'And forgetting tea!'

Tom moved back as she drew in between him and Connie. That familiar feeling came over him. 'Oh, I'm sorry,' he said, but he was thinking as he looked at Mildred: 'What a fool I am!' He was struggling with his old yet now rekindled passion for Mildred, with whom he had never resumed his violin lessons. She was still on his mind but out of reach. He felt desperately frustrated. He had been stupidly trying to avoid her, but why, for goodness sake? A feeling of non-fulfilment plagued him, and he was tense and withdrawn at times. Yet others often referred to him as happy-go-lucky, so he was able to cover up his feelings very well.

'I'll come down now. Excuse me Tom,' Connie said, interrupting his thoughts. As she and Mildred went for tea, he went back to contemplating his drawing in the design office, while puffing his pipe. He was still deep in thought. 'They should be paying more. I know I'm worth it! I'm good at this work when I set my mind to it.' Was he too easily distracted? No, not as bad as all that. Then he began to wonder how long the firm would be able to pay any of their employees. Connie was right, of course: it was important to have confidence.

It was the end of an era. Over six years had passed since Tom's first day at Fentons and this was now his final day. He was glad, though a little sad and he did have regrets, for there were many happy times hidden under the waves of misinterpretation and minor blunders. But he also remembered being made to feel that he was a whipping boy by a man with a mind so bitter that he distorted the truth. The works manager who seemed to resent Tom's very presence. But that was all past for those dark days were over and he would soon be away from the old firm and entering a new era.

He was going to work for Brown and Saxons, –'Ship designers and boiler makers' – a well established company in the London docks. He'd had an interesting interview with the man in charge of the design office, Mr Guthrey, who had eagerly offered to take him on for a six-month trial period and would be paying him almost three times as much as he was getting at Fentons.

This last Friday was a dull day in mid-January. With his personal belongings packed into a suitcase, the time came that Tom hated most of all: bidding farewell to his colleagues. He shook hands with most of the foremen he'd worked with, who had given him so much good advice, then a few grubby hands from any of his old workmates he could find. Joe wiped his hands on his overalls.

'Sorry, m'hands are grubby.' This was Joe's usual remark.

'I don't care,' Tom said with a laugh, 'there's only one last day!'

'I don't blame you for leaving, mate.' Tom thought Joe was looking even more forlorn than when he'd seen him last, only a few weeks back.

'Yes... quite glad. I'll miss the old place though!'

'Where you off to then, Tom?'

'Brown and Saxon... in the docks, London!'

'Better pay, I bet?'

'Yes, a big improvement.' But Tom didn't want to talk about money.

'P'raps we'll see you sometime... p'raps not though. You'll forget all about us when you see all them girls up there, I reckon!' A bit of the old Joe was coming out. 'It'll do you good to get away, you can't beat getting away. Wish I could, but I'm stuck 'ere now, see. You'll be better off all right!'

'You heard of Brown and Saxon, Joe?'

'Can't say I have.' Joe was scratching his head.

'Ship builders and boiler makers.'

'Oh yes... Sounds good that does. Well, best of luck, Tom.'

'Bye, Joe.'

'All the best, Tom.' And Joe got on with his work. He didn't look up. Tom walked quickly past the steps that led up to Wakely's office, not wishing to see or be seen by him.

Mr Wills was standing in Mr Glenn's office clasping a roll of drawings, while Mr Glenn was holding forth and gesticulating as if he was describing the length of a salmon he'd caught in a Scottish river. Tom hung around, glancing through the window from behind the printing machine at intervals so that he could see Mr Wills, but being careful not to be spotted by Mr Glenn. He thought Mr Wills had seen him and when he eventually came into the design office, Tom stepped out from the corner by the machine.

'Oh, hello!' Tom blurted out awkwardly.

'Are you hiding, Tom? Saw you sneaking a look at me!'

'Sorry, only I didn't want to miss you. Are you going back to the pump shop?'

Mr Wills looked at him with a fixed expression of amusement. 'Eventually, yes.'

Mr Wills was grinning and his expression made Tom smile. 'Only, I just wanted to say goodbye – and thank you for all the advice you've given me, and...'

'Advice! What advice?' Mr Wills said jokingly. Then suddenly he put out his hand and shook Tom's with a very firm grip. 'Keep out of trouble, Tom, you're bound to do well. Only watch all those strangers once you get away from Newburne. And the temptations of the big city.' He gave Tom a nudge and winked at the same time. Tom wasn't quite sure what he meant, but he took it as a light hearted warning!

'Yes, I will of course. Is Dave around?'

'No, he's not in today,' Mr Wills said abruptly.

'Oh dear, I've missed him then. Could you tell him for me I'm sorry I didn't see him.'

'Yes, I'll tell him. Come and see us sometime, if you're around!' Mr Wills spoke as he went towards the door. Then he stood for a moment, slapping the roll of drawings onto his left palm as if contemplating whether to go or stay. Then he turned and gave

Tom a reassuring smile, 'That's if you ever come back to Newburne!'

'Oh, I expect I will,' Tom said with uncertainty.

'We'll see, he said, with a nod, and he went quickly through the door. Mr Wills was a very self assured man so Tom could not imagine him being embarrassed, yet he disappeared quickly, without stopping to discuss business with anyone.

Tom had a conversation with Mr Methly who was working on an old engine room pipe layout for a refit. Only a few steam powered boats remained and like those old steam engines, he himself would soon be retiring. He smiled at Tom. 'Try to control that artistic temperament of yours!'

'Yes, I know.' Tom gripped Mr Methly's outstretched hand.

The thought of going into Mr Glenn's office perturbed Tom, as Glenn would be bound to keep him tied up while he held forth. It was hard to know the best time to go into that familiar yet foreboding room, where he had so often stood with fast-wearing patience. Eventually he chose his moment, and Mr Glenn was as verbose as he'd feared. As knock-off time approached, Tom became increasingly concerned that he would be too late to see Mildred, and he had a sickening feeling as he thought of her just drifting away with all the others into infinity. Tom's only half heard Mr Glenn's voice now: 'You'll not always have your father to lean on, you know... if you keep that best foot forward...'

At last it was over and they shook hands. It was quite dark outside. Tom wanted to bid farewell to the rest of his old colleagues but he felt uneasy; as if they were wishing him luck in a puppet-like fashion. He rushed up to see Connie, who was just packing up to go home.

'I'm sorry, Connie!' he breathed. 'Couldn't get away from Mr Glenn. You're just packing up of course, don't want to keep you'

'That's all right, panicky pants!'

'Don't like saying goodbye... but!'

'Yes, well none of us do, Tom. I hope you'll be happy in your new surroundings.'

'Yes, thanks, Connie. I'm sorry, time's getting on.' He was looking at his watch. 'Um, I expect the typists will be getting ready to go home.'

'You can go,' she said with amusement.

Tom felt embarrassed, he never quite knew what to say. 'I'll say cheerio then, and I hope we meet again.' He gently took her hand. He was thinking that it might be the last time he ever saw her. As he thought back to the night of that dance, he felt like kissing her but dared not. He left feeling vaguely unhappy.

He was now in a state of nervous disorientation. He walked towards his large packed case, then remembered that his father had arranged to pick him up outside at half past five. It was almost that time. Tom rushed downstairs to the typing office in a sudden bold effort. The door was open and he slowed to almost a tip-toe down the last few steps.

He found Mildred on her own, putting on her coat. As he stood at the doorway, she looked round and an expression of surprise gleamed from her face as she saw him standing there, looking like a lost stranger.

'Hello,Tom.'

'Oh... I see you're about to leave.'

'That's why I've put my coat on.' She looked amused.

'Yes, of course... um, I just wanted to say...' She looked straight at him as he hesitated. 'You know this is my last day, I suppose it's goodbye, but...'

'Yes, I know, Tom.' She was not smiling now. The shyness was still nagging him, he cursed himself for it. 'You're doing the right thing, I hope?' As she said that, Tom suddenly felt strangely close to her, more than he'd ever felt. He was silent for a moment, thinking: 'It's too late, you fool!'

'Yes, I think so,' Tom said.

'Where are you going?'

He told her, and Mildred said nothing for a few seconds. 'You will come and see us sometime, won't you?' Her words sounded hollow, as if she was drifting away.

'Are you cycling home on this cold night?' Tom said, feeling concerned for her.

'Oh, no fear, I'm going with Sally by bus tonight,' she said brightly.

'I see, I thought she'd gone.'Tom gained confidence. 'So she's still here then?' He couldn't think of the right thing to say, so he silently took her hand. It was so soft and gentle, she let him hold it and he didn't want to let go. A trance-like feeling overtook him as he looked into her eyes, wanting to kiss her. He was transfixed as if in a magic spell; a few seconds can give a false impression of time, but it could only have been a moment.

The spell was suddenly broken as Sally came bouncing in. 'You off then, Tom, to some new and wonderful place?' She was always the same, laughing Sally.

Tom came back to earth as he turned to her. 'Well, I don't know about wonderful, but I'm afraid I've got to say goodbye. It's too late to change my mind now!' He was not feeling happy, as if there were unseen pitfalls not far ahead.

Then Tom heard his father's voice in the hall. 'Hello, girls! I've been waiting outside in the car for a while, Tom, thought I'd better come and see if you needed any help.'

Tom had forgotten that his father was picking him up, and he was not at all pleased that he turned up at that moment. 'It's all right, Dad, I was just having a word with... well just saying goodbye. They're going home by bus!'

'By bus? That won't do, hanging about for a bus on a cold night. We'll give them a lift – going your way, aren't we, girls?' Tom wished it had been he who had made the suggestion!

'That's very good of you, Mr Hunt,' Sally said.

'Thank you,' Mildred said, 'if there's room for us with all Tom's luggage.'

'Plenty of room!' Tom said. 'I'll just go up and get my case – won't be a minute.' As he went up the stairs he was filled with emotion. His last day and he was mad with himself, sure that he'd missed other opportunities to give Mildred a lift. And it wasn't even his idea! Bad timing, he thought as he went to pick up the case.

Mr Perry was still there, smoking his pipe while looking at

the drawing on his board. It was as if nothing had changed since Tom had first seen him all those years ago. 'That looks heavy,' Mr Perry remarked. 'Can you manage?'

'Yes thank you.' He lifted the case. 'Goodbye again.'

'All the best then.'

When Tom had staggered down the stairs, they put the case in the car boot and the two women got into the back. His father was closing the boot as Tom closed the near side back door. There was quite a lot of laughter, mainly from Sally, as they got settled in.

'All right then?' Tom said. 'I'll drive.' He quickly got into the driving seat. As they drove away, it was starting to snow. 'Not a night for dogs.' Sally laughed and talked while Mildred remained silent, and Tom was glad when he let Sally out near the top of White Heath Hill, by the road where she lived.

'You can drop me at the end of the road,' Mildred said.

'No, course not!' Tom said, 'just a little detour on such a night is nothing!' He stopped outside that well remembered door and a feeling of nostalgia came over him. He jumped out and opened the car door for Mildred.

'My, this is such service!' she said. He opened the front gate and his father shouted from the car, 'Good night Mildred', as if he had been forgotten.

'Oh,' Mildred said, turning at the gate, 'good night Mr Hunt, and thank you for the lift.' Tom was sizzling inside, as he walked to the door with her.

'Don't be too long, Tom!' he heard his father shout.

'Sorry about this, Mildred.'

'That's all right, I'm very grateful for the lift.' A sprinkling of snow drifted into the porch. 'It's such a cold night, so you mustn't keep your father waiting. Hope all goes well with you, Tom.'

'Oh, and you, Mildred.' He could not help wishing he could be asked in, those old memories rolled over him. She put the key in the door; the house looked empty. 'On your own?' Tom asked.

'Dad should be in any minute now.' She was standing on the

doorstep when she gave Tom a surprise peck on his forehead. He kissed her hand in an old fashioned gesture, gripped it and turned back up the path.

'Don't forget all about me, Tom,' she said as she stood in the dim porch, and he felt as if he was abandoning her.

'Never!' he said as he looked at the lone figure standing in the doorway.

Tom turned and got into the car, waving to her as he drove off. It was a quiet drive home. Tom didn't want to talk that night; he felt that it was the worst day of his life. He could still feel the tingling of that kiss on his forehead, and wondered if there was any chance he would ever see her again.

The train rumbled on and the thoughts of that last day drifted away as it drew near London. Tom looked at those grey buildings and devastated bomb sites. He then looked at a girl sitting opposite him who had been reading Picture Post. She'd just woken from a little snooze and he smiled at her and looked back at the drab scene through the window. Maybe there are better things to come, he thought.

PART TWO

Chapter 10
Downstream

Three blasts on the ship's siren sounded the warning to those on board that the ship was about to sail. Another long blast some minutes later was the last warning, the gangways were about to be drawn away and there would be no chance of getting ashore at that point. Any potential stowaway would now have to lie low to await probable discovery later.

Brown and Saxon was a large company within the great complex of London's dockland, where there was intensive activity with a long history. It had taken many centuries to become such an important and seemingly permanent port, for there were no fears that this great area would ever begin to show signs of a fragile future. Cranes lined the docks, numerous grey girdered stems that vanished into the misty distance, swaying as they discharged cargoes or loaded the ships' holds.

The atmosphere echoed with a variety of sounds and there were many interesting features to see. Walking over a dry dock gates where a ship was being repaired, the loud rattle of pneumatic riveting and the banging of hammers against the metal fabric reverberated around the dry dock walls. There was no time to spare, for it would cost the ship owners a thousand pounds or more every day just to keep her there. After the riveting came the painting of the hull, finished with speed and efficiency. Along the dockside, where the ships were being unloaded, even the smells were memorable. Crates, bales, great timber logs of mahogany and large square bales of raw latex were being unloaded onto the dockside. And in the dark shadowy warehouses, many crates were piled high. The railway that ran alongside all the docks transported the goods throughout the country. Looking at the men hard at work, Tom, who was just new there, had an impression of great hope for the future, after the struggle of war had ended.

Ships from all parts of the world were seen with strange names, and Tom was interested in the character of the seamen that sailed with them. They would be excited by the opportunity of going ashore in a foreign country, especially if it was their first visit to England; with the exception of the Russian crews, who were never allowed ashore. The police that guarded the dock gates were thought by some to resemble prison warders; their job was to keep a strict check on all persons going out or coming in through those gates, and no-one was above suspicion. Anybody was quite likely to be called into the gatehouse for a search and questioning. Tom was sure he had a guilty expression, and he expected he would one day see a finger pointing at him. It was his opinion that the police enjoyed the power it gave them.

Brown and Saxon's chief designer, Mr Guthrey, had a firm handshake. He sat behind his huge old desk that merged with the well established company buildings. He was a short man with thin grey hair, his round face had a harassed expression and blended well with his grey suit. He spoke to Tom with words of welcome and encouragement, and introduced him to Mr Mathews, a senior designer who would willingly give friendly advice.

Tom was engaged on the drawing of ship's plans while the work of refitting progressed. He appreciated this, for it meant he could get out into the docks and on board a ship that was having major conversion work carried out. He would be measuring and sketching for several days at a time, and in the midst of great activity, surrounded by men of many skills. Then it would be back to the board again where he drew out the plans from 'A deck,' down to the engine rooms. They worked on very long tables, drawing boards on legs made specially for drawing ships' plans. The large drawing office, which was on the top floor, stretched across the building. There were high windows at each end and north lights in the roof. The room was situated near the end of the large old works buildings that dated back to the early part of the previous century.

At two minutes past half past eight, Tom signed his name in the slot of the time clock and quickly pushed down on the brass handle that recorded onto a roll of paper within the solid old time piece his time of arrival. They were strict with all the staff on time keeping, so Tom strove to get there early. If anybody was over five minutes late for more than two days running, he or she would be called into the chief's office for a little chat, and it was doubtful that any excuse would be accepted readily.

The top of a crane swung very close to the window high over Tom's board, and he'd looked with apprehension at the grey painted steel pulley as it came within inches of the window on several occasions. He felt sure that one day it would come crashing through. That day came when the square block came towards the window and stopped about a couple of inches away from the frame, and as Tom watched, he could not help thinking: I wonder if the crane driver is seeing how close he dare go, or even wanting to let the crane smash through the window, for it was getting closer at each approach. *Crash!* Tom jumped back as glass and splintered wood fell upon his plans and he turned round to his colleagues.

'It's happened! I've been expecting it for days!' Tom shouted

This calamity meant that Tom lost his nice position facing the end wall with the high window. He found himself on a table halfway down the room. This made him feel vulnerable, though he was not quite sure why! Sometimes, the atmosphere in that large design office felt to Tom strangely remote. Though the work was absorbing, he yearned for the cosiness of the smaller place that he had so much wanted to get away from a few months before, but there was not really any choice for him at the time. He got on well with his new colleagues, but he knew them only in his place of work. Some of them were so experienced, particularly in ship design, that his self-assurance felt threatened, but this feeling went away when the chief told him how much his work on the ship's plans was appreciated.

Down in the large works there was a labyrinth of workshops and stores, mostly covering very big areas. A wide expanse of smooth black flooring was devoted to the drawing in white, full size outlines of plates and ships lines, so the parts were matched to these shapes as they were made. Tom stood there intrigued for a while, holding a folded drawing and notepad.

'Watch out, mate!' came a voice from his right. He turned and stepped back out of the way as two men went by carrying a heavy plank and laid it down in front of where he was standing. 'From up top are you?' said the same voice, while the other man, who was younger, walked away. 'Not seen you around!' He was probably about fifty or more, and grinned from a bristly face under a dark greasy cap.

'I've been here a few months,' Tom said.

'You're all right up there, bet they pay you well!'

'Not that great,' Tom said, feeling irritated but putting on a smile.

'You're lucky, guv, permanent I mean,' the man said as he walked away.

Tom went out through a big door, thinking about the plight of a casual labourer without permanent work. He supposed he was lucky compared with that chap, who might never have had much education, and may have fought in the Great War. It worried him for a while. A wave of memory went through his mind for an instance as he thought of the men, the machines and those pulleys that might soon cease to turn at his old firm.

Breathtaking! Tom was standing on the gates of a dry dock. He looked down at the hull of a large ship resting on blocks and kept horizontal by heavy supporting bulks of timber firmly wedged along each side between the ship and the walls of the dry dock. All was quiet, it was dinner break, so he walked down the steps at one end and right along under the hull from the bows to the stern where he stood and looked up at the huge propeller. Standing there under the great bronze blades, a little shudder went through him as he thought of all that weight above him. The works siren blew, the men were soon back and the loud riveting started again. Painters with extended brushes commenced laying on the red oxide undercoat patching, and it was time to get out of the way. That view from under those propellers would be an unforgettable sight. He could not help thinking that the men in their large soft caps had little protection from falling objects, particularly if that missile happened to be a flying red hot rivet.

Tom became friendly with Brian, a young colleague in the design office.

'There's a Russian ship in the dry dock,' Brian told him one day.

'I didn't see it this morning,' Tom said, looking up from his plans.

'Not in this one, over on the far side.' Brian was a chap who often joked and liked to tell shaggy dog stories. 'The captain's a woman, I hear.'

'Really!' Tom said. 'Can't picture that.' He chuckled.

'Why not? Quite tough, the Russian women.'

'Sometimes I think women are tougher than men anyway!'

'Good organisers in my experience,' Brian said.

'Yes. Why not English women captains? But I just can't quite imagine it.' Tom chuckled and looked down at his ship's plans.

Later that day, Tom walked over to the other dry dock, eager to have a look at this foreign ship. The strange letters on the bow were tantalising to him and he wished he knew the sounds, so he could at least pronounce the name, even if he didn't understand the meaning. Tom was under the impression he could wander at will into any vessel, so he walked up the gangway with little hesitation. As he neared the top, a dark figure in a great coat loomed over him. The man had a grim expression that so alarmed Tom, he was frozen for a second. The man said nothing, but raised a large hand warning him off, so Tom made a hasty retreat down the gangway.

Brian was on his way back to the office and saw Tom coming down the gangway. 'What were you doing up there? That's out of bounds!'

'Did you see the bloke at the top?' Tom asked.

'Yeah!' Brian laughed as they strolled back to work.

'Scared the living daylight's out of me.'

'Serves you right!'

The staff joked about Brian and Tom, but what was the big joke? Tom thought. It was good to have a friend. Brian was three years older than Tom, good looking and outspoken, and he gave Tom confidence.

The men working on the ships started fifteen minutes earlier, which was surprising. They only had a half-hour break, but the staff had an hour and Tom thought this unfair, and asked Brian about it. 'Why do the men only have a half-hour dinner break?'

'Probably because they're on piece work.'

'Oh, I see.'

'Anyway, what the dickens were you doing trying to go on board that Russian boat? Hoping to see the captain, I suppose!'

'Well, no, I was just curious,' Tom said hesitatingly.

'Yeah I know, great big beefy woman, I expect.'

'Not necessarily.' They went through the old door and up the stone steps to the office. 'I thought it might be interesting.'

'To see the captain?'

'No, to look at the ship. You've got the captain on the brain,' Tom joked.

'Course I haven't,' Brian said with a laugh. We can't wander onto any boat, Tom, not without permission.'

'Would it be possible to get permission to go on board that Russian boat then?'

'No, not a chance.'

They were passing Mr Guthrey's office, and he called Tom in. 'Mr Hunt, can I have a word with you?'

Tom imagined he was in trouble. 'Yes, Mr Guthrey?'

'I'd like you to make me a perspective drawing of this hatch cover.' He gave him a line drawing. Tom wondered how Mr

Guthrey knew he was good at pictorial drawing. Anyway, it would make a change from ship's plans for a couple of days.

At times while he was with Brown and Saxon, no matter how interesting the work, he had bouts of depression and he was very restless. Tom put it down to frustration. He would get out of the office as much as possible and work it off. He sometimes missed the old place back in Newburne. Life had been so different then.

The secret internal struggle was always there, but he made himself keep to an orderly pattern. In his aspirations to forge a successful and rewarding career he felt restrained at times. His philosophizing and dreaming shed no light on how to cope with his own private battle. He often regarded himself as more of an onlooker than a participant in life; but he knew he had to rid himself of any idea that he was not part of the common pattern.

As the crowd of workers of all classes, from management down to the humble labourer, streamed out through the dock gates at night, they were watched. A big man in a dark uniform and a flat peaked cap stood astride in the centre glancing from side to side. A man with the power that was feared by some, a man who looked as if he enjoyed that power, like a man remembered by Tom in another place at a time in the past. And on either side of the massive egress stood other dark uniformed figures shadowed by the walls. Tom had a natural feeling of guilt as he walked out, though he had nothing to hide.

'You!.' The man in the middle was eyeing Tom with a very serious expression while pointing at his small case. 'What's in the case?'

'My personal property,' Tom said nervously.

'Open it!' the man ordered.

'No, why should I!' Tom knew it was foolish to argue with these men of power, but he felt an overwhelming impulse to resist their authority. The man yelled something rudely, and Tom was suddenly grabbed by two of the uniformed thugs who hauled him into the gate office as if he was a common criminal. His protests fell on deaf ears.

'Put the case on the table,' one man said abruptly.

'There's no need to be so rude about it.'

'Don't come that with us, matey.'

'All right.' Tom put the case on the table and one of the men started to open it.

'You leave that alone, I'll open it, it's my property!'

'Quickly then,' the man said. As Tom opened the case, he remembered that he'd brought his small cine camera in to work that day to show Brian. That worried him. 'What's this then?'

'That is my cine camera.'

'Yours, is it?'

'Of course it's mine.'

'Where did you get it then?'

'I brought it in this morning to show a colleague, not that it's any of your business.'

'It is our business, anything that's taken out or brought in through these gates.'

'But it's my own property!'

'Then you should have booked it in this morning. So where did this come from?'

'It was second hand, came from a shop in High Holborn.'

'We'll have to hold on to it and check it out.'

'You can't do that, it's my property.'

'Look, matey, you don't tell us what to do.'

'There's no need to be rude. I told you it belongs to me.'

'But we don't know that you're telling the truth, do we?'

'Look, I'm a member of the staff and I'll have to make a complaint about your rough treatment.'

'It wouldn't get you anywhere, you should know that!'

'You're not real policemen anyway.' Tom realised he'd gone too far with them and wanted to eat his words. A big beefy fist came within an inch of his face.

'How would you like to feel this then?'

'You wouldn't dare!'

'Don't tempt me, mate.'

'You've made me late, I was in a hurry tonight!'

'We've got all night, so just give us the details of where you got this from, then you can go. If the information you give us fits when we check, you can pick it up tomorrow morning.'

Tom knew he'd been a fool to antagonise them. He told them where he'd bought the camera and was allowed to go. He left feeling deflated, knowing perfectly well that you couldn't win if you argue against those men in uniform.

When he collected the camera the next morning from a man sitting at a desk in an office who was probably the chief customs officer, he was treated with the greatest of respect. 'If you'd signed it in or just left it with them without any arguments you could have saved yourself a lot of bother.'

'Yes, I know now, but they were rough with me!'

'We're sorry, but you must realise they have to be tough in the docks.' They shook hands and parted amicably.

There was a yellow haze over the dock on a warm afternoon as Tom walked along the dock side where the S.S.Chittagong was moored. She floated high enough to see the Plimsoll mark, so the upper structure was now being painted. The old wartime camouflage having been removed first, the loud rattle of pneumatic tools had died away and red oxide undercoat was being painted on the sides by men sitting on suspended planks. He stood for a while and watched, as the sunlight on the water reflected dancing patterns on the ships side. On board, the decks were being caulked and cabins refitted. Tom was fascinated by the sight of so many craftsmen converting these great ships that were once luxury passenger liners that had been stripped out during the war and used as troop ships, now being converted to take so many people away to Australia!

Each time he boarded another ship, he was enthralled to be left free to wander and explore. In one of the cargo holds he looked upon empty decks, the sunlight penetrating where the hatch covers were removed. Watertight doors were open, leaving easy access throughout the ship's hull. Following one of the propeller shafts towards the stern tube through a tunnel, a dark hideaway, Tom thought for a moment of those shafts turning continuously as the weeks went by on a long voyage. It was a claustrophobic place with a smell of gungy oil mixed with anything that might be in the bilges.

Returning forward through caverns of pipes, Tom walked on gratings around machinery and climbing the companion ways. It was an intriguing labyrinth. In the engine room there were large turbines, which were so very different from the reciprocating engines that he was familiar with during his years with Fentons. No visible crankshaft or interesting reversing gear, it all looked comparatively clean and tidy for a ship that must have been built in the 1920s. The asbestos covered pipes, gauges, wheels to operate valves and the usual engine room telegraph, reminded him of Mr Methly, poring over all those endless drawings of pipes.

In the boiler room, where work was in progress, Tom looked into the firebox of one of the boilers, where two men could be seen in a dim light. He hesitated for a second, then walked on, nodding to a man nearby. He was thinking he would hate to work down in that place, especially while at sea, though it was fascinating. Exploring further, he found himself inside the base of one of the two funnels, an enormous oval column, full of ventilation ducts. He climbed the steel ladders, up to gratings at various levels and it seemed a long way up. When he reached the top, he looked over the rim and felt like a man making observations from a castle. There was the most splendid view across the docks to where other funnels could be seen among the cranes, shimmering through the haze in the warm sun.

With his back to the sloping aft side of the great oval rim, it was so much larger up there than it appeared from the quayside. Seeing a temporary ladder secured on this side for maintenance work, Tom climbed over, deciding it was a good way down to the upper deck. Once over the rim, he held on about to descend. 'Must hold on tight!' he said to himself. The funnel's slope towards the stern made it a little tricky, not helped by the fact that the ladder moved slightly. He looked down, and saw that he was over the open hatch, a long drop down to the bottom of the hold, well below the water line. Clinging on shakily in a cold sweat, he got back over that rim. For a while he stood, calming his thoughts before making his way back down inside the funnel. He was feeling a little foolish at getting so panicky.

People from all parts of the country wanted to get away from a crumbling old world to seek a better future. They were drawn by the excitement of travel to the other side of the world, a dream world in the sunshine. Tom was doodling on a piece of paper while his thoughts drifted, when he sensed someone overshadowing him. Brian had stopped by.

'You look busy,' he said with a smile.

'I was deep in thought.'

'Dropping off to sleep, you mean,' Brian joked.

'It's pretty humid in here. No, I was thinking about all these people popping off to Australia. Wouldn't you have thought English people would prefer to stay in this country?'

'Why shouldn't they want to make a new life for themselves?'

'Mm. Would you want to go to Australia then?'

'Not at the moment, but people have always emigrated.'

'They only pay ten pounds, I think – just over a week's wages and off they go into the blue. The Aussies only take skilled people, don't they, Brian?'

'I don't know,' Brian said thoughtfully.

'Would have thought we need the skills here!'

'I don't think it makes much difference, it's only likely to be a small proportion of the population.'

'I was thinking about it, that's all – worrying I mean.'

'You always want something to worry about, Tom!'

'Oh, only a bit,' Tom said with a smile.

When Brian had gone,Tom looked down at his almost finished plans, then went to the ship. On board the S.S.Maltan, where the refitting was almost completed, Tom thought his plans seemed finished, but there was still some checking to be done. He walked about the ship with folded prints, three large, long drawings that had taken him some weeks to complete. There was a special smell on board ship which added to the atmosphere that Tom enjoyed, a mixture of cooking, new paint and oil. He walked through the main galley where there was always a considerable hubbub, with an increasing number of white coated cooks busy at the long metal tables and large boiling pots. Extractors roared above, it was warm in there and Tom wondered what it was like as they crossed the equator. He came to the bakery and looked in as a man was just taking some rolls out of the oven.

'That's a good smell,' Tom said.

'Yes,' said the baker, 'have one!'

Tom took a roll and devoured it.

'You must be hungry then?'

'No, it's just that there's nothing like new bread.'

'You're right there, mate.' The man beamed from a reddish face that seemed to blend well with the crust on the rolls.

The stewards were all Goanese, very smart in their white coats and black trousers. Tom measured up all the cabins in their quarters at the forward end of the ship. They sometimes offered him a cup of tea, which was gratefully received, though the tea was always the same on the ships, made with dried milk; the milkman didn't deliver to ships, even in the docks. Once he got into a difficult conversation with an Indian who knew little English, but he managed to tell Tom how many children he had back home, from the youngest to the oldest, by placing his hand at five different heights.

At the aft end of the ship were the Lascars from the East Indies. Tom never found out exactly what they did, except that they were manual crew workers, and he thought they were probably mostly stokers. They seemed quite primitive to Tom. They dyed their hair red and ate with their fingers, Tom watched one of them take his food on a large chapatti and crouch down to eat on the deck by an air duct. Their quarters also had to be measured up for the ships plans. Tom entered their domain with slight trepidation. But he found the lowest of them all, as regarded by some, to be the friendliest of them all and he was greeted by broad smiles with surprisingly gleaming white teeth. Tom's instinct was to be as friendly towards them as they were to him. There was much laughter, and in spite of the distractions, making his work tricky, one of them held the tape for him. They sat round a large pot from which they took meat and ate it off the bone. Before he could leave them, he was given a cup of tea, then a piece was torn off a chapatti and a morsel of meat on the bone was thrust at him, which made him feel a little ill. He declined their offer, though it was most difficult, as they were so very insistent.

It was a Friday, and the Maltan was due to sail. Tom was filled with enthusiasm. His plans had been delivered and he was feeling restless, he wanted to get out there and go on board. He was intrigued to experience the pervading aura that always takes over when something new or a change is about to take place. A boy behind him in the office started to whistle, interfering with Tom's thoughts, so he went out into the passage to look out of the window near the top of the stairs. The Maltan's three funnels and masts were just visible behind the old slate roof of a welding shop and stores.

'Mr Hunt!' Mr Guthrey shouted, and Tom looked round to see him at his office door. 'You're not busy now!'

'Curse it,' Tom thought, 'is he telling me or asking me?'

'Yes, Mr Guthrey!'

'Would you do this for me.' Guthrey held a tracing of a small steam trawler. 'Put a title down here would you.' He was pointing to the left bottom corner. 'Special Surrey.'

'Yes, I'll do that straight away, Mr Guthrey.'

Tom soon got that finished and Mr Guthrey asked him to have two prints made. These were done by a girl they called Sandy, who was in charge of the printing. Tom got on well with her; she had a great sense of humour and always laughed a lot with him. She had straight sandy hair, so he was not sure whether Sandy was her real name or a nickname because of her hair, which Tom liked very much.

'Boo!' Tom said as he peeped in on Sandy.

'Oops!' She turned round from the machine. 'Tom, you made me jump!' She put her right hand on her bosom.

'Only me, Sandy, am I that frightening?'

'Course not, just me! Oh dear.' She laughed.

'You busy?'

'No... not terribly. What are you up to Tom?'

'Not up to anything, Sandy, just want a couple of prints for His Worship, Mr Guthrey, two weenie ones!'

'Give them here then, seeing it's you!' She slipped them in between a batch of prints she was making.

'Smashing!'

'Am I, Tom?'

'I didn't mean, er... well, course you are!'

She laughed at his embarrassment, turned and patted his hand. 'You're funny Tom.'

'You know me, Hunt by name and hunter by nature.'

'Oh, huh...You!' she handed him the warm, damp prints.

'Thanks, Sandy.' He looked into her big blue eyes as they smiled at each other. He quickly left the room, feeling entranced.

He asked Mr Guthrey if he could go over to the Maltan as it would be the last chance of seeing her before she sailed. He agreed and Tom walked over there after he had finished dinner. As Tom walked up the gangway, he looked at the gleaming, newly painted hull and up at the white upper structure. It was all so clean and even the gangway was newly painted. At the top, a man in a smart uniform looked at him and Tom hesitated.

'Oh, I'm from Brown and Saxon.' The man looked down at the folder of drawings he was carrying.

'I see, sir, you have a pass I presume?' Tom had to search to find which pocket it was in. He was not used to being challenged, as he was free to walk on board during all those weeks he'd worked on the plans. 'On business then? don't forget we sail in two hours, you won't want to find yourself on the way down to Tilbury will you sir.'

'No, not likely,' Tom was wondering what would happen in such a case. 'Just some checking on these plans.'

It was very shipshape now, though there were a few men having to sail down to Tilbury while completing some unfinished work. A few of the passengers were now on board, though the bulk of them would be boarding at Tilbury. As he looked over the side, he saw a few groups of people, some waving and a few still boarding. Better have a quick look round, he thought and made his way to the upper decks.

Tom slowly walked round on one of the upper decks, taking his time. He dwelt upon the prospects for those escaping to a new life. Then he went up to the next deck and from between two life boats, looked out onto the dock, over to the ships on the other side. He leaned on the rail and looked down at the flickering water. His mind turned to thinking about his time at Fentons. He missed some of his old colleagues, and he was wondering if they missed him. Was there any more future in his present work than there was there? He dismissed these thoughts, for though he liked the ships, he was sometimes afraid that his personal life would interfere with his work. Turning away, he went back down to the deck below. At the forward end of this long promenade deck, he went through a door, down a few steps to where he found himself in the children's nursery or play room.

As there was no one else there, he sat on a seat, but a few minutes later, an attractive woman came in to the nursery with two young girls.

'Good afternoon,' Tom said with a smile and immediately opened a drawing to look businesslike.

'Oh, we mustn't disturb you,' she said with concern.

'You're not disturbing me,' Tom said. 'Carry on!' One of the girls climbed onto a rocking horse and as the woman sat down on the same seat as Tom, she gave him a nice smile.

'Off to Australia then?' Tom said for something to say.

'Had to get away,' she said, looking flustered.

'I see... er your daughters?'

'My two troubles,' she chuckled.

'I wouldn't mind going to Australia, but I think I'd want to come back sometime!'

'You're working then, are you?'

'Yes, a bit of checking before she sails away with you all!'

'There's only the three of us,' she said, surprising Tom.

'Oh, er... you mean?'

'Yes, I'm divorced, no need to be embarrassed.'

'No, I'm sorry.'

'Don't be,' she said, and lit a cigarette.

'What will you do out there?'

'My sister lives in Brisbane, she's asked me to come.'

'Oh, that's good, you've got somewhere to go then.'

Three blasts on the ship's siren sounded the warning to those on board that the ship was about to sail. Tom and the woman looked at each other, then it was silent.

'That means, you've got to go ashore I suppose?'

'No hurry,' he said, defiantly.

'But are you staying on board then?'

'Yes, to Tilbury,' Tom found himself saying. Another long blast sounded the last warning. Tom felt he was being foolish, but was mesmerised. The gangways would be drawn away and he'd be on his way downstream and no turning back. In a sudden panic, he realised he had no idea how long it would take to get to Tilbury.

Chapter 11
Sailing Down to Tilbury

It was quiet in the office, on a warm afternoon, with hardly any sound other than the soft rustling of papers from a gentle breeze that aerated the room, with the windows open at each end. Brian looked at his watch, he was thinking about the Maltan; should be about to sail now! He walked up the passage to look out of the window towards where the Maltan was docked. Tom had gone over there about an hour before. He saw a blast of steam, then the sound reached him of the siren, three blasts were blown. So Brian decided to have a wander over to see if he could find Tom, he thought he would probably be standing on the quayside, watching the ship leaving from where she'd been lying for all those months.

Brian hurried along and as he neared the ship, he saw that the gangways had just been drawn away. There was no sign of Tom, the ropes were being winched up and the tugs were skilfully moving the ship out from the quay. It was then that Brian spotted the solitary figure come to the rail, high up on the deck below the life boats. Brian cupped his hands up to his mouth.

'Tom!' he shouted, but he didn't seem to hear him. Again he shouted and he saw Tom look at him and wave. Brian was bewildered and surprised to see him still on board, so he shouted, 'Tilbury then?'

'Yes!' Tom just nodded, said no more, then disappeared from the rail.

Over on the port side, Tom looked out across the gently rippling waters of the dock to the ships on the other side, glinting in the sunshine. The ship was slowly moving out as the tugs did their work. As he watched with interest, he was wondering what it was like to be a stowaway, and decided he was never likely to try. He looked towards the nose tug as the ship neared the huge open metal lock gates. There were several barges in the dock and Tom wondered if the tug was going to touch them as they were two and three abreast along side some of the ships. Tom was clutching his drawings tightly and hoped he looked business like. He thought of the attractive woman, mother of two children that he'd met in the nursery. She had long, straight black hair as did one of her daughters, who was riding on the rocking horse. Tom had come out on deck to see if the gangways had been pulled up, but he did not hurry and was too late to go ashore. Then he saw Brian, a small figure on the quayside, shouting. Tom quickly answered and turned away. After a while he looked back into the nursery, but there was no one there. A feeling of emptiness and slight sickly panic swept over him. He took a few deep breaths as he had done so often to steady his agitation.

He stood at the ports looking out over the bow as the tugs hauled the ship steadily through the open gates into the lock.

Time passed. As the ship was slowly lowered to the level of the river, it was after high tide, but the water level in the dock had to be constant; high water times varied considerably at different times of the year. Tom had read about the floods that occurred at times when the water level rose on an extra high tide. Eventually, the tugs eased her out into the river, all twenty two thousand tons and hauled her nose round to continue down stream. Two red sailed barges steadily approached, a beautiful sight as they passed on the port bow. The clock on the bulkhead behind, was now at half past five, well over an hour since the gangways were removed.

Back along the promenade deck, Tom looked across marshes, where it was so bleak, he thought of Charles Dickens. There was nobody about on the deck, but he thought he'd better justify his stay on board, so he went down and walked about the ship making some notes on the plans. It was surprising how much he found to put in that could be added later, though they wouldn't get the amended plans till the end of the return journey, in over three months' time.

He found his friendly baker, just as if he'd always been there.

'You still on board? Running away to sea, are you then?'

'Getting off at Tilbury.' Tom was hoping the man would offer him one of those fresh baked rolls again, but no such luck and he couldn't bring himself to ask. He walked on, back up to one of the lounges and sat down by a table and made a few notes. By this time he was feeling fed up with the drawings, mainly because he was getting hungry!

'Hello!' Tom recognised the soft and slightly husky voice. It was the lady he'd met with her two daughters in the nursery.

'Oh! hello,' Tom smiled.

'You all finished then?' She sat down beside him.

'Yes, you don't know what time we get to Tilbury I suppose?'

'No idea,' she said, 'one of the stewards would know.'

'Trouble is, I'm a bit hungry.'

'Hang on,' she said, and walked away. She was soon back with a plate of sandwiches. 'Tuck in, the steward said we should get to Tilbury about eight to half past.'

'Thank you, this is good of you. Are you going to have one?'

'No, I'll be eating later.' She brushed aside her hair.

'Oh... yes of course. I must owe you for the sandwiches?'

'No, nonsense! You never intended to stay on board, did you?'

'Well... what gave you that idea?'

'I guessed!' Her eyes came close to Tom's, making him wish he didn't have to get off at Tilbury. He was lost for words. 'Come on, you're not eating. My name's Cathy, by the way.'

'I'm Tom. It's a pity... such a short meeting.'

'That's how life goes, you'll find out one day.'

'Oh, I do know that, I think,' he said with a smile.

'I'll be starting a new life where I'm going. You've got a lot to learn yet, I should imagine, Tom. You seem very shy, if you don't mind me saying so.'

'I expect you're right.' He was looking into her dark eyes. 'Where are your two girls?'

'I've put them to bed early, they were tired.' She paused. 'There's a little bar through there – perhaps you would join me in a drink?' She was getting up from the seat.

'That would be nice.' Then: 'Oh dear...um, I'm afraid I haven't got much money on me!'

'I shouldn't let that worry you, it'll be down to me.'

'Oh, if you're sure...'

'Come on, I like company.'

Saying no more, Tom picked up his drawings and followed her. She had him under her spell, lured by her charm.

'What do you normally drink Tom?'

'Oh, just a small beer please.'

'Charge that to my account, fifty seven B'

'Of course Mrs Leapman,' the steward said, and Tom thought he gave her a funny look.

'That will do, steward, thank you,' she said, with a look of annoyance 'We'll go and sit over there where we can look out through the ports.'

'This is nice,' Tom said, feeling more confident as they sat down at their table.

'He's a funny one that!' Cathy whispered, leaning over the table. 'Over familiar.'

'Yes... I thought so. Is he bothering you?'

'No, I can deal with him. It's because we're emigrants, Tom.'

'Oh! But you've only just started on a long voyage, and you've got weeks ahead of you. Are you going to be all right?'

'Of course, Tom, it was my fault. I was up here soon after we boarded.' She still spoke in whispers. 'Left the children in the nursery, a lady who calls herself the Nanny looks after the children, but she can't be everywhere. Think that steward is an old hand at looking out for women on their own, doesn't bother me though now I've got the measure of him.'

'Well, I sincerely hope so... for your sake, Cathy. I won't see you once we get to Tilbury. Wish I was staying on board now, all the way to Australia.'

'That would be a laugh!' And she laughed loudly, mainly for the steward's ears, Tom thought. 'Where have you got to get to from Tilbury?'

'Forest Gate. I'll get a train I suppose, if I've got the fare.'

'Can I help you?' She leaned over and put a warm hand on his.

'No! of course not. I was joking. I should buy you a drink.'

'This evening's on me,' Cathy said as she got up and went to the bar. Tom saw her talking to the steward as he refilled the glasses. She was gesticulating, as if she was putting him in his place.

'I thought the steward served drinks at the table.'

'I wanted a word with that one, Tom.'

At Tilbury, they berthed at a long floating landing stage, where the rest of the passengers would come on board.

'It's been very pleasant meeting you, Cathy, and I wish you luck. It seems a shame, I mean we most likely will never see each other again!'

'It was nice meeting you too. Now mind you get that train all right.' She squeezed his hand with both of hers.

'Wish we'd met before you decided to go to the other side of the world.'

'Go on, don't be silly,' she said. 'I'm twice your age, you've a lot to learn. Enjoy life while you have the chance and good luck to you.' He got up to go. 'Don't forget your drawings!'

'Oh thanks!. I'll say goodbye then, and I hope things go well for you.' He went out and along the deck, it took him a while to find the crew gangway. He was feeling sad, and a little stupid, but he remembered her words that he should enjoy life while he had the chance.

At the bottom of the gangway, away from where the passengers were boarding. a uniformed officer was examining papers.

'Have you got your papers?' The man held out his open palm.

'Yes,' Tom said firmly, 'I was working on board.

'Where are you from then?'

'Brown and Saxon.' He took out his pass, and the man eyed it.

'Bit off beat, aren't you?'

'Just a last bit of work on these plans. I have to get back to Forest Gate.' The man looked at his watch and smiled as he looked at Tom and the others waiting behind to go ashore.

'You'd better hop it then, hadn't you? Go through the crew gate on the right.' He pointed with his thumb behind him, indicating across the linking girder bridge as he looked at the next man's papers.

There was a cool breeze getting up as he walked over the bridge and the lights were just coming on. Walking with late workers and crew, he felt rather like a piece of wood drifting along in a stream, with a few floating leaves moving in the same direction. He thought about those people going all the way to Australia in the hope of finding a better life. Would it be? Maybe for some. Tom was anxious about getting back to Forest Gate. As he looked Eastwards across marsh lands, The Old Fort was just visible where mist was forming, looking bleak in the twilight. Uniformed officers were at the gate, watching those stragglers with eagle eyes.

'You!' said a tall, dark blob in a peaked cap, pointing at Tom. 'Where are you from, what have you got there?'

'Brown and Saxon, these are ship's plans I've been checking.' Tom showed him his pass. 'I have to get back to Forest Gate.'

'Yes, I see.' He looked closely at the pass and the drawings, squinting in dim light. 'How come you were left on the ship?'

'I hadn't finished, so I stayed on board.'

'You should have had a permit, you know, to stay on board.'

'Oh, yes, I suppose so. The checking took longer than I thought... I got carried away!'

'Carried away all right!' he said sarcastically. 'You'd better get a move on then!'

The railway station was just a little way from the gate that Tom had emerged from. The train terminus was at the point where passengers to and from the ships went through the customs building. The booking office was closed, so Tom enquired about trains that evening, from a man at the customs.

'Not tonight, last one went twenty minutes ago. You'll have to get a bus to the town station.'

As Tom left, he saw an old bus leaving with the men who had come out of the gate. He put out his arm as he ran to attract the driver, but he was too late!

'You was unlucky there,' a man said.

'Blast! Any buses to the town station tonight?'

'Should be in fifteen minutes, goes round the houses though, get there quicker walking guv. Where you trying to get to?'

'Forest Gate.'

'Should make that all right, keep up Ferry Road, about a mile to the station, there's plenty of trains from there.' He pointed to the bleak road.

Holding on to those ship's plans, Tom strode out at a fast pace as he was not wearing an overcoat, it was chilly and he wished he'd come off the boat with more haste. He passed a sign to the Worlds End, an isolated pub near The Old Fort. Light from a window was the only sign of life. He walked over the railway and up a hill. There were streets, some of which were named after far off foreign cities that were part of the old British Empire.

He was beginning to worry because it would be quite late when he eventually got back to his lodgings. He was thinking he would be locked out as the old lady, Mrs Blackburn, hardly removed from the Victorian era, bolted the door at ten and he would not be able to get in without a disturbance. The thought of that made him shudder.

He could stay somewhere in Tilbury and get an early train on Saturday morning to get to work. There would be some explaining to do. But at the thought of spending a chilly night in some station waiting room, he was past caring. The unmistakable fragrance of fish and chips wafted into his nostrils and he was suddenly aware that he was hungry. Following the delicious smell, he soon saw the glowing sign at the shop. He walked past the serving counter through to the cafe at the back where the tables had red and white squared oil cloth. He was served by a lady who called him deary. Time didn't seem to matter as he enjoyed cod and chips.

The street was not very interesting, though there were a few shop windows, and he began to feel cold again. So when he saw a public house on the other side of the road, he quickly crossed over. He could hear a piano being strummed and there was laughter which lured him inside, even though in his pocket he had only about two pounds left to see him through. The usual Friday night's merriment made getting to the bar no mean feat and two men drinking pints stood aside.

'Let the chap get in; he's probably thirsty!'

'Better serve this gent first Flo,' said another.

'Oh, thank you,' Tom said.

'Yes, love?' said the voluptuous barmaid smiling brightly.

'Bitter please!' Tom shouted above the noise.

'Pint of bitter it is.' And she was pouring him a pint before he could say a half. He was dazed by the general hubbub. As she pulled the beer pump he had a titillating glimpse between her breasts.

'There you are, my love, ninepence please.' She was laughing and glancing about as remarks were shouted. 'Thanks, dear.'

'Come on Flo,' came a voice next to Tom as a man tapped his glass on the counter. I wonder how she stands it, he was thinking. The Friday night, pay day revelry. He would have to wait till Monday for his not too princely sum, having missed his pay packet.

'You're not from round here are you?' said the man with the empty glass. 'Thanks Flo.' She took his glass.

'No, I've... been working.'

'Thanks Flo, I love you!' He slapped the money on the bar and picked up his refilled pint. 'Brought your work with you have you then?' he said, looking at the plans Tom was carrying. 'Office work is it?'

'Ship's plans, I came off the Maltan this evening.'

'Emigrant ship!' He half emptied his glass.

The man at the piano struck up again, obviously a popular character there playing in his own unique way, an octave tremolo between thumb and little finger on his right hand while thumbing away discordantly with his left. He knocked out a recognisable tune in this way which was almost drowned anyway by the loud singing that started up. They sang vigorously, as if to detach themselves from a burdensome and stressful survival.

'OK, Flo,' said the man next to Tom, 'and our friend here.' pointing at Tom's almost empty glass.

'No thanks, really.'

'Go on, have another pint,' the man pressed him.

'Well,' he finished up the glass, 'if you insist!'

'I'm Mickey, most here call me Mick though. What do we call you then?' He was looking Tom straight in the eye.

'I'm Tom.'

'Right, Tom. Staying in Tilbury are you?'

'No, at Forest Gate, I'm stranded here!' Tom took a mouthful of beer. 'Too late to go back there now, I'd be locked out.'

'Locked out!' the man chuckled.

'Well, the old girl who runs the boarding house, she's a bit old fashioned and locks the door at ten or soon after.'

'Go on!'

'Never said I was going to be late, missed the meal and...'

'Huh, you don't want to let them scare you. Why not phone?'

'It's a bit late now anyway, I'll have to stay somewhere.'

'She sounds a bit of a witch, Tom, a bloody witch, mate.' The singing suddenly got louder as more joined in, including Tom's dubious drinking crony, who turned his back to the bar, sang raucously and spilt some of his beer. Then he drank up the rest. 'Another one, Tom?'

'No thank you.' He put his hand over the glass. 'I should buy you one really,' he said, though he thought Mick had already had too much; he was already holding another beer that someone had bought for him.

'Tom Tom the piper's son!'

'No look, I must go, to see if I can find somewhere to stay. In the station waiting room if necessary.'

'That!' Mick swayed a bit and put his arm round Tom. 'That won't be necessary, just listen to me now, this is on the level. I can help you.'

'Oh, can you?' Tom said, feeling embarrassed. Mick spoke right into his right ear, there was so much noise in the bar.

'I thought you were,' he hesitated, 'looking for something.'

'Yes, well, it's a matter of where to stay!'

'Give us your plans,' he scribbled in pencil an address. 'There you are, number twenty four, Nell will fix you up, say Mickey Boy sent you.' He gave him some directions. 'Trust me! You'll be all right there, Tom.'

As Tom walked briskly along the street, he wondered what he'd let himself in for. He found number twenty four in part of a terrace of tall houses, went through a gate that squeaked, and he was looking at a shabby green door with glass panes in the upper half and an upright letter box knocker. He knocked and waited, but he heard no sound, so after a minute, he knocked again, a little louder. A light went on in the hall, and a woman's voice behind the door called out.

'Who's there?'

'Mickey Boy sent me!' Tom called through the letter box.

'Hold on a minute.' She unlocked the door, and opened it about two inches. 'Well?'

'He said to ask for Nell. I was wondering if...'

'I'm Nell. You're a bit young aren't you!'

'He said you could fix me up, for the night I mean.' She opened the door wide, and he could see she was wearing a pink frilly house coat.

'You'd better come in, hadn't you, no sense in standing out there in the cold.'

He stepped inside and she locked the door. It was a narrow

hall and he slightly brushed against her as she turned.

'Thank you.' There was an aroma in the house, a mixture of perfume and mustiness.

'Come along then.' Tom followed her through the hall and he saw she had long black hair, but when she turned round in the light at the foot of the stairs, he could see she was older than he had first thought and over made up. 'So you just want somewhere to stay then, nothing else?'

'Well yes, I came down the river on the Maltan... working, and I can't get back to Forest Gate tonight.'

'You just want a room for the night then, and you haven't any luggage?'

Tom gave an embarrassed laugh.'No, just these plans of the ship, that's all.'

'You're lucky, you know, there's a spare room you can have. Come into the kitchen and have a cup of tea, love.'

'That's good of you.'

'I was going to make some, sit down then.' She pulled out a chair and Tom sat at the table. 'This is not a good place to be stranded in you know.' She poured the hot water into the tea pot and put it on the table.

'Have you lived in Tilbury long?' Tom asked.

'Years, I've been 'ere... what did you say your name was?'

'I didn't, it's Tom,.....Tom Hunt.' She poured the tea.

'I've had a hard time of it, my son was killed in the war.'

'I'm sorry... but, his father?'

'He was a rotter, left me before the war, it's been bloody hard, meant desperate measures, see!'

'I'm terribly sorry.' Tom was lost for words.

'You're a nice young man, and I'm as hard as bloody nails so don't go feeling sorry for me, mate.'

'I'm sure that's not true.' Tom drank his tea, trying not to think too deeply of Nell's plight. Tom hated the expression 'old bag', there was too much sadness there. Desperation had led a woman down that road, from which there was no turning back. He shook away those thoughts.

'I must get back, I've got a client waiting, I'll show you the room, you'll be all right there.' She led him to the top floor and a small room at the front. 'The lav's at the other end of the landing.' She turned and went quickly down to the next floor, he heard a door open and close and all was quiet.

It was a bare room with an unshaded light bulb, old lino on the floor no rug and no curtains. It was also stuffy as the window was closed. Standing on a chair, the only other piece of furniture apart from the iron bed, Tom managed to open the top sash window down a few inches. There was a dark blue blind but the cord was broken. He reached this by standing dangerously with one foot on the bed end rail and the other foot on the window sill. He thought of the consequences of slipping and falling towards the window as he struggled to move the blind which had been allowed to fly up at some stage, becoming wedged between the roller and the top of the window. When he pulled it down it would not stay there. In desperation, he folded two of his plans that he'd been guarding with such care, and wedged each tightly in between the ends of the blind batten and the window frame. He hated uncovered windows at night.

He walked softly along the landing, on boards that had no floor covering but were stained black and creaked. In the lavatory there was no wash basin, but he dared not creep down to find a bathroom. Back in the room, he removed his shirt and trousers then switched off the light at the door, which left him in darknes. But the bed was just on the other side of the door. The sheets felt rough and he hoped there were no bed bugs!

That night, Tom dreamt of Connie and of other people he'd known at Fentons. A loud bang, which could have been a door slamming, disturbed his sleep. Then, it was as if he'd woken up, it was light, there was no blind at the window, and in the far corner there stood a pair of crutches. He heard the door open and he turned to see a very tall woman dressed in black, standing looking at him. He buried his head under the bedclothes and did not move for a long time. When he eventually looked up, the blind was still down, and faint light was showing. He decided that it was a vivid dream and not a ghost. He had no idea what time it was as it was too dark for him to see his watch. He drifted off to sleep again and woke much later to some noise downstairs. It was quite light.

When he made a move and removed the folded plans from the blind, it shot up and he was wide awake. To his horror, he had overslept and it was almost nine o'clock. He should have been at work! He quickly put on some clothes and went down to the next floor and found a bathroom with a squeaky door handle. It was the dingiest and the most untidy bathroom imaginable, with an old fashioned stained bath. The gas geyser over the end looked very intimidating to Tom. He washed in cold water, there were some towels and he picked one that looked clean enough.

Unshaven and clutching his plans, he ventured downstairs where he found Nell in the kitchen. She was wearing a flowered cotton dress, a red belt and pink carpet slippers.

'Morning!' Tom said, trying to appear bright.

'Cup of tea, ducks?' She was just pouring two cups, and placed them on the table.

'Yes please,' Tom nodded. 'Overslept, I'm afraid!'

'Hungry, are you?'

'I am a bit.'

'Would you like some bacon and fried bread?'

'If you can spare it, that would be fine thanks.'

'I wouldn't ask you if I couldn't spare it, would I?' She laughed and pushed her hair back over her shoulder. There were a few grey hairs that Tom hadn't noticed the previous night. He wondered if she was alone in the house.

'Is...?' Tom indicated towards the door. 'I mean upstairs...'

'Don't worry, Jack's gone, comes here every Friday and clears off early.'

'Thought I heard a door slam.'

'Sorry about that, love, he don't give a bugger!'

'Oh... that's all right, it really didn't matter.'

He enjoyed the bacon and fried bread, and had the strange

feeling that he almost didn't want to leave, but Nell was from a world so unlike his. Though his was not greatly happy, it was by no means a hard one.

'I want to say thank you very much for putting me up.'

'Glad to have been a help to you!'

'How much do I owe you?'

'Shall we say five bob, love.' She put her head on one side and came quite close to him with a wry smile that made Tom feel a little ill at ease.

'Oh, that's fine.' He felt for the money in his pocket and put two half crowns into her palm, whereupon, she put her other hand onto his, holding tightly and trembling.

'You can stay a while if you want to. I like you.' She turned and coughed.

'Er... thank you, I really must go.'

'Yes, I know dear, call sometime if you want to!'

As Tom left the house that morning, he was almost overwhelmed by a feeling of dreadful sadness, for Nell seemed like a woman so beaten down by life, yet she had survived the hardship. No wonder she was a bit rough. And Tom had sensed a deep kindness beneath that coarse veneer. But Nell would probably never crawl out of that rut, and that thought made him shudder.

Tom found a phone at the station and made the dreaded call to his office. As luck would have it, Mr Guthrey was not in that morning and he spoke to his senior designer colleague.

'Hello Mr Mathews, Tom Hunt speaking.'

'Good morning! Where are you?'

'I'm at Tilbury!'

'Tilbury?' Mr Matthews gave a laugh. 'What are you doing there?'

'I came down on the Maltan. I was working on those additions to the plans, and... well, I didn't get off soon enough.'

'That was crazy! So you stayed in Tilbury then?'

'Yes, didn't Brian mention it? I mean, he saw me leaving!'

'No, he didn't tell me.'

'Now I have to make my way to work somehow.'

'What, at this time! Not worth it, see you on Monday, Tom.'

'If that's all right.'

'Yes of course, and have a good weekend.'

'Oh, yes... thank you, see you on Monday then Mr Mathews.'

Tom made his way back to his lodgings at Forest Gate by train and bus, feeling quite pleased with himself. He sat on the bus, enjoying the journey on that sunny Saturday morning. He wasn't worried about how he was going to explain to Mr Guthrey what had happened – it probably wouldn't be necessary.

Chapter 12
Stoneleigh House

Freedom! Tom was thinking as he rode on the bus from the station. He thought of life as a pattern that was full of unexpected surprises. There were rules of behaviour to be adhered to, though he was not always very good at it. His adventures from the day before had been a lesson. Life is seldom fair or free. We have no choice of background; we are born, and it may be into a life of struggle or great fortune. Honesty was important, but at times it had got Tom into trouble. If all people were honest, then hypocrisy could not exist!

Saturday was his favourite day. When he escaped from work at twelve, it was as though the weekend would last for ever, it was magical. Getting a day off midweek was not the same; it lacked that magic. So finding himself free all day Saturday was a bonus, though he did not feel the elation he always felt when he broke off with the others at midday. For a moment he thought of old Mr Fenton, and his apprenticeship days.

The bus slowed. This was his Forest Gate stop. As he walked past the shops, and large houses dating from an age of architectural splendour, Tom contemplated what Mrs Blackburn's attitude would be if she knew where he'd spent the night. She would probably get the wrong idea, as she was from a bygone era and lived the lifestyle of that time. He doubted she would understand the problems of real hardship. But what did he know of her life? He could be quite wrong! Tom was not naive, and knew about vice and such things, but he would rather her not know the details of the previous night, even though it was all quite innocent. Though Mrs Blackburn presented the image of a strict Victorian lady, it was rumoured, jokingly, that she shared her bed with Mr Robinson, an elderly lodger.

Mr Gallagher, an Irishman aged about forty, with a small moustache, hornrimmed spectacles and a smart grey suit, was at breakfast early. 'Thank you Jessie,' he called down to the kitchen as he took his boiled egg, bread and butter from the dumb waiter. He managed a shoe shop, was good humoured and well liked. Not all those who lodged at Stoneliegh House worked on Saturday. He was soon joined by Dr.Desiri, an Indian doctor who partnered a practice at the other end of the street. Though they were from widely different cultures and occupations, the amiable conversation between them was often very humorous.

'Good morning, Doctor,' Mr Gallagher said brightly.

'It's a nice morning, yes indeed,' Doctor Desiri replied as he went to the dumb waiter. 'Any sign of young Thomas Hunt?'

'Would you think he's run away?' Mr Gallagher said in his lilting Irish tone.

'Perhaps he would stay with a young lady?'

'Anything's possible, Doctor.' Then Mr Sheet walked in. 'Top of the morning, Mr Sheet, nice morning!'

'Morning.' Mr Sheet said dully. He was still half asleep.

'Any sign of Tom Hunt?' Mr Gallagher asked.

'I didn't hear him come in, I thought I'd better not knock on his door as I went by in case he was having a lay in.'

'I don't think we should trouble ourselves over him, he can take care of himself, to be sure!'

'Left the country, I imagine!' said the doctor with a grin.

Fortunately for Tom, who had no overcoat, it was a warm morning. The sun was glinting off the window panes of the large suburban houses dating from the late Victorian era. As he turned into the tree-lined road, he was wishing he had managed to phone the night before. He paused for a moment when he reached Stoneliegh House to take in a few deep breaths, then walked up the tiled pathway with his eyes fixed on the doorway at the top of the steps that led up over the basement. As Tom stood in the porch to get out his key, Mr Sheet opened the door. He hesitated with a look of surprise to see Tom there, then his expression changed to one of amusement.

'Good gracious!' We were all wondering where you'd got to.' Tom hesitated, still clutching his plans as they stood there smiling at each other. 'Hello Mr Sheet, I got stuck on a ship, I had to do some last minute work on the Maltan, went down to Tilbury.'

'To Tilbury?' Mr Sheet said with amazement. 'We wondered where you were as there was no message. You spent the night there then, did you?'

Tom explained what had happened, and Mr Sheet looked amused. 'Was Mrs Blackburn very annoyed?' Tom asked.

'No. I don't think so, I think she was worried!'

'Is she around?'

'I think she's in the kitchen, you'd better go and see her before she rings the police and reports you missing.'

'That would never do, I'll go and find her.'

'I wish you luck,' Mr Sheet said with a laugh. 'You better have a shave,' he added, pointing at Tom's chin. 'I'll see you later and you can tell me all about it!'

Tom got on well with Mr Sheet, but although they often got into pleasing conversation, they never discussed Mr Sheet's line of business. That remained discreet. Tom thought he most likely worked in a local government office. Nor were they on Christian name terms, though that was quite conventional. Mr Sheet was a short plump man, balding and a bachelor, though Tom thought probably not by choice. He was always falling for different women; it was a favourite topic of conversation among some of the men guests. Mr Sheet professed to be a teetotaller. One day, when he and Tom were discussing parties, he said he became intoxicated just by the vapours from the drinks!

There was no one in the hall. Tom went up to his room at the top and put the plans safely in a drawer. He was glad of a good wash and shave at last. With some feeling of trepidation, he went down to the basement kitchen in search of the lady of the house. He found Jessie on her own, putting some plates away and she turned as Tom came in. He always felt a magnetic attraction towards her; she radiated charm.

'Hello, Jessie.'

'Good morning,' she said with a nice smile. Unlike Tom, she showed no sign of shyness as she walked towards him.

'Is Mrs Blackburn, er...' He was suddenly mesmerised as he looked into her sparkling eyes and he dried up.

'She went upstairs just now,' Jessie said, still smiling.

'Oh, I've just missed... I'll look for her upstairs.' They stood facing each other. Tom was dumbstruck for what seemed ages, though in reality, it could only have been a second or two. She was so very pretty, with her long, light blond hair, a pale smooth complexion and a smile that matched the brightness of her eyes.

As Tom went back up the dark basement stairs, he felt ruffled by his lack of confidencewith the young maid. In the hallway he paused for a moment's thought, then sauntered slowly towards the garden at the back. Jessie lingered in his memory, a vision in her light green dress and frilly white apron, with dewy blue eyes. He wanted to go back down to the kitchen, just to see her again, but he couldn't think of an excuse. What would he say?

His thoughts were suddenly shattered when he saw Mrs Blackburn come to the foot of the garden steps. She was carrying some flowers. 'Oh! there you are Mr Hunt!' she said, with an enquiring smile that Tom found a little daunting.

'Hello Mrs Blackburn,' he hesitated, 'I'm sorry if I worried you, but...'

'You should let me know if you're going to be away!'

'Yes, I know, but I didn't know I wouldn't get back.'

'Get back from where? You should have phoned!'

'I would have, but I was stuck on a ship, working late!'

'I see, Mr Hunt. Well, I hope this won't be a regular occurrence. I have to know where my guests are, you should know that.'

'Yes I understand, but it was late and there was no phone where I was.'

'No phone? I hope it was a decent place,' she said with an expression of curiosity.

'No! I mean yes, but there was no phone there.' Tom gave an embarrassed laugh.

'Well, you're here now. We were a little worried that's all, we have to have codes of behaviour, there are standards, I'm sure you know all about that, Mr Hunt.'

'Yes, of course, but it was really difficult this time!'

'Yes I'm sure. You'll be out today, will you?'

'Yes, and I will be here for this evening's meal if...'

'For dinner? As long as we know.' She gave a little smile.

'Thank you, and sorry again over last night.'

'Go on, we'll say no more about that!'

Later, Tom telephoned home and told his parents he would probably stay with them for a day or two in three weeks time, at the start of his summer holiday. There was a rota system for the staff at work and he would be off for a fortnight, but had made no special arrangements. He thought he might go for a cycling tour for part of the time, as he could afford little else. Making a phone call from Stoneliegh meant asking the operator the cost of the call and filling in a record book that was kept on the phone table in the hall, name, date, time, length of the call and the cost – a strict house rule!

Stoneleigh House was an imposing, grey-walled detached house with a shaded frontage facing north. It was a splendid example of Victorian architecture, with a basement and three floors above. Vast numbers of these fine houses were built, where large families resided and they afforded an army of servants, albeit tradition tells us, they worked for a pittance, though many were quite proud. It is strange how it all came about and how it vanished, dissolved with the collapse of a way of life. These large dwellings were gradually being used as boarding houses or hotels. The side entrance led to where the sun shone on the path and garden at the back, with white stone steps down to the basement kitchen door.

The front door opened onto a wide hall with a fine staircase on the right. To the left, the main room was divided by heavy folding shutters; the lounge at the front was furnished in mahogany, and included a red velvet chaise longue and matching curtains. The dining room was at the back with a dumb waiter hatch to pull up from the kitchen, this also had fine mahogany furniture in the best of Victorian taste. The large table could seat up to twelve when fully extended. The room dividing shutters were seldom closed and often two fires were lit during the winter. The front room on the right of the hall was called the music room, it was over furnished, and almost crowding out the grand piano. Down the hall and beyond a door leading down to the kitchen, there was a small room on the right, used as a library, study or morning room where there was a small table.

Peter Gordon was in the library studying engineering, busily writing on sheets of foolscap, with his books spread around him, swotting for an exam. Recently demobbed from the Royal Air Force, with his dark pointed moustache, he looked typical of his generation. He glanced up at the window where a beam of sunlight showed up the tiny particles of dust in the air. The door opened and Tom came into the room.

'I'm sorry,' Tom said, as he saw the smart-looking gentleman with the moustache, working at the table.

''That's all right, you're not disturbing me,' said Peter, with an outstretched hand. 'Peter Gordon, I'll be staying here for a while. You're a resident I presume?'

'Yes, – I'm Tom Hunt!'

'Glad to know you Tom – Peter Gordon, but call me Peter.'

Tom nodded and smiled, then hesitated as he looked at the papers and books on the table. 'You're very busy, I mustn't stop you!'

'Glad of a break, old man,' Peter said, lighting up a pipe.

'Oh, yes I see,' Tom paused. 'What are you studying?'

'A lot about general construction, strength of materials and that kind of thing.'

'Are you a draughtsman?' Tom asked.

'Good lord no, I'm far too interested in engineering to be a draughtsman!'

'Oh?' Tom said, feeling a little put out. 'Well, that's what I do! And it covers a wide field of experience in design with an engineering background, lots of study and practical work... I'm sorry you don't...' Tom slowed down and stopped talking as he looked along the book shelves.

'I understand the importance of good design, I can assure you of that. What I'm studying is civil engineering. I leave pure mechanical design to experts like yourself.'

'Yes, if you say so.' Patronising. boffin, Tom thought.

'Look, you seem the sort of chap that takes things to heart too much. The world's a tough place! I've been out there!'

'Yes, I know you probably have,' Tom said, and squinted through the glass doors of the book case. ' I'm sorry. It's a strange world, don't you think?'

'Yes – and no need to be sorry. You need to have a philosophy for life.'

'I see,' Tom said, not understanding what he meant.

'I've had enough studying for today!' Peter said suddenly. 'All work you know, won't do!' He looked at his watch. 'Yes!' He gathered up papers and slipped them into his briefcase. 'What do you do with yourself on a nice Saturday then?'

'I don't usually decide until the day,' Tom said.

The door opened, and it was Jessie with flowers arranged in a pot. 'Oh, excuse me,' she said and smiled radiantly as she looked at Tom. 'Hello there!'

Tom felt a tingling sensation as again he looked into her eyes. 'Hello again!' he said.

She turned to Peter Gordon. 'Sorry to disturb you both.' She walked between them and placed the flowers on the window sill, while Peter eyed her up and down.

'You're not disturbing us at all,' Peter said.

'No, not at all. They're nice.' Tom was trying to get the words in as Peter interrupted.

'And such a pretty bringer of flowers too! Where have you sprung from then?'

'Helping my aunty. She likes to have flowers in the house, it makes the air smell nice and fresh, don't you think?'

'You refer to Mrs Blackburn, I presume. Your aunt, the owner of this fine house?' Peter Gordon smiled, gesticulating with his hands parted.

'Yes, you guessed right, Mr Gordon.' She gave a self-assured smile as she arranged the flowers.

'That's very nice...'

Tom was interrupted again. 'You like it here, do you?' Peter Gordon said.

'Of course, I often visit,' said Jessie.

'And she keeps you busy too by the looks of it!'

'I enjoy helping, it's not something I have to do, Mr Gordon.'

'Oh; Peter please. Most people call me Pete! And what do they call you then?'

At that moment Mrs Blackburn called from the hallway. 'Jessie dear, come and give me a hand will you!'

'Coming, Aunty.' Jessie looked at Tom. 'Bye,' she said in a gentle whisper, giving him a little wave with spread fingers.

'So it's Jessie. I think she likes you, Tom,' Pete said after she had gone.

'Do you think so? I thought you were trying it on a bit.'

'Nonsense, old chap, I don't know what you mean!' he smiled.

'Well, I mean flirty!'

'Don't be ridiculous that's not flirting. You seem to be very much misinformed about life. I was just being friendly. She's not interested in me anyway, that was obvious:'

'I'm not very good with girls, never know what to say.'

'You shouldn't be so self-conscious, that's your trouble.'

'Yes, I know, it's silly of course,' Tom said, 'don't know how to get over the problem, I've always been... a bit slow!'

'Don't think too seriously about life, that's my advice If life was just a dream, it wouldn't worry you would it?'

'But it isn't a dream, so I get a bit nervy.'

'I should go for a walk if I were you, and forget about it.'

'Have you got a girlfriend?' Tom asked suddenly.

'Yes, in Bristol. She's marvellous, I'm crazy about her, and she's coming up to London. We're meeting in town later today.'

'Oh, that's good, I'm sorry if I...'

'Think nothing of it, Tom.' Peter was fumbling in his briefcase. 'There you are, Tom, a smasher isn't she!' He handed Tom a photograph.

'Yes, I've got to agree with you there.' She was stunning, a real beauty.

'That's Jean, she's a teacher.'

'I think you're lucky!' Tom nodded approval as he handed it back. 'How did you meet her if she lives in Bristol?'

'Simple. I'm from Bristol too, but we met in the Air Force. She drove lorries in the war!'

'Like Princess Elizabeth?'

'The war was pretty well over by then,' he smiled, 'but Jean was an Air Force driver for three years.'

'Were you... a pilot?' Tom was hesitant.

'Yes,' Peter said abruptly.

'Oh, was it very bad?' Tom felt he was intruding.

'I don't talk about it,' he said firmly.

'No, I'm sorry.' Tom didn't mention it again.

It was a warm day and Tom was anxious to get out into the sunshine. Up in his room at the top of the house, he took two pounds from a tobacco tin that he kept at the back of the top drawer of the dresser, to replenish the money he had left over in his pocket, about ten shillings. Downstairs, he looked into the music room. Old Mr Robinson, the most permanent resident, and reputedly Mrs Blackburn's loyal companion, was sitting there in a leather chair with the morning paper. Cigarette smoke curled up and he looked round at Tom through thick glasses over his cigarette-stained bushy moustache.

'Good morning, Mr Robinson.'

'Hello, young fellow. We've not really been introduced have we or was it when you first arrived?'

'I think so, in the hallway!'

'Oh yes, of course, stupid, we've not had much chance to have a little talk and get to know each other have we. Huh!' he laughed.

'Well, no.'

'You were missing last night weren't you?'

'Working late.'

'Oh... now you're back then.' He coughed.

'Yes.' Tom hesitated. 'It's a nice day.'

'Glorious!' he coughed again and stubbed out the cigarette.

'It's quite cool in this room though.'

'That's why I like to sit in here.'

'I'm just off for a walk.'

'A good idea, don't get lost will you!'

'That's not likely around here. I'll see you later then Mr Robinson.'

'Yes, dear boy.' He turned back to his paper.

Tom walked at a fast pace to work off his nervous energy, and kept up a steady pace for more than an hour. He walked onto a common where he stood by a lake and gazed across the sparkling waters where children were playing with their model boats.

He was suddenly surprised by a voice nearby. 'Hello, Tom.'

The plump man standing a few yards away seemed vaguely familiar. He was wearing a dark blue suit, and had a black beard and glasses. Tom knew he couldn't be a stranger, for he addressed him by his first name. The bright eyes, voice and humorous smile struck a faint chord, but Tom could not quite place him.

Chapter 13
A Visitor from the Past

'You don't recognise me, do you?'

Then it clicked. Of course! Tom thought back to his years at Fenton's.

'Tom Hunt, I presume?'

'Yes,' Tom said with a smile. 'Hello, Mr Wills.'

'How are you, Tom?'

'Very well thankyou.' They shook hands. 'I'm sorry, I didn't recognise you straight away.'

'It's the beard,' Mr Wills chuckled, his gleaming white teeth contrasting with the black facial hair.

'Oh yes, it's so unexpected; I mean our meeting here!'

'Yes!'

'Strange coincidence! Am I dreaming?'

'No!' I'm just as surprised to see you! How's work then?'

'OK thankyou.' They laughed together. 'I thought it was your double, um... with a beard!'

'Huh! I'm visiting a firm near here.'

'I see,' Tom said.

'Doing some business for the firm, hoping to get a contract to supply Merton pumps.'

'Oh, to a local company in this area?'

'Procters,' Mr Wills said with his usual quick smile.

'I've not heard of them.'

'They're in Leytonstone, they do gas and water engineering installation work.'

'You came up last week then?'

'Last night! I'll be going to see them on Monday.'

'I see, you've come up in good time then.'

'It so happens that I have an uncle near here. I'm staying with him.' And Mr Wills told Tom a little about his widowed uncle, whom he hadn't seen much of in recent years. 'He needs company, though I think he's managing all right now. He went off quite happy this morning after breakfast, on an organised day trip somewhere. He wanted to cancel it as I was staying with him., but I insisted he go.'

'Yes, naturally. So you're on your own then?'

'Doesn't bother me.' Mr Wills cleared his throat loudly.

They stood there looking across the lake. Tom was beginning to feel hungry now. 'Really nice here you know. My uncle lives over on the other side of the common.'

Mr Wills nodded in that direction. Tom thought of Mildred, and remembered the absurd feelings of guilt he used to have years ago. There was a pause in the conversation that seemed to echo across the lake and the sky. The silence made him feel enclosed in a strange time capsule, though it was just for a second or two.

'Are you still with Fenton's?' Tom asked.

'Yes,' Mr Wills said a trifle sharply, as if it should have been obvious.

'Oh, and what's it like there now?'

'Quiet.'

'And how is...?' Tom paused as he thought of Mildred. 'Er, how are all the others?'

'All right!' Mr Wills was always fairly economical with words.

'How's Mr Methly?' Tom asked.

'He's dead!' Mr Wills answered, as if Tom should have known.

'Oh, I'm sorry, I didn't know!' Mr Wills could be rather abrupt, but then this was his character. He smiled often, was always calm and obviously didn't take life too seriously.

'You weren't to know,' Mr Wills said and offered no more, so Tom didn't ask.

'Is Miss West still there?' Tom asked quickly.

'Yes, think she's built into the firm.' He had a more serious expression, so Tom just nodded and looked across the sparkling water.

As they stood before the lake, there was a lengthening break in the conversation. Tom's thoughts went back to the past. It was six years since that first violin lesson with Mildred. He thought back to his apprenticeship days. Even after all those years he had only ever known his boss as Mr Wills, for his senior colleagues were known to him only by their surnames.

Tom felt a sudden cool breeze from across the lake. He was desperate to break the silence, as he could not stop thinking about food.

'Do you know where one can get a bite to eat?' asked Mr Wills.

'You must have read my mind,' Tom said with relief. 'I'm famished myself, but don't know where the nearest cafe is.'

'Perhaps you'd like to join me, see if we can find a cafe or something – that is, if you've no other plans?'

'Yes, OK,' Tom said with enthusiasm and they walked round the edge of the lake towards some buildings and shops. 'What about that pub over there?'

'Shouldn't think you could get food there.'

'I was thinking, maybe we could see if they have sandwiches and we could have a drink at the same time, couldn't we?'

'Huh,' Mr Wills proclaimed loudly, 'can't think of anything I'd rather not do.'

'Oh, I see.' Tom tried not to appear disappointed.

'I'd rather have a cup of tea myself, there must be a cafe where we can get some dinner.' Tom thought back to years ago, of Mr Wills, without the beard, standing with Mildred in that little washroom drinking cups of tea. And asking her to come to the pictures.

'There's a likely place!' They'd just rounded a bend and across the road, there was a sign painted in white letters, on a small cafe window. 'The Cookery. Meals all day from breakfast till tea time,' Mr Wills read aloud. 'Shall we try there?'

'Yes, OK.' Tom hoped the food would at least be as good as that in his works staff canteen.

The meal was adequate: meat and two veg, followed by apple pie and custard, plus a cup of tea. It cost them two shillings and sixpence each, and they paid separately.

It was still very warm when they came out into the bright sunshine. 'Thank you for your company Tom,' Mr Wills said, holding out his hand.

'Oh, glad we met,' Tom said smiling. 'I'll be coming down to Newburne in a couple of weeks, so we may meet again then.'

'We'll see. The best meetings are those not arranged.'

'Yes, in a way.'

'Sorry I have to leave you, but I must do some shopping for my uncle.' Tom could see Mr Wills was anxious to get away.

'Well, best of luck on Monday!'

'Thank you, Tom.' And he walked away quickly.

It had been a strange experience, for such a meeting was surely a chance in a million. As Tom walked back to Stonliegh House by a round about route, he looked down at the pavement passing under his feet, then up to the endless sky through flakes of cloud and the blue beyond. His thoughts were of the mysteries of time and space. He liked to think of the past as not lost for ever. Tom was trying to come to terms with the uncertainties that lay ahead. He predicted drastic changes and feared for the future. He resisted the thought of some universal plan; surely it was just coincidence! Otherwise it would give a new meaning to the notion of time. If one's fate was already mapped out, it would mean it had already happened, and if the future was there, then, the past would also still be there. That would come back to his old argument again: that time only exists for us. Tom felt that could not really make sense. He smiled at his thoughts. No use brooding over it, nobody really knew, though Perhaps Albert Einstein came the nearest to understanding the universe and the infinity of time.

Back at Stoneleigh House, Tom met Mrs Blackburn coming

out of her room on the first floor landing. 'Hello, Mrs Blackburn,' he said, pretending he was delighted to see her.

'Good evening, Mr Hunt,' she said 'Remember supper is at eight!' She had the glimmer of a smile.

'Yes, I won't be late.'

Mr Gallagher and Mr Sheet were chatting as they entered the dining room. 'Have you got your wireless fixed all right?' Mr Gallagher asked.

'Yes thank you,' replied Mr Sheet with an amused smile. 'It's better now than when I bought it!'

As Tom came into the room, Mr Gallagher said, 'Ah, the hunter returns!'

'Good evening,' Tom said brightly.

'Have you had a good day?'

'Yes, I did. I met someone from my old firm in Newburne, by chance, hadn't seen him for over two years. I didn't recognise him at first, because he'd grown a beard.'

'Trying to disguise himself, I expect,' Mr Gallagher said.

'I can't picture you in a big beard, Mr Gallagher.'

There was laughter around the table. At that moment, Mrs Blackburn came in with a tall, slender young woman.

'May I introduce Miss Lovell, she's a new guest.'

'How do you do,' was murmured from the table.

'Good evening,' Miss Lovell said with a very Irish accent, and she sat down at the table opposite where Tom was sitting, giving him a big smile.

She was very pale, with straight black shoulder-length hair that shone. Her slanting eyes were accentuated by the fact that her eyebrows were smooth and almost hairless. Tom was quite intrigued; he had not been aware that some women would actually go to the trouble of plucking out the hairs, in fact he thought it a pitty to remove a natural feature. He hardly said a word during the meal, so enchanted was he by this strangely beautiful woman. Each time their eyes met, he became more spellbound, which was torture for him. He did not wish to embarrass her, so he was quite relieved when the meal was over.

Later that evening, feeling more relaxed as they sat on the red chaise longue in the sitting room, Tom and Miss Lovell chatted about local history. She was a teacher, it turned out; she showed Tom some interesting books and they spent some time poring over maps. She expressed such interest in the docks and ships that Tom said he would see if he could arrange to take her over to one of the large passenger liners some time. The charming Miss Lovell really was having an impact on young Tom.

It was getting late and Tom was suddenly jerked back to cold reality when Mrs Blackburn came into the room. 'You two still here?' she said disapprovingly.

'I better go up now,' Miss Lovell said, gathering up her books and maps as she stood up.

'I'll say good night then,' Tom said, also getting to his feet. He nodded and smiled at Mrs Blackburn and Miss Lovell as he left the room.

'Good night, Mr Hunt,' Mrs Blackburn said without turning. Tom glanced back through the door, but Miss Lovell was talking quietly to Mrs Blackburn and did not look at him. He went to bed that night thinking too much about the genteel little teacher and not getting to sleep very easily.

On Sunday morning, Tom pulled the curtains open and looked upon the start of what could be another very warm day. The London Stock bricks on the house next door were a bright yellow, with a deep shadow cast by the sun on the lower half . His room only got the sun in late evening as his window faced west. It was half past eight and he hurried down to the bathroom. He slipped a small sketch book and a pencil into his trousers pocket as a matter of habit and got to the breakfast table soon after nine, as most of the guests did on a Sunday, with the exception of Mr Sheet who was never at the breakfast table on Sundays. Mr Gallagher was in a particularly bright and joking mood and Tom was enjoying the repartee between him and the doctor. He was also thinking about Miss Lovell, who was not at the table.

'Where has our new young lady guest got to this morning?' Mr Gallagher said.

'Tired I would think,' said the doctor.

'She's very.... er... pale,' Tom said. He had stopped himself from saying 'beautiful', though the word was on the tip of his tongue.

'Perhaps a little anaemic, yes!'

'Pale and interesting, Doctor,' Mr Gallagher said. Tom was beginning to feel restless, then Peter Gordon came into the room, anxious to join in the conversation.

Tom quickly finished his toast. 'If you'll excuse me,' he said sharply and got up.

He stood on the garden steps that led down from the back. The sun was already quite warm. Sitting on the top step and feeling more relaxed, he got out his sketch book and made a study of tree branches. Someone came out of the door behind him.

'Hello there.' Tom knew the voice and looked back. Mr Sheet was in his dressing gown. 'That looks interesting.'

'Just a little sketch. Nice day again, Mr Sheet, going to be pretty warm, I think.'

'Hum.' He turned and went back inside.

After a few minutes, Tom went back into the house, and as the library door was ajar, he looked in. Mr Sheet was sitting at the table having breakfast, still clad in his dark red silk dressing gown.

'Sorry, I didn't know you were in here Mr Sheet.'

'That's all right, come in and sit down.'

'A very late breakfast?' Tom said.

'I always have a late breakfast on Sundays.' He spoke with an amused expression and Tom felt at ease with him. While they talked, Mr Sheet tucked into a boiled egg and Tom sketched him. The man's crouched repose as he concentrated on this Sunday ritual of a lone late breakfast; the dark red of his dressing gown and half-bald head against the greenish striped wallpaper and an old vignetted photograph – all this appealed to Tom. It would be a good subject for a painting, if he ever got round to it.

'I hope you don't mind me sketching,' Tom said.

'No, go ahead, doesn't worry me in the least.'

'Do you like Sundays?' Tom asked.

'Yes of course I do, don't you?'

'I sometimes feel bored on Sundays.'

'Do you know what I do? I take a ride on a bus.'

'Where do you go then?'

'Just anywhere! It doesn't matter and doesn't cost much, it takes you out of yourself.'

'Yes, seems a good idea,' Tom said. 'You never know who you might meet, do you?'

'Very true.' Mr Sheet shook his head and smiled. 'But I don't bother about meeting people, there are some people I'd rather not meet.'

'Yes I think I know what you mean.' Tom had to smile at some of Mr Sheet's ideas.

After the usual heavy midday meal, Tom took Mr Sheet's advice and caught a bus to Epping, then went for a long walk that took him out of the town and across country. Eventually he found a church with a square wooden tower and a short curved slated spire was topped with a golden ball. He spent some time sketching the church among the trees.

It was getting late when he tried to find his way to a bus stop. The path he took led him through a dark gloomy wood. There were creaking sounds as the branches moved in the breeze A lonely, panicky feeling suddenly seized him, and he walked on through the wood at an increasing speed, though not quite getting into a run as the wood grew denser and darker. He was afraid he was lost, and that the path would take him nowhere.

Then the wood began to get lighter and he found himself in an open field. He discovered a track that led to a green, where there was a good path leading straight across to some houses with lighted windows. He was relieved to see a bus stop as he came out onto the road.

When he got back to Stoneleigh House, it was too late for the usual cold Sunday evening salad, and he had to make do with what he could raid from leftovers in the kitchen. The other guests must have had an early night. Tom was glad.

Chapter 14
A Peculiar Enterprise

During the following week, Tom spent some of his time on the S.S.Chittagong, but he was mainly in the office. Now that the Maltan had sailed, he felt a sense of loss, as if it was 'his' ship. There was little mention of his adventure down the river except a joke with his good colleague Brian, who was quite eager to hear all about it. Mr Mathews came and spoke to him quietly.

'Just a word, Mr Hunt. I shouldn't say anything about your trip down the river on Friday. Mr Guthrey didn't know about it so just keep it under your hat, OK?'

'Is he likely to ask?'

'No, why should he? You'll be needing this.' He handed Tom his pay packet.

'Thankyou.' Tom tried to appear casual.

In the afternoon, dark clouds formed and there were rumbles of thunder. The office became very dim and the lights were turned on early. 'We're in for a downpour by the looks of it,' someone said. There was suddenly a bright flash of lightning and the most almighty bang of thunder. Sandy screamed and disappeared into the darkened print room.

'Hells bells!' Brian said. 'I think the Martians have arrived.'

'The lights are still on anyway,' Tom said. Heavy rain was falling on the glass North light roof windows.

'Hope it doesn't leak!' Brian said, looking up. The sound on the roof grew louder as it turned to hailstones.

'Will the glass hold?' Tom shouted above the continuous roar. Lightning flashed and there was another loud thunder crack that rattled across the heavens. They both went to the end of the passage to look across towards the docks, a murky scene obscured by the downpour. A bright bent shaft of lightning shot down at a little distance by the warehouses as if it might have struck a ship's mast.

'See that!' Brian said.

'Yes!' Tom shouted as the thunder boomed. They stood there for a while as the storm continued and the air cooled with a strong smell of rain, like no other smell. Tom thought of the previous Friday when he'd been walking about without a raincoat. If this storm had happened then... 'Wet ships plans,' he murmured to himself.

'What's that?' Brian said.

'Just thinking about last Friday.' He looked out onto the bleakness.

A strange feeling of excitement came over Tom as the lightning flashed and the thunder rolled across the chilling scene. He felt small within the vastness of the universe, where all the elements which make up everything are forms of electrical force, of which we are a tiny part. A feeling of coldness swept over him as he pondered the mysteries of this world in which he was an onlooker.

Tom turned to find his colleague had gone. There was a minor panic up one end of the office; Mr Mathews was mopping up the floor and Mr Guthrey in his grey suit was just intervening.

'Any wet drawings?' he said, pretending to look worried.

'No, just a wet floor. The heat of the sun must have cracked the roofing.' He looked up, then put a bucket under the drops.

'We'll get a man up there, when it's dry enough.'

The hailstones had stopped but there was a steady downpour of rain. Tom went back to his work, leaving the others standing around the offending droplets as if this were a debate of great importance. Tom smiled to himself.

Mr Mathews had just answered the phone.

'Tom Hunt. Telephone!' he called out.

'Coming!' Tom said.

Mr Mathews left the phone on the table and came towards him. 'A lady with a musical voice – a Miss Lovell,' he said with a smile. 'She sound's very nice!'

'Thank you,' Tom said, excited yet curious to know why she should be ringing him at work, as he hardly knew her. The black instrument waiting there on the table took on a strange character of its own, as he thought of Miss Lovell with her ear pressed to the other end of the line. He picked the receiver up carefully, as if it were her he was holding.

'Hello... Tom Hunt speaking.'

'Hello, Mr Hunt, this is Miss Lovell, sorry to bother you at work,' she said in a clear Irish voice.

'That's all right.'

'You mentioned the other night that you could arrange a visit on board a large passenger liner. The children have expressed interest and would love to do this if possible. Can you fix a day?'

'Yes, of course,' he found himself saying, while thinking: what have I let myself in for? He knew she was a teacher, but he had not been thinking of a school outing when he casually said he could take her on board a passenger liner. 'Which day were you thinking about?'

'I know it's short notice, but can it be this Friday?'

'Yes, I'm sure that can be arranged.' Tom was putty.

'That's fine, I phoned you to get it arranged as soon as possible as it's getting near the holidays. You can confirm it when I see you tonight.' Her voice went gently up and down like soft waves in twinkling sunlight; he was mesmerised.

'Yes, leave it to me...'

'That's wonderful. Goodbye then, Mr Hunt.'

'Goodbye.' He wished she'd call him Tom. His heart throbbed, for he'd got himself into an awkward situation. He didn't even know if it would be allowed. Suddenly he wondered how many kids she would bring, he'd forgotten to ask.

'Hunt,' Mr Guthrey called, 'come into my office, will you.'

'Yes, right coming.' Tom immediately wondered if he was

going to mention his absence on Friday afternoon and Saturday morning.

The rain was still steadily pouring as Tom hurried into the chief 's office.

'Sit down will you.' Mr Guthrey, behind his large mahogany desk, put his hands together and looked at the window. 'This rain is what my garden needs, but too heavy, it'll beat everything down.' He was talking as if he'd just asked Tom in for a friendly chat.

'Do you have a large garden Mr Guthrey?'

'Medium sized.' He was still rubbing his hands together and looking out of the window. Then he turned to Tom. 'Anyway, I've not called you in to talk about the weather and gardens.' He held his hands tightly together and put on a serious expression. 'I'm expecting a man this afternoon, Mr Rogers from Rogers and Cooper Marine. He's coming at half past three.' Guthrey looked at his watch. 'He could get held up by this storm of course.'

'Yes, it's pretty rough out there.' Tom looked at the window as sheets of rain rattled against the glass.

'I'm impressed by your work on the ship's plans, and you handle perspective drawing very well.'

'Thank you, Mr Guthrey.' Tom was relieved that he was not in trouble, being always apprehensive.

'How would you like to take on something more challenging?'

'Yes, whatever you say, of course.'

'Mr Rogers requires a large perspective drawing of a new barge, and I took it on to say we would be able to help him. This could also do a bit of good for you. All right, Mr Hunt?'

'Yes, well thank you.' He was glad to be praised but at the same time, he had some qualms about the challenge.

'You'll have to go along to his yard to measure the barge and make drawings. I think you can handle that, don't you?'

'Yes, it sounds interesting. When do you want me to start?'

'Probably Friday, I'll let you know when he comes in.'

That's put paid to Friday, he thought, as he walked out of Mr Guthrey's office. The chief's trust in his work gave him confidence and he couldn't check a broad smile.

'What are you smiling about?' Brian asked.

'Oh, just thinking.'

'What did old Guthrey want? Couldn't have been bad news by the way you're smiling.'

'No, it wasn't! It was quite interesting in fact.'

'Come on then, what was it all about?'

'He wants me to see a chap this afternoon about a drawing of a barge, that's if he gets here through the storm.'

'Well, I can't see that's much to smile about' Brian said.

'No... not that! I thought I was going to be on the carpet, that's all.' Tom spoke quietly. 'It was good news instead, it should be interesting.'

'What, an old barge!'

'It's not an old barge. It's a new design, and it will be a change for me anyway. Guthrey is expecting this chap Rogers any time now, though he'll probably be held up by the rain.'

'Rogers, did you say?'

'Yes.'

'If he's from Rogers and Cooper Marine, a small yard up Wapping way, he's a crook. Been in trouble with the law over all kinds of roguish and fraudulent shady businesses. Smuggling as well. I wouldn't want to do any work for him. I don't know how it is he's not in prison!'

'I don't believe you,' Tom said with a smile. 'I know you're pulling my leg.'

'God's truth, Tom, I'm not joking.'

'Oh! But I can't tell Mr Guthrey now that I don't want to do the job, can I?'

'I'm surprised at Guthrey not knowing he's a rogue.'

'But I don't know about him, Brian. He's a boat builder as far as I'm concerned.'

'You've not lived around here long. You weren't to know.'

'True,' Tom said with a nod.

'Best of luck then, Tom. Rather not be in your shoes!'

Tom was now feeling some trepidation, but he didn't see how he could get out of it.

Four o'clock passed and there was no sign of Mr Rogers. Brian stopped by, sharing Tom's anxious anticipation.

'I don't think your spiv will show up this afternoon.'

'In this weather, it wouldn't surprise me.'

'How's he getting here?'

'In his car, I think...' Tom saw Guthrey coming down the side of the office and Brian walked away.

'If you'd come in now, Tom, Mr Rogers is here.'

He was introduced to a stockily built man, a rugged character with greying hair and a bushy moustache. He wore a brown raincoat and a dark trilby hat, which he did not remove as he stood with Mr Guthrey at his office doorway.

'Pleased to meet you,' Rogers said with a voice that was not quite a pure East London accent. He gave Tom a firm handshake, looking at him with expressive eyes shadowed under bushy brows within a well worn face. 'So you're going to produce the picture for me?' He broke into a smile.

'Yes... I hope so.' Tom quickly put on an air of confidence.

'Mr Hunt can start whenever you wish,' Guthrey intervened.

'I was going to suggest he came to my yard this afternoon. Course I'm later than intended, what with the road being flooded. I came a different way round the houses, but if the young gentleman would care to come along now, the old jalopy's outside.' He looked towards the window. 'The weather seems to be brightening up a bit! How do you get here then, bus is it?'

'Yes, well trolley..'

'So, you can ride with me now then.' Tom looked back at the clock. It was half past four.

'I don't finish till half past five and...'

'You can go along with Mr Rogers now if you like,' Guthrey suggested.

'Yes,' Tom said, 'if that's all right.' He was thinking that it would make him late for the evening meal.

'Very good then, when you're ready,' Rogers said.

'Yes, I won't be a tick.' Tom hurried down the office.

'Oops!' said Sandy. She came out of the print room as Tom darted for his coat. 'You're in a hurry!'

'Sorry, Sandy, I've got a chap waiting.'

'Oh, look at you! Rushing around like no one's business,' she said with a light in her eyes.

'Yes, well can't stop,' he said and Sandy gave a burst of laughter as he rushed away, putting on his rain coat.

'There's no need to rush,' Rogers said with a look of surprised amusement.

'No, I suppose...' Tom was over reacting with excitement.

'Thank you, Mr Guthrey,' Rogers said as they shook hands. 'I'll look after your man.'

'I'm sure you'll be happy with the result,' Guthrey said.

'We'll be off then, come on Mr... er?'

'Hunt, Tom Hunt.'

'I'll leave you to it then,' Guthrey said.

'These old stone steps have seen a few feet boy, judging by the wear.' Rogers led the way, while Tom looked down at the top of the black trilby hat.

'Yes, I suppose it's Edwardian really!'

'No, older! In these places, I can feel the atmosphere.'

'And the ships have changed through the ages.'

'You're not from round here are you?'

'No, but I was apprenticed in marine engineering..'

'There we are, a beauty ain't she.' They were approaching his car which was parked in the yard, where gusts of wind swept across large puddles left by the heavy downpour.

'Yes, looks pretty powerful,' Tom said as he looked at the large, grey car.

'SS Jaguar, laid up a while in the war, not for long though.

'For business?' Tom said as they climbed into the car.

'Yea!... I have contacts.' Rogers pushed the gear lever.

'I see, so you got by?' Tom thought of his father's car standing on blocks for most of the war.

'That's right. Some are still struggling, but not me boy.' He glanced at Tom and put on a crafty expression.

'Oh...' Tom enquired no further. 'Must have been bad; the blitz, I mean!' The car bumped over cobbles and railway lines.

'Yea, boy, rough at times, we got the brunt of it, hardly touched Tilbury, but the big hotel was destroyed by incendiaries. Would take more than Hitler to knock out London's docks.'

'I would say so,' Tom said, not finding it easy to imagine what it must have been like. He'd only read and seen it in the papers and newsreels at the pictures, and it had looked very bad.

Tom was enjoying the ride in the well sprung car, taken gently over cobble stones and crossing a few railway lines before approaching the dock gates.

'Here we are.' Rogers handed his temporary pass to the man on his side while Tom showed his permanent pass and was given a humourless nod. Rogers was making a few remarks to the man. 'Yes, it's looking a bit black over there still,' he was saying. Tom thought of the gate men as cut out characters, dark and foreboding symbols of authoritarianism.

They continued onto a straight cobbled street with railway lines along one side.

'They always worry me,' Tom said. 'Make me feel guilty.'

'What do you mean, guilty?'

'The police on the gate.'

'They don't bother me, boy. You've nothing to hide have you?'

'No, not likely! It's the way they eye me up and down.'

'You don't want to let them worry you. Remember, they've got a tough job to do, they're more than ordinary customs officers. They have to deal with some pretty rough characters at times.'

'Yes, I know,' Tom said as he thought of Brian's disclosure of the man sitting beside him, mixed with his own particular experience of tough handling by the same police.

'You in a hurry?' Rogers said.

'No, not really....'

'Not really! What's that mean?'

'I'll be expected for my evening meal, usually at half past six.'

'Oh. Whereabouts are you staying?'

'Forest Gate.'

'Some good houses there.' He took his eyes off the road and glanced at Tom. 'An old aunt of mine lives about there, used to stay with her as a boy.' Tom worried as the car wobbled. Rogers seemed to be looking at him more than at the road.

'Look out!' Tom said as they narrowly missed a van.

'You don't want to worry when you're with me, boy.'

'No... of course not,' Tom said anxiously. 'It's a fine car this,' he added, hoping he was expressing confidence.

'Yes, my great pride; she's a beauty!'

Rogers had stopped talking for a while and Tom was glad of that. Their route seemed complicated, a mystery tour by high grey walls and some streets of terraced houses. They passed through areas bearing the scars of war. Grey, hollow shapes still filled with rubble and charred beams, that were once shops, warehouses and homes, now open to the sky from where the devastating horrors had emerged. This part of the scene depressed Tom and he wondered how long it would take to clear up the mess and rebuild. His mind wondered back in history and he thought about the great fire of London in 1666, when the whole city was destroyed, but that was another age and London had suffered devastation of various degrees in the past. All was rebuilt – though not necessarily in the best way!

Tom's questioning mind tended to dwell on the past, which now appeared less daunting than the uncertain present with all its problems. His telephone conversation of that afternoon with Miss.Lovell came to mind, a problem he'd got himself into by not handling a simple situation properly.

'Oh dear!' Tom said, thinking out loud.

'What's on your mind then?'

'Sorry, it's just a little private matter.'

'Oh, can I be of help at all?'

'No, I wouldn't think so.' Tom was silent for a moment. 'The thing is, Mr Guthrey mentioned that you would want me to start on your work this Friday, and...'

'No!' he said. 'Friday this week? I don't know what gave him that idea. What ever suits you, Mr Hunt. You can have a look now and come back next week.'

'Oh good, will any day next week be all right?'

'Monday suit you?' The car swung left into an open gateway, between high, old reddish brown doors leading into the yard. There was a drab old building with big letters painted on the wall: 'ROGERS AND COOPER MARINE Ltd.'

The tatty door slammed behind them with the rattle of a chain weighted by a piece of metal. The light was dim as Tom followed. They walked by old brown steel plates with rivet holes round the edges and on the other side, old boilers resting on heavy oily bulks of timber. The floor was a mixture of black earth and broken concrete where there were puddles fed by drips from the leaky roof. They emerged from the jumble.

'There we are,' Rogers said. They were looking at the straight stern of a large dark reddish brown hull under construction which dwarfed them. There was hammering somewhere inside the steel shell but Tom couldn't see any workmen.

'Very impressive. I see the propeller is fitted. Isn't it more of a ship than a barge?'

'It is a self-propelled barge. I designed it as a good commercially viable project to carry goods by river and sea.'

'Yes, I see. I was thinking of barges that are towed by a tug!'

'No, no boy, this will replace the old sailing barges, all welded construction and powered by an oil engine. Don't have to rely on the wind.'

'Yes, I see,' Tom said thoughtfully. He had a regard for the old sailing barges. 'As long as the engine doesn't conk out.' Tom gave a nervous laugh as he realised he was being tactless.

'Conk out?'

'Of course not really... umm, I'm sure it must be reliable.'

'Why should you be sure? You don't know about my engine. Well do you?' Rogers sounded offended, making Tom feel even more embarrassed.

'No, I don't... sorry.' Tom said uneasily. There was a pause as Tom thought of sailing barges and wondered what to say.

'It's the future that counts in business. It might interest you to know that in this very yard, or hereabouts, they used to build the old wooden sailing barges back in the past, long before the Port of London Authority was formed. Steeped in history this area is. See this,' Rogers turned and pointed down to a pile of old wooden pins stacked against the wall. He picked one up and handed it to Tom. 'Feel that? Hard as rock.'

'Yes, and heavy too. What are they?'

'Pins, dowel pins that held the wooden ships together. You find them in the mud where the old boats have rotted away and all that's left are the pins, fossilised.'

'Interesting!'

'You can take one or two if you're interested.'

'Thank you,' Tom said, not knowing what he could do with them but slipping two into his raincoat pocket anyway. 'Sailing barges are not a commercial proposition nowadays, I suppose.'

Rogers said no more to that and stepped onto some balks of timber bedded into the muddy floor. 'Anyhow, come and have a look up here.' He walked along the side of the boat on wet planks towards a ladder and Tom followed. 'Mind you don't slip.'

'OK, whoops!' Tom cried as he almost slipped off the board.

'Careful now, Mr Hunt, I did warn you.' Tom watched him climb up the ladder and step over a low gunwale. 'How's it going, Albert?' he heard Rogers say to a man up there. 'Coming up then?' he shouted down to Tom. 'It's quite safe.'

'Yes, OK!' He felt a bit shaky as he started to climb the ladder which was tied by a rope at the top. As he gingerly climbed up, he could hear Rogers talking to the man and not looking back down the ladder at him. Tom was thinking about the tricky task he would be tackling next week. He climbed over the gunwale with no help from Rogers who carried on talking with Albert, while holding a drawing as they discussed the work.

'If you weld the brackets to the frames each side here,' Rogers said, pointing and moving his finger across the folded drawing, 'the curved tee bar will drop in...'

'That's what I had in mind, governor.'

'Yes right!' Albert joined the other man and Rogers turned to Tom. 'You're up then.'

'Yes.' Tom forced a slight laugh. The narrow, wet steel deck surrounded an open hold and it was none too safe up there.

'We're well on the way now. Some work on the for'rd deck and the engine room aft before we're finished.'

'When will the launching be?' Tom looked towards the open end of the building where the slipway sloped down to the river. There was a yellow light in the clouds. Tom instinctively looked at his watch; it was almost six.

'Three weeks from now, give or take a day or two, time enough for you to get what information you want and finish the drawing, am I right?'

'Yes!' Tom felt sure he would be under pressure.

'These chaps are working overtime, bound to be finished on time. I just want to pop along to the office now, so I'll leave you to have a shufty for a while, alright?'

'Yes, but...'

'Take care on wet decking, don't want any accidents, do we?'

'I was wondering.'

'What's on your mind, Mr Hunt?' Rogers' face turned to a grin and Tom felt intimidated.'

'It's just that, if I'm going to be late I should phone.'

'I'll only be five minutes. Have a good look round, and then I'll give you a lift somewhere.' He went down the ladder and as he walked along the boards, an attractive young girl with shoulder-length auburn hair and wearing a raincoat came from a corner door.

'The phone for you, Mr Rogers!' Her voice was soft East

End nasal Cockney with a silken tone. She spoke to Rogers for a few seconds.

'Christ, not him again,' he bellowed and they both vanished through the doorway.

At the end of the slipway, Tom noticed that a small boat had just come in and moored. There were two men, one of whom stepped out while the other man handed out two heavy looking boxes judging by the way they lifted them. They carried them up by the darkened wall away from the slipway and into the door where Rogers and the girl had gone. They soon reappeared, and Tom crouched as they quickly walked down to the boat and cast off.

He walked carefully up to the bow, where the deck sloped upwards at a slight angle. He stopped and looked down into the large hold which had an unusually nice finish, with a double skin. As he walked further and onto the bow, he had a fright as he almost stepped into a dark square hole cut out in the prow decking that had no walls, an added hazard in the dim light. He thought a hatch cover would be constructed there, and for a while he stood still on that prow feeling a little shaken.

As Tom looked out through the slipway opening, a faint light was approaching over the water that had become misty. As it got nearer the light showed up brighter and he could see the port and starboard, red and green lights. He made his way back towards the stern, and near where he'd climbed the ladder. From there, he watched the boat as it came right up to the slipway and two uniformed men got out. It was a river police patrol boat this time. Tom kept out of sight again as the men walked inside the building and disappeared through the corner door.

He walked back to the aft end on the other side, where the men were working with the aid of lights below the wheel house. This was the living accommodation: a cabin for eating and sleeping, galley and toilet. A door led through to the engine room aft.

'Good evening,' Tom said to the men who were working in

the engine room. One of the men looked up, nodded and carried on working. Then the other man glanced up.

'Watch your step up there, it's bloody dangerous.'

'Yes, I know.' Tom went back to the ladder, and peered at his watch. It was twenty past six and there was no sign of Mr Rogers. Tom was wondering how much longer he could hang on, and decided to get back down the precarious ladder.

He was half way down, when the river policemen reappeared at the corner door. Tom reached the bottom of the ladder, and one of the policemen shouted, 'We'd like a word with you sir!' The two policemen clambered over wet balks of timber towards him, and he thought of his experience with the dock gate police. 'I presume you're employed here, Sir?' the first policeman said.

'No, but I'm about to do some work for Mr Rogers.'

'Tell us your name please?'

'Thomas Hunt, and I...'

'How long have you worked for Mr Rogers?' the other policeman asked.

'I met him for the first time this afternoon,' Tom replied. 'I work at Brown and Saxons.'

'I see, Sir, thankyou,' the first policeman said, writing in his notebook.

'But, what's this all about?'

'Just checking. Have you got your pass, Sir?' Tom quickly got out his Brown and Saxon pass and handed it to the policeman. 'Yes, this seems to be in order.'

'I was only asked to do some measuring,' Tom said as he took his pass back.

'This is a formality, that's all, Sir.'

'We can contact you if we need you,' the other policeman said as they stepped back over the balks. Tom watched them as they walked down to the police boat, two dark figures.

He caught sight of the auburn haired girl as she came through the corner door where the light was quite dim.

'Mr Hunt!' she called out.

'Yes, here!'

'You won't mind if I don't come over there?'

'No, of course not, I'm coming up anyway!'

'Mr Rogers said he's sorry he's been held up, he'd like you to go up to the office.'

'Oh, yes all right,' Tom said as he approached her.

'Watch how you go there!'

'So they keep telling me.'

'Well it is muddy.'

'I've just been questioned by the police; what's that about?'

'Don't ask!' she said, leaving Tom none the wiser. 'I've got to go now, I'm half an hour late as it is.'

'I'm late too!'

'Oh dear... Go through the door and up the stairs, it's straight through to Mr Rogers' office. Now I must fly.'

The staircase was on the right as he went through the door. The narrow wooden steps creaked, and were just about wide enough for one person. At the top of the stairs was a passage with a door on the left. The office door ahead was slightly ajar, and as he approached, Tom could hear Rogers in heated conversation on the phone. He stood near the door, apprehensive at the thought of entering. Rogers' voice had gone quieter, but Tom was just able to hear part of what he was saying. 'I've had a visit from the law, asking questions. Look, Alf, they must have followed your mates. There's trouble so watch your step if they come and see you... Well, they mentioned your name but I knew nothing, get it? Let me in for it, I tried to hide them with drawings... I don't care what you do. If you've got any more stens dump them if necessary.' He slammed the phone down.

In that dim passage, the door looked ominous now to Tom. He took a deep breath, but as he went to the door, Mr Rogers opened it in a hurry as if he'd forgotten Tom was on his way up.

'Oh, Mr .. Tom, yes.' He looked very flustered. 'You'd better come in,' he said, pushing the door open wide.

'Thank you.'

'Sorry you had to wait. Trouble with a client. You wouldn't want to know about that, son.'

'No, I...'

'That's business.' He walked towards the window. Rolls of drawings lay on a long table. He stood in silence for a few seconds with his back to Tom. 'Look at these drawings.' He unrolled a large print and held it open, resting it on the other drawings. 'There you are, a general arrangement. You might find it interesting.'

'Yes, that's what I need,' Tom said and glanced anxiously at his watch.'

'Well I'm sorry, you can tell Guthrey the job's off!'

'Off? But...'

'Yes. Thats business for you. I'm afraid I've brought you on a wild goose chase. My problems, mate.'

'Oh dear, that's...' Tom was lost for words.

'I don't mind telling you, I'm bloody fed up with things as they are at the moment. You try to help people and they let you down. Believe me, son, look after number one. No one else will.'

'I'm sorry,' Tom said.

'Don't waste time being sorry. I'll phone Mr Guthrey tomorrow morning. You can find your way out?' Rogers still stood looking out through the window. He hadn't turned his head and Tom slipped out quietly. He descended the long narrow stairway, and wondered if there was another way out. Rogers seemed oblivious to the fact that it was getting late, in spite of Tom's frequent glances at his watch. He was obviously in trouble with the law and had forgotten about the lift he'd mentioned.

Another police boat had arrived at the end of the slipway, and Tom saw three dark shadowy figures with torches making their way up the side. Tom hid behind the stern of the barge till they disappeared through the door. He groped his way out by the way he'd entered with Rogers, but it was almost pitch dark in places. He wished he had a torch.With great relief he swung open the door to the yard, dimly lit by a street lamp near the main gate. He looked at Rogers' car still there, and resisted the urge to jump in and drive off. It was a fleeting thought as he noticed the ignition key was left in place.

It was a dismal evening and dark clouds hovered as Tom walked along a damp cobbled street. He reflected on his brief 'promotion'. His thoughts were mixed, for it would have been quite a challenge, even if he would have been working for a crook. He thought of the men working to a deadline, and of the auburn-haired girl. It would be a pity if that work had to be abandoned and they would all be out of a job.

So, it would be back to drudgery again. Life seemed full of 'roads to nowhere.' Eventually he reached a road on a bus route. A few spots of rain began to fall as the sky darkened, then, after a long wait, the lights of a bus drew near. Tom sat upstairs and it seemed an endless journey, though he enjoyed looking down at the lighted shop windows that lent a cosy cheer to the dull evening journey. He lit up his pipe and thought of his fruitless afternoon, then dismissed it as all part of life's puzzle, where the pieces don't fit together.

It was after eight when he walked up the steps of Stonliegh House. He looked into the dining room where he found only Mr Gallagher and Doctor Desiri still there.

'Well, look who's here.' said the doctor.

'Missed supper again,' Mr Gallagher said.

'Yes... I was working late.'

'We thought you would have another night out on the tiles,' said the doctor.

'Oh, no such luck.'

'I think you're in trouble with Mrs Blackburn,' Mr Gallagher said 'You know how she likes to keep tabs on us.'

'Oh yes?' He was sure they were joking.

'You have to make peace with her,' said the doctor.

Mr Sheet was in the study reading. He looked up from his book as Tom entered. 'Hello there,' he said.

'Is Mrs Blackburn around?'

'I think she's gone upstairs. She might be in the kitchen.'

'Is she annoyed with me?'

'I shouldn't think so. Why should she be?' He chuckled.

'I missed supper, again!'

'Yes, but I don't think she's annoyed. Why don't you go down to the kitchen and see if you can scrounge something.'

'Perhaps I will.'

'I think there was some toad-in-the-hole left.'

'OK, I'll go and see.'

Tom opened the basement door and went down the dark staircase. He listened for voices, but only heard the sound of pots and pans being moved. Jessie was humming as she tidied up. She looked round as Tom came into the kitchen.

'Hello!' she said with a smile. 'You missed supper again!'

'Yes. I was held up unexpectedly.' His eyes felt dreamy again as she looked at him and a warm feeling came over him.

'You must be hungry,' she said with concern.

'Yes, I am rather – is there any left over?'

'Not a morsel, they ate every scrap, always do,' she said with a cheeky expression in her bright eyes.

'You're pulling my leg – I hope?'

'You know I wouldn't do that, Mr Hunt.'

'No? They laughed together and Tom was suddenly aware of a feeling of closeness between them, as if time had paused at that fragile, magical moment.

'Why don't you sit down, and let me find you something to eat. There's some toad-in-the-hole left. I can pop it in the oven and warm it up for you.'

'Thankyou, if it's not too much trouble.'

'Would I suggest it if it was too much trouble?' She pulled out a chair from the table, placed a knife and fork on the table, then went to the old gas cooker and opened the oven door. *Woof!* it went as she lit it with a taper. There was an ancient kitchen range which still gave good service at times and had probably been there since the house was built, and now only used in the winter. 'It won't take long, Mr Hunt.'

'Call me Tom.' She shut the oven door and came away.

'If you want me to.'

'Yes.. why not? I call you Jessie.' He was conscious that she seemed older than him, though she was younger.

'There's heaps of food here,' she said, changing the subject. 'Could be some black market! My aunt's pretty crafty, you know.'

'Is she likely to come down to the kitchen?'

'No, she's upstairs... with Mr Robinson most likely,' she laughed.

'I see,' Tom smiled, thinking of them sharing a bed.

'I won't be staying much longer,' Jessie said turning towards the oven. 'My aunt has arranged to have a French girl come and work in the kitchen.' She opened the oven.

'Oh! That's a shame.'

'Why? I never can stay very long.'

'I think... well, I think you're very nice.' He hesitated.

'Do you? I'm not always nice. You hardly know me!'

'Sorry, I was just...' His words petered out.

'That's all right.' She laughed.

'Where will you be going then?'

'Back to stay with my parents for a few days.' She placed the plate of food in front of Tom. 'That should fill the void. There's some potatoes and cabbage.'

'Thank you.'

'Then I'm going to spend a fortnight in the Lake District with my friend.'

'I hope you enjoy it, the scenery's wonderful.' Tom felt downcast and it must have shown, for she looked concerned.

'I will be staying here again sometime, I expect. I go back to college after the holiday, but I might be visiting my aunt at Christmas.' She put some apple pie and custard on the table. 'I expect you can manage that after.'

Mr Sheet stood in the fading evening light of the music room. He gazed out through the window, as he often did, a silent, vigilant figure, a staunch silhouette watching his latest dream girl, standing guard as if he imagined some fate would befall her, should he move away from his post. But she was saying a long goodnight to another, and though he hoped it was only a passing friendship, he knew his infatuation was just another dream.

Mr,Gallagher and Dr.Desiri were sitting on the chaise longue, engrossed in convivial conversation to while away the evening.

'In your line, it must be hard to please,' the doctor said.

'It's mainly seasonal. The weather is a big influence. It's hard to get people to spend money on good shoes. I tell them it's cheaper in the long run to buy a strong pair of Oxfords.'

'You could fix me up with a pair of first class shoes then?'

'Of course. My sole business.' The doctor chuckled. Tom came in with a bemused expression, as if deep in thought.

'You look a little pale,' the doctor said, 'as if you have much care. I hope you are not in trouble again?'

'No, it's nothing,' Tom said.

'Did you manage to get something to eat?' Mr Gallagher said. He did not hide an expression of amusement.

'Yes, I saw Jessie in the kitchen, and she fixed me up. It was very good.' Tom hesitated, then pointed with his thumb, back towards the door, and whispered, 'Why is Mr Sheet standing in the dark, in the music room?'

'Sh!' Mr Gallagher put his finger to his mouth and whispered. 'His latest dream love. He watches over Jean while she says goodnight to her boyfriend, just waiting for her to be safely indoors.'

'Jean? Who's Jean?'

'Miss Jean Copley. She's another schoolteacher. You must have met her.'

'Oh yes, sorry,' Tom said as he realised who she was. He had only met her once, a plump and jolly girl with wavy golden hair. There was a sound from the front door and a few seconds later, Jean Copley poked her head round the door.

'Hello everybody.'

'Hello, Jean. Had a good day?' Mr Gallagher asked. She stepped briskly into the room with a big smile.

'Yes, but what a storm we had this afternoon.'

'Tremendous!' Tom said.

'You've met Mr Hunt, haven't you?' Mr Gallagher said.

'Yes, of course, Mrs Blackburn introduced us last week.'

'You'd been to a show,' Tom said. 'She introduced you as Miss Copley... I mean, not Jean.'

'I wouldn't let that worry you.' She laughed. 'I'll say good night to you gentlemen. See you in the morning.'

Dr.Desiri and Mr Gallagher were both smiling broadly.

'I think she has a liking for you,' said the doctor.

'Why do you say that?'

'We can tell by the way she talks to you,' Mr Gallagher said.

'Ridiculous. She's just said good night to her... her friend?'

'Just a passing cloud.' Mr Gallagher had a jaunty expression.

'Well, I expect Mr Sheet hopes so,' Tom said.

'He likes to have dream. He would run away I am thinking,' the doctor said half smiling, yet serious.

'Yes, I suppose so,' Tom said, yawning. 'Oh dear, it must be this humid evening after that storm.'

'Is your work very wearying?' Mr Gallagher asked.

'Can be at times.' Tom chuckled. 'Especially on days like today.'

Chapter 15
The Outing

On Thursday morning, the sun shone on the breakfast table where Dr Desiri was busily eating.

'Morning doctor. Sunny again!'

'Good morning; but it is so much cooler.'

'After all that heavy rain I suppose.'

'It was nothing much. When I think of the monsoon, it rains much harder and goes on for many days, yes and twice as hard.'

Tom, standing by the dumb waiter hatch, called 'Good morning,' down to the kitchen.

'Morning Tom. Sausages or a boiled egg?'

He liked Jessie remembering his first name. 'Just a boiled egg, thanks Jessie.'

'I'll call up when it's ready.'

'You seem to have a way with the ladies,' the doctor said.

'Oh no, you don't know how shy I am!'

'I would say that's the secret. Women like shy young men, they enjoy power over man.'

'Do they?' Tom said with disbelief. 'Have you seen Miss Lovell this morning?'

'No; you can see she is not down yet!'

'Yes, of course,' Tom said, 'a silly question!'

Mr Gallagher came into the room. 'The top of the morning,' he said as he walked to the hatch.

'Breakfast coming up,' Jessie called.

'That was quick!' he said.

'It's my breakfast,' Tom quickly intervened.

'Good morning Mr Gallagher,' Jessie called as Tom took his

breakfast from the hatch.

'Good morning Jessie, how are you?'

After having had a restless night, Tom was not in the mood for idle chatter and finished breakfast quickly. As he went into the hall, Miss Lovell came down the stairs.

'Good morning Mr Hunt,' she said quietly. Tom thought she looked very pale and fragile.

'Good morning.' He hoped she would not sense his unease. 'Sorry I missed you last night – I had to work late, it was unexpected!'

'Don't worry.' She stood surprisingly close to him at the foot of the stairs. She seemed to be trembling and Tom suddenly wanted to put his arms round her slender waist. It was difficult for him to push those arousing thoughts from his mind. 'Only, I was wondering about tomorrow – the docks?'

'It's all right, just passes to collect.' He glanced at the ceiling.

'Is it all arranged?' She seemed to perk up suddenly.

'Yes, of course!' Tom said automatically. He was again making promises without knowing if he could arrange anything.

'That's very good of you.' She walked towards the door. 'So, what will the arrangements be then?' Tom felt a shiver go down his spine. He was almost lost for words.

'Tomorrow afternoon, if you could meet me at the north gate. Or I could meet you here if you like, with... how many will there be?'

'Six children, but there's no point in you coming back here. Your first suggestion is the best.' Just tell me which bus to get and what time you want us there.'

'Yes, of course. Will I see you tonight?'

'If you're not late again,' she said with a slight smile.

'I shouldn't be. We can sort it out this evening then.'

'I can't thank you enough,' she said and slid through the door into the dining room, still smiling.

On the journey to work that morning Tom's mind was a mix of delight and anxiety. He gazed at the familiar sights on his bus ride, for they all looked strangely different. He felt extra sensitive to these everyday scenes, and the play of the morning light on buildings and windows looked as if he was seeing them for the first time. But when he arrived at work his stomach was churning. What a pickle! He knew he had only himself to blame, though his justification for making such hasty promises was because he was a victim of circumstances, especially if there was a powerful sexual clement..

'How's things with you this morning then?' Brian said. Tom looked to his right to see his colleague munching a sandwich. 'What's the next instalment in your adventures?'

'Oh, nothing much! No breakfast this morning then?'

'Have to admit I overslept. No exciting adventure then?'

'No such luck,' Tom said shaking his head. 'I must see Guthrey, but he's in his office with the door closed.'

'Perhaps he's having a little sleep and is not to be disturbed.' Brian chuckled.

Mr Guthrey sat at his desk in the morning light, with his head down, reading a letter. A breeze rattled the window and he looked up, rubbed his hands together then rested his chin on them, tightly clenched. His mind was troubled. He had been with Brown and Saxon for almost thirty years, having joined the firm when he came out of the Navy soon after the end of the war in 1918. The firm was doing well, even through the depression during the 1930s, but now he was thinking about the future, which appeared uncertain. On his office wall there were framed pictures of ships, mostly passenger liners, but one was a naval battle ship from the Great War era. A large photograph of a ship with four raked funnels had a white ivory inset in the bottom of a mahogany frame with black letters that read 'Mauritania, 31,000 tons'.

There was a knock at the door and Mathews looked in. 'Morning,' he said with a broad smile. He always emanated cheerful confidence.

'Come in, would you, and take a seat.' Mr Guthrey was not smiling.

'Oh, do I detect trouble?'

'I don't know really,' Guthrey said forcing a slight smile. 'It's a formal letter from the London office. Here, read it and tell me what you think.' He handed the letter to Mathews, who read it through, then shook his head and smiled.

'Only says they may have to close the boiler-making shops.'

'You can be sure they wouldn't send info of that kind out unless it was absolutely on the cards.'

'Yes, I think you're probably right. Shouldn't affect us though, should it?'

'No, not perhaps straight away, but some staff will have to find other work eventually; with no new design work coming in from what is, after all, a major part of our business. And my concern is with the men that will have to be laid off, some very good craftsmen that have been with us for years.' He looked towards the window. 'I don't know what's happening to business in this country, do you?'

'There's nothing we can do about it anyway.'

'No.' Guthrey paused for thought. 'No, perhaps not. What concerns me is that extra men were taken on only a few months ago... and after scraping through the war! It was a different story when I joined the firm, we had everything going for us, business was booming.'

There was a knock on the door and Tom looked in. 'Oh, I'm sorry,' he said when he saw a discussion in progress.

'Not now, Mr Hunt!'

Tom quickly retreated. 'You look a bit ruffled,' Brian said, as he saw Tom emerge from Guthrey's office.

'Do I? Well, there's a serious discussion going on in there.'

'What about?'

'How should I know, I came away quickly.'

'Best to keep out of the way then.'

'I've got to go in and see him soon.'

'What about? Going to ask him for a rise?' Brian walked away, not realising that Tom was so tensed up. Eventually Mathews came out of the chief's office, and Tom thought he had a serious expression as he walked quickly up to his special area at the top end of the room. It was his domain, where the long drawing office was made narrower to accommodate the print room where Sandy worked. She spent most of her day in semidarkness. Tom was wandering up to have a word with Mathews, when Sandy rushed of the print room holding a bundle of drawings and spoke to Mathews animatedly. Tom hesitated, not wishing to interrupt yet another conversation; but he slowly approached. Sandy thumped the drawings down onto his old plan chest and stood looking at them, then at Mathews.

'Look, I don't normally make a fuss, you know that, but just dumping it on me like this!'

'Calm down, Sandy, Mathews said. 'I agree with you,' he said with a smile. 'Don't let it worry you, I'll see Mr Guthrey.'

'Oh, I suppose I'll be in trouble then!'

'No you won't, I'll see to that, just leave it with me.'

'Thank you Mr Mathews – I'm sorry. Oh dear, it's just one of those mornings.' She quickly disappeared into the print room.

'Dear oh dear,' Mathews said, breathing a sigh. He turned to see Tom standing behind him. 'Oh! You gave me a start hiding behind me like that. Did you want something?'

'Yes, I just wanted to see Mr Guthrey about something'

'Well, why come to me then? Go and knock on his door.'

'Yes, of course, but I was wondering if he'll be in a good mood, only he was a bit serious with me when I looked in.'

'He's got things on his mind. I should leave it for a bit if I were you.'

'Oh dear!'

'Look, I've got to see him again about those drawings left by your friend Mr Rogers last night. Bit of a cheek, don't you think?' He was pointing at the bundle of drawings on his plan chest which were tied up. There was a scribbled note with them; 'Two sets of prints, Rogers.'

'Yes, I see.' Tom was thinking: *they'll not be needed anyway.*

'He left them on the table by the time clock, and someone put them in the print room.'

'Oh, and she thought he wanted prints. They look like tracings,' Tom said. 'But I can see they're prints on cloth.'

'Yes, of course, they *are* prints. Sandy got the wrong end of the stick and I see why she was in such a fluster about it. I didn't look at them properly myself, that makes me look a fool!' Tom was used to looking at prints on cloth from his days at Fentons. They both had to laugh. 'I'll pop them into Guthrey's office.'

'It's a bit awkward for me really,' Tom said slowly.

'Why?'

'Oh nothing, I have to see him!'

'That's up to you. I'll give these drawings to him now anyway and you can see him when you like.' Tom was on the point of telling Mr Mathews that the job for Rogers was off, but decided to wait and see what Guthrey had to say. It seemed that Mathews was unaware at that stage. The morning dwindled further while Tom waited and nervously glanced at the clock, wishing he could have seen the chief earlier.

When at last Guthrey was free, Tom found his office door open, and knocked very gently. Mr Guthrey looked up from the drawings left by Mr Rogers.

'Can I have a word with you please?' Tom said.

'Yes, of course, come in and sit down. Tell me how you got on with Mr Rogers. The drawings are interesting!'

'Well, I'm afraid it was a waste of time. You see um...'

'Waste of time?' Guthrey said with a puzzled expression.

'He had an argument with someone on the phone, then told me the job was off.'

'That's strange!'

'Yes, I thought so, and he left me to find my own way back to my digs, after promising me a lift!'

'Oh, I see... that's a bit off, and he gave no explanation?'

'No, he just had this argument over the phone. The river police called on him, more than once; I kept out of the way!'

'Oh dear! Sounds ominous. Leave it with me to sort out.'

'He said he'd phone you this morning. So he didn't?'

'No, I've heard nothing from him.'

'I wanted to ask you...' Tom paused.

'Yes, go ahead!'

'It's a teacher, I mean a lady teacher I know.' He hesitated for a second, as in his mind he saw the pale Irish face and dark hair.

'A teacher?' Mr Guthrey said.

Tom quickly surfaced. 'Yes... would it be possible for her to bring a party of children to look over one of the large passenger liners tomorrow afternoon?'

'A party of children? Good-gracious, how many?'

'Six,' Tom said quickly.

'I can't give you permission anyway. You'd have to go to the shipping line office – but I can give you the afternoon off.'

'Yes... thankyou Mr Guthrey. Can it count as time off in lieu of the late night, instead of a Saturday morning as arranged?'

'Make it a long weekend! That's supposing you can get a permit at short notice. Have you a particular ship in mind?'

'Well, I was thinking of the Canton, that very fine-looking white P and O ship that came in a few days ago.'

'I don't know if that would be possible,' he said with a doubtful expression, 'but you can only ask. Take a walk over to their office now and let me know how you get on.'

There were no problems. It turned out, to Tom's relief, to be a straightforward formality. In fact they welcomed parties such as groups of school children with their teacher. Having filled in a form and presented his company pass, he was issued with a paper to take a party on board the Canton. 'An officer on board will take you all on a conducted tour of the ship,' he was told with a smile.

Tom left work that day feeling much more at ease, like a man who had just climbed a mountain. In the evening, Miss Lovell was at the supper table, and Tom could not avert a feeling of apprehension. Mrs Blackburn introduced two more guests at the dinner table, a lady and gentleman.

'This is Mrs Hoskins, we play bridge together.' Mrs Hoskins was plump, aged about fifty or more and had a miserable expression. 'And Captain Cobb, they're friends.' He had a grey beard and was probably a little older than Mrs Hoskins. She gestured with her hands as they sat down. Tom struggled through the meal with polite conversation and he tried to avoid looking straight at Miss Lovell.

As they left the table after the meal, Tom saw Miss Lovell go out into the hall. He was seized with the feeling that she'd forgotten all about the arrangements he had made for her, though reason told him that this would surely be unlikely. He said, 'Excuse me' and rushed out of the door to catch her.

She was talking to Peter Gordon. 'I can't say how long I shall be staying, Mr Gordon.'

'I sincerely hope you'll be with us for a while. It's not often we have someone so attractive as yourself staying, and we have to have time to get acquainted.'

'There will be time for that, Mr Gordon,' she said with a slight smile.

'Do call me Pete, that's what my friends call me.'

'But I'm not your friend, am I?'

Tom walked slowly up to the front door, where he turned over the pages of the telephone directory.

'There's no reason why we shouldn't be though.'

'No, but I have to be given time to get to know people.'

Tom was feeling irritated as he slowly turned the pages of the directory without looking at them.

'But you don't want to be formal do you. I can't go on calling you Miss Lovell?'

'I don't see why not, do you?'

'That's your prerogative my dear, yours entirely.' Peter whispered close to her ear, gesticulating with his finger.

'Yes well, all right; I'll call you Pete then.' Tom couldn't help feeling prickly at Pete's apparent arrogance.

'Fine, so what do I call you then?'

'It's Betty.'

'OK, I'll see you around then.' Tom glanced round and saw him go upstairs.

Tom put down the directory and walked towards her. She gave him a strange smile and beckoned him into the music room. She had a tremendous effect on him, as if she was possessed with divine power. He felt hypnotised; he had no wish to resist. Pete would never have any such deep feelings, he was thinking.

They stood facing each other. 'And what have you arranged for me then, Mr...?'

'Oh. it's all arranged... I take you and your small party on board the Canton.' He felt his voice faltering as he looked straight into her cool Irish eyes.

'I'm most grateful to you for all your trouble, and we'll see you at the... did you say North gate at two o'clock tomorrow afternoon?'

'Yes, I've made a note of the trolley bus to get from here.' He handed her a piece of paper. 'It takes about twenty minutes, so...'

'That's very good, it will be no bother and you've drawn me a little map!'

'Thought it would help.'

'Yes, we'll be looking forward to it very much. Please excuse me.' She moved to the door. 'I have books to mark.' She went out, leaving Tom standing with a dreamy smile.

It seemed a long Friday morning for Tom, as he made every effort to keep his mind focused on his work. He felt elated, though this was mixed with a touch of anxiety, which often affected him when his normal routine changed. The thought of seeing Miss Lovell was thrilling, but he was also looking forward to visiting a different ship. In the staff canteen, he talked more boldly than usual with his colleagues and there was much laughter. His friend Brian was intrigued to know what he would be doing that weekend, starting with the afternoon off. 'Why the secrecy!' he asked. But Tom was cautious not to divulge his carefully planned arrangements.

Everything went smoothly to plan. He met Miss Lovell with her puplis, three boys and three girls. They were at the gate at five minutes before two that afternoon. The sun was warm and it was a hazy view across the docks to where the Canton was berthed, a faint shimmering white shape with a single yellow funnel. It was a long walk between docks and warehouses, the children bristling with excitement, as they pointed at the cranes and bales, interested in so much activity. At the gangway, they were met by a smart young uniformed seaman. He took them on a very thorough tour of the ship, from the top deck, which included the bridge, even allowing two of the boys to be helped up the ladder inside the foremast to the crows nest, then down to the engine rooms, the cold storage rooms and kitchens.

Because Tom's arrangements had gone so well that afternoon, he was buoyed up with an exaggerated feeling of importance, like a man who owns everything. But the children were tired during the walk back through the docks, when the excitement had worn a little thin. They had a lengthy wait at the bus stop and Tom suddenly came down to earth, feeling deflated. When the bus came, the children rushed up the stairs and to the front. Miss Lovell kept them in order while Tom could only look on with a smile. She took the children back to the school to be picked up by their respective parents, while Tom made his own way back to Stonliegh House.

There was no sign of Miss Lovell at the table that evening, which was, in a strange way, a relief to Tom. Later, he got into conversation with Mr Gallagher.

'You seem to be getting on very well with Miss Lovell.'

'Oh, do you think so?' Tom was irritated by the question, if it was a question. 'Well, I hardly know her!'

'Don't you? She seems a quiet girl for a teacher.'

'As a matter of fact, I took her and six of her school children into the docks this afternoon.'

'Did you now? So you're doing well then?'

'It was quite fun, but it was an outing for the children. And I will say, she handles them strictly, she's not always quiet.'

'I've come to realise that a woman's character is hard to assess, I'm almost forty you know, and still a bachelor.'

'Yes!' They fell silent for a while. Tom had already guessed that much. He changed the subject. 'Have you stayed here for long?'

'Over three years. Mr Sheet and I have been here longer than anyone. In fact, I think Mr Sheet's been a resident nearly five years!'

'That sounds pretty permanent to me.'

'Nothing is permanent, nothing at all.'

'No, I know.' There was another silence. 'And where does the old lady fit in then?'

'Who do you mean, not Mrs Blackburn?' he said with a laugh.

'No, the little old lady who has an afternoon nap on this sofa (he was referring to the chaise longue they were sitting on).

'You mean Millie!'

'Millie?'

'Mrs Millie Gaylor. I would say she's what you might call an old family retainer who's always lived with Mrs Blackburn.'

'Mrs Blackburn does speak sharply to her at times. I've seen how mad she gets with her when she's slow to understand her and she gets impatient.' Tom paused for thought. 'It's as if she resents her, she does help in the kitchen and around the house, but she seam's terrified of Mrs Blackburn.'

'Oh, she probably is. Familiarity breeds contempt, you must know; the trouble is that she is so absent minded and does silly things. I'm afraid it's a question of intolerance, you can be sure of that.'

'I think that's terrible!'

'Yes, I feel a little sorry for her myself, but at least she has a home here.'

'But Mrs Blackburn is so strict though,' Tom whispered.

'She does put on a stern face, but that's just her way. She's really very kind you know.' He chuckled. 'She just likes to feel she's keeping everything in order, including us!'

'Yes, I see,' Tom said with a yawn and stood up. 'I'll go up now. Good night Mr Gallagher.'

As Tom went up the stairs, he met Mr Sheet coming down

in his dressing gown and carrying a towel. A shadowy figure in the fading light had just passed the door to the bathroom on the upper floor.

'Hello Mr Sheet,' Tom said. 'Going for a late swim?'

'On my way to the basement.' He chuckled. 'I always use the bathroom down there, less likely to be disturbed.

'Oh, I didn't know there was a bathroom down there.'

'Yes, beyond the kitchen. I like to take my time, regular Friday night routine.' He uttered a kind of bubbly giggle.

'Like a secret hideaway?'

'If you look at it that way.' He continued down the stairs.

'I'll say good night then.'

Tom liked Mr Sheet's individuality. He was a character who was easy to get on with and spoke interestingly about any subject.

That night as he lay in bed, he thought of Miss Lovell, his latest crush. 'Call her Betty, you fool!' he scolded himself. But he knew almost nothing about her, nor she him. Would she even care? he wondered as he drifted off into an uneasy sleep.

Chapter 16
A Daunting Weekend

A free Saturday morning was an unusual pleasure and Tom sat in the garden. It was peaceful and the sound of traffic was faintly heard behind bird song. At least, until Mrs Blackburn appeared at the top of the garden steps. 'Oh, this is where you are Mr Hunt,' she said and went back indoors. 'Strange woman,' he thought. He'd never seen Mrs Blackburn and Mr Robinson at the table in the early morning; he imagined them at breakfast in bed together.

Later Tom looked into the music room where he found Mr Robinson reading the paper, smoke rising from his cigarette.

'Good morning,' Tom said and Mr Robinson turned to look at him. 'I'm sorry, I won't interrupt...'

'No, only reading newspaper rubbish!' he said with a chuckle, and coughed harshly.

'Are you OK, Mr Robinson?'

'Oh, I'm all right old boy. Just reading about the Palestine question. All about the illegal Jewish immigration.'

'Illegal?'

'Yes! Putting them into detention camps in Cyprus. Brimming full it says in the paper... Newspaper talk,' he mumbled.

'Sounds bad to me,' Tom said thoughtfully.

'No use us worrying.' He took another puff, coughed and stubbed out his cigarette.

'I don't read the papers much, Mr Robinson.'

'Don't blame you – not at work this morning then?' he said stifling his cough.

'No, some time off in lieu of overtime.'

'Ah.' He nodded. 'Have you planned anything in particular?'

'No, nothing special.'

'Sit down and have a chat if you're not in a hurry.'

'If I won't be disturbing you.'

'No, not at all, I welcome the chance to talk to someone.' He looked at Tom through thick round spectacles, his bushy moustache stained with tobacco smoke. 'I've hardly got to know you! How do you like this area then?'

'Very pleasant around here, also the docks are interesting.'

'Yes.' He hesitated. 'I was in engineering you know!'

'Were you! What kind of engineering?'

'Designing; hospital sterilising units.'

'Oh yes, was it... I expect that was interesting work.'

'It was, yes I developed many new ideas.'

'How did they work, did they use steam?'

'No, it was a system of boiling in beautiful specially designed stainless steel boxes, there were various types and sizes, but that wouldn't interest you.'

'Most things interest me, I mentioned steam thinking of my connection with steam engines, though that was marine work and very different. I thought steam, I mean super heated and under pressure, was used in sterilisation as it is so much hotter, though I suppose it would be impractical in a hospital, wouldn't it?'

'I don't know, dear boy, I've been retired for quite a while now and you never know what new ideas are coming up. However, that sort of temperature would be quite unnecessary, the heat in our sterilisers would kill any known germ.'

'Yes...amazing,' Tom said uncertainly.

Mr Robinson lit up another cigarette, puffed and coughed.

'I gather you work for a company within the docks?'

'Yes, at Brown and Saxon.'

'To do with shipping I presume?'

'I've spent most of my time making new ships plans' while they are being refitted to take emigrants to Australia would you believe it. I find them a good firm to work with though. They're also well established boiler makers.'

'You're on firm ground with an old well rooted company.'

'Should be I suppose.'

'I'm sure you are, you should do well.'

'Thank you, I hope so.'

'I heard you had a trip down to Tilbury?'

'Yes, it just happened that I was left on board but I enjoyed the experience.'

'Deliberate, was it, on your part?' He gave Tom a crafty look.

'Well, let's say I didn't try too hard to rush off. I got into conversation with a lady who was emigrating to Australia with two young daughters, that's how it happened.' Mr Robinson started to laugh, then he coughed from the blue haze of cigarette smoke. 'It was quite innocent really!'

'Yes, I'm sure it was, been in situations like that myself.' They laughed together. Tom thought Mr Robinson could tell him an interesting tale or two sometime. 'I was adventurous when I was your age.' There was a pause. 'You're interested in art, I gather?'

'Yes,' Tom said, 'I like to paint and sketch.'

'So you dabble in art. I used to dabble in art, you know.'

'But I do take it seriously!'

'What do you think of this modern stuff, all this abstract business. I don't care for that rubbish. Do you?'

'I don't understand all of it, but it depends on what you mean by modern or abstract. Some of that kind of painting is quite interesting, could be a hidden secret or meaning that only the artist who did the painting understood, or doesn't even understand himself what he was trying to say.'

'That's more likely I should think.' He laughed, coughed and stubbed out his cigarette. 'Damned cigarettes, should give them up really.' Tom could only smile and nod in agreement. 'I had a game once.' Mr Robinson paused with a bemused expression as he looked at Tom.

'What kind of a game?'

‘Oh, I got a large canvas and worked on it, to see if I could fool some of these art people. I just let myself go and painted anything I thought of.’ He waved his hand around as if he was making an invisible painting in the air. ‘I put in grottoes, I put in strange creatures, and a mass of colour, a waste of paint, ha!’ he gasped out a laugh. ‘Put it in a local art show and guess what, my boy?’ He coughed. ‘Highly commended!’

‘That was good, so they were very impressed then.’

‘Yes, yet I had the laugh on them.’ He chuckled. ‘But it was in bad taste on my part really I suppose.’

‘It was quite a joke though,’ Tom said and laughed. ‘So you’re saying you fooled them?’

‘That was my intention anyway, but perhaps I did achieve a worthwhile painting completely unintentionally.’ He smiled.

‘They obviously didn’t think you were joking.’

‘May have proved something.’

‘Yes!’ Tom looked at his watch. ‘I have to go now and get a hair cut,’ he said as he stood up. ‘I’ve enjoyed our chat.’ He went to the door and Mr Robinson waved his hand from his armchair in a silent gesture.

The barber’s shop on a Saturday morning was usually quite busy, but Tom liked the atmosphere there. He found the *snip snip* of the scissors as the two barbers clipped away at the customers’ locks very soothing, as was the quiet talk, and the gentle rustling of newspapers. Blended with the pleasant smell of hair dressing oils, it made him feel relaxed.

He glanced at a newspaper the man next to him was reading. It was a local and his eye caught a headline on the front page: ‘PRISON SENTENCE FOR BOAT BUILDER.’He just saw the name Rogers, and something to do with the black market and smuggling guns. ‘Crikey!’ Tom said in an involuntarily loud whisper and the man with the paper turned round. ‘Sorry, I was thinking aloud!’

‘Next please,’ said one of the barbers who was very tanned as if he’d spent much time in the sun rather than in the shop.

'Thank you,' Tom said as the barber put the apron round him and gently tucked it into his collar.

'How do you like it cut, sir?'

'Not too short please.' The scissors and comb were worked softly over his hair, while Tom's mind was on that newspaper headline. He knew Rogers was up to something. There was so much black marketeering going on, though many people took advantage of this and he didn't think it a terrible crime. But guns! That was more serious and he wondered where they would be bound for. Rogers was in serious trouble, and Tom wondered if he would ever get his barge built.

There had been no sign of Miss Lovell since their visit to the docks. It was as if she had never come back at all the night before. Tom was daydreaming about her. He came down to earth as the barber talked about his holiday in Clacton and the heavy thunder storm after the heat wave.

A mirror was held behind Tom's head.

'How's that sir?'

'Yes, that look's fine, thank you.'

'Anything on the hair sir?' The barber was massaging Tom's scalp with his fingers, which felt wonderful.

'Yes, just a little please.'

The charge was one and threepence, and Tom gave the barber one and sixpence saying, 'Keep the change.'

Walking along the sunny pavement that Saturday morning, Tom felt refreshed and free. He gazed into the window of a car sales shop where there was a 1924 Rolls Royce, a smaller model than usual and priced at three hundred and ninety pounds – a lot of money for a car over twenty years old, but it was a classic as far as Tom was concerned. He thought it would be marvellous to be the proud owner and to take pride in keeping it in good running order. But that was just another of his dreams, for he had little money.

'Would you be thinking of buying that car?' He was startled by the clear Irish voice and he turned to see Miss Lovell.

'Good morning, I...' Tom's muscles jolted as he looked at

those slanting eyes that sparkled as she smiled. 'If I could afford it, it's a grand old car!'

'Do you drive, Mr Hunt?'

'Only my father's Rover, when I visit home.'

'Well now, that's something.'

'Yes, do you, er...?'

'Drive a car?' she intervened.

'Yes, perhaps back in Ireland?' Tom asked.

'No never, my father has a Ford V8 but I don't like driving.'

'Oh, you can always get a bus.' Tom smiled and looked back into the shop. 'Are you doing anything special this weekend?' Tom asked, still eyeing the car in the window.

'Now, I don't know what you mean by special – I like to have a rest at the weekend.' He turned and looked straight at her.

'Well, I thought I might take a bus ride this afternoon, but I don't particularly want to go on my own, so if you'd like to keep me company...?'

'Well now, I'm not sure I would be very good company.'

'Oh, that can't be true. I was thinking of perhaps Epping, and we could find a tea shop there?'

'That would be nice, but...'

'Look at the weather,' Tom said glancing up at the sky. 'It would be a nice trip.'

'All right then, it would be pleasant.' Tom had surprised himself by asking, and was even more surprised at her acceptance. 'I'll come and keep you company, but that's all, no commitments,' Miss Lovell warned.

'No, of course not!' Why did she have to say that, Tom thought, but he shrugged it off. 'See you later,' she said.

The world suddenly seemed a little different. He felt stimulated with excitement as he crossed the road to the pub where he sometimes had a beer. But he stood there for a while, wondering if he should have a drink. He feared that this strangely fascinating teacher would not approve, so he didn't go into the pub, but had a snack in a cafe. As he sat over a cup of tea with his confidence boosted, he resolved to make a good impression upon this lovely, enticing lady.

They talked for most of the bus journey, although she was surprisingly formal for she continued to address him as Mr Hunt. Tom carefully avoided addressing her by any name., but decided he would somehow have to tactfully reproach her at a suitable opportunity. It was as though, all the time, she wanted to keep her distance from him, but he was sure that had not been the case when they first met and she'd showed such interest in the docks and ships. He even wondered if he'd blotted his copybooks by something he'd said.

'There are a lot of trees, Mr Hunt.'

'Yes, it's all part of Epping forest.' He hesitated. 'Look, do we have to be so formal? Is there any reason why I can't call you Betty?' Tom said rather clumsily.

'Well, I suppose not,' she said surprisingly brusquely. 'All right then...'

'Tom, of course.'

'Yes, Tom.' She then broke into a smile, which seemed a good sign.

'Good! I hope you don't mind me suggesting it, now we can be normal.'

'I didn't think we were ever otherwise.'

'No!' Tom imagined he'd handled it badly. He felt strangely distant from her, and lapsed into silent thought. 'Why,' he thought, 'should there be awkwardness? Perhaps she's very reserved and afraid of getting involved.' He looked straight ahead, and there was no conversation for a while.

'We must be just coming into Epping now,' she said suddenly, breaking the silence.

'Yes – this is Epping, we can get out at the next stop and have a look round the town.'

They spent a happy hour walking about the small town, looking in shops and gardens. She took a knowledgeable interest in architecture and remarked on the number of interesting wooden buildings there were. They found a little tea room where they spent almost an hour, with a pot of good tea and homemade cakes.

Afterwards, they decided to go for a walk away from the town and into the parkland, about half a mile back in the direction from which they had come into the town. They crossed a park where there were woods and lakes, a delightful place to enjoy a long walk.

'Oh, there's a large house!' Tom said. They had just come out from some trees that surrounded a rather grown over lake.

'We'd better not go that way,' Betty said, 'it would be private property.'

'Wait a minute Betty, it's a ruin – look, you can see the sky through the windows.

'It must have been the most dreadful fire I would say.'

'Yes, many years ago though, look at the weeds, and there are even small trees growing inside. Shall we take a closer look?'

'We must take care, Tom, it's probably dangerous!' They walked towards the building, which was a huge mansion gutted by fire. The wide gravelled drive that swept round to the front entrance was a mass of weeds, the double doors were intact and barred entrance to the dismal shell. But curiosity got the better of Tom and he persuaded Betty that they could make their way round to the back of the house through the shrubbery.

They looked upon what must have once been a magnificent and well laid out garden. It was approached from the classical edifice where the ground floor led out onto a traceried stone balcony with curved steps on either side. Tom thought of Victorian ladies and gentlemen coming down the steps and walking in the gardens by pools with fountains and statues. These could be seen, half covered by the garden plants and shrubs that had turned into a wild jungle of exotic growth.

Looking up through that once fine opening into the shell, it was a sorry sight to see fireplaces high up in the blackened wall where there were once floors, but now even the rubble was shrouded with brambles. Tom thought of all the servants that would have worked there, suddenly perhaps in a night of terror fleeing desperately from the great blaze that engulfed the building with merciless destruction.

On one side there was a great conservatory with a black and red tiled floor, where cast iron decorative gratings covered the heating pipes. The plants had gone mad, making it difficult to go very far. Mixed exotic plants that still survived were entangled with sycamore trees that had broken through the glass roof. It was surprising that much of the original glass set into the cast iron was still intact. Tom was thinking of the gardener who would have taken great pride in looking after the plants in such a large conservatory.

In another part of the garden, on a wall, they came upon an inscription that was carved in Latin on a commemorative stone slab which Betty translated. Tom was very impressed. She stood up from where she had bent down to read the carved letters, she was close to him as they looked at each other.

'I think that was very clever. I've forgotten most of the Latin I studied at school.' He gave her a little kiss on the cheek, and she looked surprised.

'Now why did you want to do that?' She turned and walked away quickly, leaving Tom puzzled and he followed her.

'What's the matter Betty? I was impressed with your translation.'

'You know what's the matter.' She was walking even faster now as Tom followed her onto a path and caught up with her.

'No, I don't know, damn it, I'm only human.' It made Tom think, no wonder some chaps say women are so hard to understand. He was very puzzled to know why just a kiss on the cheek should suddenly change her attitude from friendly to hostile. 'Look, what's the matter, Betty?'

'Don't pester me. The less said the better.' Tom could not help wishing then that he'd kissed her passionately on the lips. Would she have screamed? he wondered.

'I'm sure there are plenty of buses,' she said coldly as they waited at a stop. Tom felt chilled and hurt. On the way back, they hardly spoke. Tom found the frustration almost unbearable, especially after such a pleasant and interesting afternoon. For him the day had been marred by her attitude. He felt depressed by her company, wondering what he'd done wrong.

At the dinner table that evening, Betty was more taciturn than usual. It was the polite conversation that Tom had become so accustomed to. At least she had politely thanked him for the trip out when they got back, but he was quite naturally not feeling very happy with her manner.

Betty left the table promptly after picking at her meal, while most were still chatting and finishing theirs. Tom felt as if he was under a stifling veil which dulled his senses and blunted his self-esteem. It was like a nightmare and the guests and surroundings seemed unreal.

'You're quiet, MrHunt,' said Mr Gallagher, 'are you with us?'

'Yes, just deep in thought!'

'I'm thinking he is most likely dreaming of love,' said the doctor.

'Why should you say that?' Tom had a sickening feeling.

'Was it a pleasant afternoon outing?' asked Mr Gallagher.

'It was interesting.' Tom said. 'There's a great house near Epping that was gutted by fire a long time ago, must have been very terrible.'

'1918 I think, if it's that big house near Epping,' came a voice from the corner. It was Mr Sheet. Tom hadn't noticed him there reading the paper.

'Yes, that's right,' Tom said. 'Do you know the name of the place?'

'Copped Hall, I think, a big estate. That's all I know.'

'Why was it just left like that?' asked Tom.

'I don't know, perhaps they went broke.' Mrs Blackburn had been hovering about round the table as she was helping Jessie to clear the dinner things, then she came and sat near them.

'You took teacher with you?' said MrGallagher.

'Yes, Betty,' Tom paused, 'She was, um... company, and found it interesting.'

'You mean Miss Lovell!' Mrs Blackburn said pompously.

'Well, I call her Betty, we're on Christian name terms.'

'Miss Lovell it should be,' Mrs Blackburn said with a very serious expression. Tom thought her remark astonishing and hypocritical, for clearly in his mind he recalled knocking on Mrs Blackburn's bedroom door one Saturday afternoon to tell her he would be out that evening. He'd heard her shout what he thought was, 'Come in,' but she must have said, 'coming'. He had opened the door and was surprised to see her and Mr Robinson in bed together! Tom had said a quick sorry and retreated immediately. Of course, no more was said about the incident, as if it never happened. Mr Sheet had been quite amused and didn't seem at all surprised when Tom told him about his unwanted entrance. He simply said, 'well, I don't suppose it matters at their age,' and they had a laugh about it.

Tom, rolled around in bed that night, trying to come to terms with his struggle. Someone had once told him not to make mountains out of molehills, but he never thought they knew what they were talking about. He knew he made mistakes, but he wondered how he was supposed to know how to handle some situations; there were no guidelines. Finally he fell asleep and dreamed he was swimming with Betty, just the two of them in a beautiful pool. It was a sexy dream and a complete contrast from reality; especially as Tom couldn't even swim!

Sunday morning was dull, drizzly and much cooler. So after breakfast, Tom went up to his room to write a letter to his old school friend Henry Hayes, to be forwarded to where he was stationed. He was hoping Henry could get some leave and spend a holiday with him. He'd not heard from him for quite a time and never had a reply to his letters.

After some time, probably slightly over an hour, Tom became aware of an increasing smell of gas. He was worried and went out of his room where the smell was much stronger. As quick as lightning, Tom ran down stairs to the hallway. He was surprised to find the lounge door open and he saw Millie, the old lady, asleep on the chaise longue where a gas fire had been lit, in spite of the season. He closed the door quickly and ran down the hall towards the basement door, where the smell was strongest and he opened the back door leading to the garden to take a deep breath of fresh air. Mr Sheet came out of the study as Tom turned back and he nearly knocked him down.

'Steady on!' he said. 'Oh, can you smell gas?'

'Sorry, that's why I'm rushing.'

'Oh, oh dear!'

'Don't follow me,' Tom shouted as he put a handkerchief to his face, opened the basement door and rushed down the dark steps. He was immediately aware of a very distinct hissing sound, it was coming from an unlit gas stove with a tap turned fully on. He turned it off then flung the kitchen windows and the door wide open.

Standing outside at the foot of the stone steps, he wondered how such a thing had happened. It could have been disaster. A chilling thought, with only himself, Mr Sheet in the study and Millie asleep with the lounge door open and a gas fire burning at the wrong time of the year. It was a cool day, but Tom felt apprehensive, for it could have blown the house sky high! 'Deliberate?' Tom thought. No, surely not!' He thought that Millie may have left the tap on as she was absent-minded and deaf. He thrust suspicion from his mind. When he went back upstairs, he found Mr Sheet standing in the hall in an agitated state.

'Is it all right?'

'I've left the door and windows open down there, it's clearing anyway, and you've opened the front door.'

'Yes of course, but is there a gas leak? Shouldn't we call in the gas men?'

'No, don't panic, a tap on the stove was left turned on.'

'But who...?'

'Your guess is as good as mine. Could have been Millie I suppose, being absent-minded! For goodness sake don't say anything about this to Mrs Blackburn, you know how she goes on at Millie. She might turn her out or something – best to keep quiet about it.'

'But...'

'Don't say anything Mr Sheet, we'll just have to keep an eye on things, that's all.'

'Yes, I can see that.'

'Where's Jessie this morning?'

'She was here at breakfast time, but she went out with Mrs Blackburn. She'll be leaving us soon you know. Pity!'

'Yes, I know,' Tom said. 'Where is everyone this morning?'

'I think doctor Desiri went out with Mr Gallagher.'

'Mum's the word!' Mr Sheet nodded and returned to the study.

Millie was still asleep when Tom quietly opened the door. He could still smell gas, so he turned off the gas fire and opened the French windows. The air was cool and moist after night rain and low clouds drifted across the sky. He did not think it was likely that anyone in the house would get gas poisoned, though he worried about Millie laying motionless. A chill went through him when he thought of the explosion there might have been.

The smell of gas had almost gone and Tom closed one window. The room did not seem cold to him so he wondered why the fire had been on. Then Millie stirred and Tom spoke to her softly. 'Good morning, are you all right?'

'I must have dozed off. What time is it?'

'Gone eleven,' Tom said, looking at his watch.

'Oh dear, I should be helping in the kitchen.' Tom heard the front door open. It was Mrs Blackburn and Jessie. They came into the lounge.

'Still resting Millie, I see,' Mrs Blackburn said sharply.

'I just thought I would lay down for a few minutes...'

'You really do spend far too much time on that sofa, you need some exercise Millie.' Tom thought this was very unfair to such a timid and frail old lady.

'Don't worry,' said Jessie, 'I can manage quite well.'

'I'd better come down and help you,' Mrs Blackburn said, 'see if we can make a start on the Sunday dinner. It's going to be late today!' Mrs Blackburn left quickly, followed by Jessie.

'Stay there Millie,' Tom said as she moved to get up from the sofa. 'Now they've gone, I have to tell you something.'

'Yes!' She was trembling and Tom was very concerned as to whether it was through nervousness or physical weakness.

'I don't want you to worry, but please do be careful with the gas, I found one of the taps left turned on.'

'Oh dear, but I'm sure I wouldn't... what will Martha say?'

'Martha? Is that Mrs Blackburn?' Tom asked.

'Yes, she'll be so angry.'

'I won't tell her and I'm sure no one else will. Did you want the gas fire on in here?'

'Oh, no thank you, Mr ... Hunt, it's not cold!'

'No, of course not.' Tom was mystified, but left it at that. He did not want to worry her as he felt she might be confused.

'Stay there, Millie, best place on a day like this.' Tom said it with a broad smile and he got a gentle smile in return.

'Thank you... you're a very good young gentleman.'

In the hall, the front door opened and Betty came in, followed by Mr Gallagher and Doctor Desiri.

'Good morning,' Tom said, startled. 'All of you together then?'

'No, we met at the gate,' Betty said. The two good-humoured men went into the sitting room, while Betty went to the stairs.

'Will you be free this afternoon?' Tom asked.

'I have some work to catch up with,' she said bluntly.

'I see, I thought you might keep me company, but... I'm sorry.'

'No. I'm busy, I've got to go, if you'll excuse me,' she said as she flew up the stairs making a quick escape. Tom felt quite hurt, as if he'd been kicked in the groin.

In the sitting room, Millie slowly got herself into a sitting position as Mr Gallagher and the doctor entered the room.

'How are you this morning Millie?' Mr Gallagher asked.

'Oh, Mr Gallers...' she said confusedly. 'Oh dear, I think I'm in trouble.'

'I'm sure you're not.'

'Oh yes, I left the gas turned on in the kitchen, and I will be in trouble.'

'Please Millie,' said the doctor, 'do try to relax, I am sure you are not going to be in any trouble.' Tom. came into the room with a long face.

'You look as if you've just seen a ghost,' Mr Gallagher said, addressing Tom.

'No... it's nothing,' he said with a vacant expression.

Chapter 17
Great Humiliation

The car driven by Doctor Desiri, was a 1937 saloon. The map net suspended from the roof was stuffed with a few medical journals. Tom sat in the back, enjoying the ride and the entertaining conversation between the doctor and Mr Gallagher. When the doctor had suggested that Tom needed cheering up and might like to come for a ride with them, he'd jumped at the idea.

'I'm hoping you're a good navigator, Gallagher, my friend?'

'Now would I be leading you on a wild goose chase, Doctor?'

'I am joking you know, these roads I find I am not familiar with, that's all.'

'There's my church, Doctor! Turn left and park up this road.' The car was parked and Tom went with then into the church. His first participation in a Roman Catholic Mass. It came as a surprise to him, as they had not mentioned going to church.

The service was delivered mostly in Latin. Tom thought of his studies at school but he was unable to understand what was being said and wondered how many in the congregation understood the unfamiliar words. He presumed his senior friends were both Catholics.This new experience was full of mystery and he was intrigued by the ritual. He thought of Betty; she was most likely Catholic and seemed a good Latin scholar. Tom's religious convictions were removed from ritual or any kind of dogma, but he believed there had to be a reason for the puzzling pattern that governed the universe. Near the end of the service the priest spoke in English. 'I want you to give to the collection, and when I say give generously, I mean you should give just a little more than you can really afford.' Tom wondered what he could really afford as he put his hand in his pocket. He found a few coins to put in the black collecting bag as he took the brass rod handle protruding from each end and passed it on.

The doctor drove them a short distance and stopped in the High Street right outside the shoe shop where Mr Gallagher was the manager. The sign across the frontage in gold letters on a black background read 'BEST'S SHOES.' As Gallagher unlocked the door, Doctor Desiri turned to Tom.

'I think we are greatly privileged, as it is Sunday!'

'Oh yes,' Tom said, who had not spoken since leaving the church.

'Come along in, gentleman,' Mr Gallagher said.

Tom watched as the doctor tried on several pairs of what looked like very expensive shoes.

'Those look attractive yes,' the Doctor said as Gallagher opened another box.

'Very special and imported from Ireland, would you know! Would you like to try them?'Tom was thinking he could do with a new pair himself, but he kept quiet, as he had to watch the pennies.

'These I would say are very well made,' the Doctor said as he put them on. Tom was thinking, there weren't the shortages in Ireland, even during the war years.

'How do those feel?' said Gallagher. The Doctor was walking and stepping up and down.

'Yes, I would say I can do no better than choose these.'

'Good!'

'Yes, very comfortable indeed, these feel.'

'Those are top quality, Doctor, well made and a good style.'

'You wrap them up, yes,' the doctor said as he removed the shoes and handed them over.

'There we are,' Gallagher said, closing the shoe box lid, and the doctor took out his wallet.

'Now we settle up!'

'No need to worry today, Doctor, best left to a week day.'

The doctor put his precious shoe box in the car and they

crossed the road to the pub. When they entered, Tom was quickly aware that the manager from Best's Shoe Shop opposite was one of their regular customers, for the barmaid had his favourite stout poured before he could get to the bar.

'How are you today, Mr Gallagher?'

'Topping. I have to say you're looking gorgeous this morning, Elsa.' She was a big woman of about forty with auburn hair and well made up with blue eye shadow.

'Go on... silly old flatterer.'

'Now you have to let me get these,' said the doctor, pushing to the bar. 'A large scotch for me and you Mr ...'

'Tom's the name,' Tom said quickly.

'Oh yes, Tom of course.'

'I'll have a glass of bitter thank you.'

'Pint is it?'

'Just a half please, Doctor.'

They stood at the bar chatting, while the number of customers mounted around them and voices were becoming louder.

'Tell me,' said Gallagher addressing Tom, 'what was poor old Millie so very agitated about this morning?'

'You won't mention it to Mrs Blackburn, will you,' Tom said. 'She'd be furious!'

'Why, what was happening?' said the doctor.

'Could have blown the house up,' Tom said, then watched their open-mouthed expressions as he told the whole story.

'That was an act of bravery, Tom,' said Gallagher. 'Saved us all from extinction.'

'Hardly that, I acted on the spur of the moment. Anyway you were both out!'

'Yes, I was showing Gallagher my surgery, Mr Tom,' said the doctor.

'Do you imagine it could have been Millie?' Mr Gallagher said.

'Don't ask!' Tom said. 'We'll have to watch that it doesn't happen again. I've never seen Mr Sheet looking so pale with sheer fright!' There was some amusement, though they were naturally worried.

Tom tried to get a round of drinks but Gallagher stepped in first, and Tom soon found he had a pint in his hand instead of a half. 'Where did Betty, er Miss Lovell, get to this morning?'

'She went to early Mass,' said Gallagher.

'Oh, I see... well, she wasn't very sociable this morning. I think she was trying to avoid me.'

'She's a strange girl, and perhaps she is concealing a deep secret,' Gallagher said with an enigmatic smile.

'That seems unlikely,' Tom said thoughtfully. 'I feel let down and wonder what she's got against me!'

'I can't imagine she would be against you,' Gallagher said, and they laughed. Tom thought they were laughing at him.

'She's about to finish for the holidays,' Tom said and drank up his beer. 'She's pale and looks tired sometimes – and we don't often see her at breakfast.'

'She would be sleeping, Mr Tom, sleeping!' the doctor said. Meanwhile, Gallagher was getting another round of drinks.

'She goes to bed early most nights though,' Tom said. 'But I suppose she might be busy marking books till late.'

'Here we are, that will surely warm the cockles!' Tom had noticed Gallagher drink up a quick scotch, then pour another one into his beer. Tom suspected his own beer was also laced with scotch, but he was beyond caring.

'I think she has mesmerised you with a hypnotic power,' the doctor said. 'And you have gone very faint. That will do no good at all, yes I think so, Mr Tom!'

'I thought she liked me,' Tom said suddenly, a lost expression on his face.

'Best not to get too serious with women,' Gallagher said. 'I think there's no doubt about it, you're a romantic fellow. You hardly know her, is that not so, Tom?'

'Well, we were getting on fine but then she suddenly went cold on me.' He paused to drink. 'And I was surprised when Mrs Blackburn got so funny with me when I called Miss Lovell

Betty. Surely that's none of her business, is it? Seems strange to me. Can't win, can I?'

'You must not let her worry you, Mr Tom,' said the doctor. 'She is a woman, set in her ways.'

Tom glanced down just in time to see that his glass was being laced with tots of whisky from both sides, but he pretended he didn't notice, as the ambience all around him was getting very warm and friendly. Customers were singing into a microphone at one end of the bar. It all became strangely unreal as Tom watched some, who thought they could sing, go to the microphone to render a song, accompanied by a pianist who would play anything requested. Tom thought they were doing well as he stood there slightly swaying while holding his glass of laced beer. He was no longer counting how many he'd had or noticing who supplied them. His well-intentioned friends were probably trying to draw him out of his apparent state of malaise.

Tom was amazed to see Mr Gallagher take the microphone, a leaning figure in his smart grey suit, with the light reflecting in his glasses, in contrast to his dark moustache. He looked very different from usual. Tom could never have visualised him singing in a pub, or anywhere for that matter. He sang a couple of songs, 'I'll take you home again Kathleen' and 'The Mountains of Mourne'. Though it was not a great performance, witnessed through the mists of inebriation, it was appealing enough.

The next thing Tom remembered was sitting in the back of a car. Everything seemed to be made of rubber, including the houses and trees, as he swayed on the back seat. He was deluding himself, thinking he would appear to be quite sober on arrival at the lodgings. At the dining table, he tried hard to behave in a completely normal fashion, but in fact he was ridiculously over polite. As he looked at the plate of roast beef and Yorkshire pudding placed before him, everything on the table appeared to move away, followed by a sharp crack on the back of his head. It was the floor! 'I wonder how that happened!' he slurred as he looked up at those peering down at him.

He was helped up to his room, and was vaguely aware that

it was the doctor and Gallagher assisting him. So he was in good hands, and felt sure they'd take the blame, though he would still be in disgrace, whatever they said. Now that had really done it. Betty wouldn't want to know him now. This was the main thought in his befuddled mind while he laid there on his bed. He remembered the look on her pale ivory face as he'd joined the table, and he even remembered she was wearing a check dress. As he tried keeping his eyes closed the room would float up and up, looping the loop, so he had to open his eyes widely. Eventually he went to sleep and he was surprised to find that it was getting dark when he woke up hours later.

The stairs seamed to creak more than he'd ever noticed before as he crept slowly down, still feeling woozy and also apprehensive about who he might meet. He could not help feeling annoyed with himself for being so stupidly taken in and made to look a fool, though he did not dismiss the fact that two fellow lodgers, twice his age, had let him down. They were to blame. It was, he thought, a good experience and enjoyable while it lasted; but was it worth it?

The house was very quiet as Tom went down into the hall. He looked into the music room, which was dimly lit only from the fading daylight. He was surprised by the faint figure of Mr Sheet sitting in the corner behind the grand piano.

'I thought there was nobody in here,' Tom said.

'Oh hello.' Mr Sheet gave a little laugh. 'Are you all right?'

'Yes... well, not too bad.' Tom paused while Mr Sheet was still chuckling. 'I was, er... sorry to cause trouble!'

'I thought it was rather funny myself.'

'I don't suppose Mrs B found it funny though.'

'Oh I don't know. I wouldn't let it worry you.' He continued to chuckle. 'You must be hungry, or are you off food?'

'Not completely, got a bit of a head though.'

'That's not surprising,' Mr Sheet said with amusement. 'You missed supper but you could always go down to the kitchen.'

'Yes,' Tom said, hesitating. 'But Mrs B might be down there!'

'I think she's upstairs.'

Tom looked out of the window as the street lights were coming on. 'Do you like sitting in the dark, Mr Sheet?'

'I find it rather pleasant, it concentrates the mind.'

'Do you mind me talking to you?'

'No, of course I don't.' He gave a little laugh. 'Did you want to talk about something special then?'

'Well, I've been a bit of a fool, but on the other hand, it wasn't without reason. You know I've been going out with Betty?' Tom spoke very softly.

'Betty Lovell, um...Yes, you seem to get on well together!'

'But the problem is, she's gone right off me, I know it sounds a bit silly, but... since I gave her a little kiss on the cheek – and believe me, that's all it was – she's strangely distant. I always thought she liked me!'

'Women are like that, in my experience. Never had much luck myself.' Tom couldn't imagine Mr Sheet involved in a romance. 'It doesn't bother me now though.'

'But I love...' Tom began. Well, I thought I loved her!'

'You could fall in love with Princess Elizabeth but that wouldn't get you anywhere.'

'But I do love Princess Elizabeth!' Tom insisted, and Mr Sheet chuckled.

'I think you're in love with love, that's your trouble.'

'Aren't you, Mr Sheet?'

Down in the kitchen, Jessie had just finished doing some of her ironing. She picked up the pile of clothes and went to open the kitchen door. As she did so, the latch went up and the door came towards her, which made her jump back and almost drop the carefully folded pile. Tom apologised, thinking again how stupid he'd been. Yet Jessie was always cheerful and easy to get on with. 'Are you on the scrounge again?' she smiled.

'Well...' Tom managed a laugh.

'You're hungry now!' Jessie said with a bright and amused expression.

'I could manage a slice of bread and butter, if possible.'

She was still holding her pile of ironed clothes, so she put them down on the table.

'Of course it's possible, and how are you feeling now, apart from being hungry?' She was looking back from the table as she spoke, with a smile. 'Your performance at dinnertime was really staggering!'

'Oh dear, not too brilliant, was it? I... it was stupid.'

'I wouldn't let it worry you – a lesson learned though!'

Tom was now thinking: *why fall for a moody woman? Jessie's nice and gives me a warm feeling inside.* She took out a loaf of bread and put it on the table. Jessie always joined the rest of the guests at the dining table after sending up the food on the dumb waiter.

'This is no holiday for you,' Tom said. 'I mean your aunt making you work in the kitchen.'

She gave a burst of laughter. 'She doesn't force me to work, she pays me and it's good domestic experience anyway.' She paused. 'Mr Gallagher and the doctor were most concerned, by the way. In fact they went to great lengths to assure my aunt that it was entirely their fault. Will two slices be enough or do you want more?'

'Two will be OK, I think.'

'I'll make it three!' she said.

'But I must be in your aunt's bad books now!'

'On the contrary, I think it's your two friends she's displeased with, Tom.'

'That's a relief, but on the other hand, I feel I've got them into trouble. Where are they now?'

'Probably skulking in their rooms!' Tom had to laugh. 'There you are.' She finished buttering the bread.

'Thank you, Jessie, you're very good to me.'

'It's no trouble, Tom.' She was smiling and he could see she regarded the episode with amusement.

'It's been a strange day. There was nobody about this morning first thing and...'

Jessie sat down. 'Yes, I heard about your quick action over

the gas leak. Sit down, Tom, there's no point in standing while you eat.'

'It wasn't a leak,' Tom said as he sat down opposite her. 'I hope your aunt didn't know about it. Don't you think she's a bit hard on Millie?'

'Yes, I think she can be. I knew it wasn't a leak and I'm sure no one told my Aunt. Pity in a way, she would thank you!'

'Yes, but who told you then?'

'Mr Sheet, he was quite agitated.'

'Well, as long as he doesn't spill the beans!' added Tom.

'I shouldn't think that likely. We'll have to watch Millie though, she shouldn't be helping in the kitchen really.'

'Yes, you're right of course.' They were silent for a while. 'Haven't seen Peter Gordon around,' Tom said.

'He's off somewhere this weekend. Can't stand the man, he's very arrogant.'

Tom agreed but he was cautious in his reply. 'Do you think so?'

'I wouldn't trust him, but that's only my opinion.'

''It takes all sorts.' Tom finished his last slice of bread. 'Mmm – I was thinking...'

'What are you thinking about?'

'Only that I wish you weren't leaving us!'

'Oh Tom, I can't stay with my aunt all the time.'

'No, of course not.' And Tom gave a restrained laugh.

Later during that week, soon after the evening meal, Mrs Blackburn approached Tom with a very grim expression. 'Miss Lovell is waiting to see you in the music room.'

'What does she want to see me about?'

'She wishes to make a complaint about your behaviour.'

'What am I supposed to have done?'

'You'd better go and see her, hadn't you. I really cannot tolerate this sort of thing in my house.'

Tom began to get very nervous, as he had no idea what it was all about. He just thought he was being victimised because of the previous Sunday. 'She can come in to me if she has something to say,' he asserted.

'It's a private matter, Mr Hunt, so will you go. She's waiting to talk to you.'

'Yes, I'll go and see her, but I'm sure it's no bloody business of yours. Busybody!' he found himself shouting at her as he left the room. He caught a glance of Gallagher and the doctor as he went by them. He saw their surprised expressions, but he also detected a suggestion of amusement on their faces.

The music room door was closed and Tom opened it gently. 'Hello Betty! What's this all about?'

'Come in and sit down,' she said coldly. Tom felt he was being spoken to as if he was one of her young pupils who had misbehaved. He sat in the armchair next to where she was sitting.

'What's wrong then, and why is Mrs Blackburn so...?'

'I was utterly humiliated at the dining table this evening.'

'In what way?'

'You were staring at me all the time. Every time I looked at you, you were looking straight at me.'

'I'm sorry, I didn't realise I was.'

'Yes you did, you know very well, it was deliberate.'

'But, you've been so cold towards me. What am I supposed to have done? Perhaps I have feelings about you that I can't help and I didn't know I was embarrassing you.'

'I have no feelings for you. Do I make myself clear?'

'Yes, but we were getting on well, I mean as friends.'

'I have no wish to continue that friendship, that's final!'

'Why tell Mrs B? That wasn't necessary.' Tom walked to the door. 'Now I'll have to leave this house, I'm very upset!'

The doctor and Gallagher were in the sitting room engaged in mundane conversation with nothing further from their minds than Tom's predicament. Mrs Blackburn came into the room. She had gone upstairs after her fracas with Tom and commiserated with her old friend Mr Robinson. He would always be meekly in full agreement with her. He would not dare to appear otherwise.

'That was the last straw, I cannot tolerate that kind of ill-mannered profanity in this house.' She was standing before them with her face very red and a most severe expression.

'He is a very sensitive young fellow, in a fluster too!' the doctor said. 'Please try not to be too hard on him.'

'That's as may be, Doctor, but he'll have to leave.'

'I feel sure he'll apologise,' Gallagher said.

'Yes, yes,' the doctor agreed.'

'We'll see about that!' Mrs Blackburn stalked out.

As Mrs Blackburn entered the hall, Tom had just left the music room in a very agitated state.

'I hope you're satisfied, Mr Hunt!' There was a momentary stunned silence as they looked at each other. Her face was still very red and distorted, while Tom looked at her as if he was about to explode.

'No, of course I'm not satisfied, it's all your fault anyway.'

'Just what are you talking about, young man? You come in drunk on a Sunday, you cause a disturbance, upset Miss.Lovell and the other guests in the house. You'll leave at the end of the week, Mr Hunt.'

'Don't you worry, I've already decided to look for another lodging.'

'Good, then that's settled.'

'No, legally I'm entitled to a month's notice. You should know that.'

'After the way you spoke to me, I would have the right to turn you out this minute.'

Tom went to the stairs. 'I'm going to start packing to leave, and I'll go as soon as I can find somewhere.'

'Don't ask for a reference, you'll not get one from me.'

'I'm not employed by you, Mrs B, and these are not Victorian days, you know.'

'You'd better be more polite if you find somewhere decent, that's all I can say.'

'If it hadn't been for me on Sunday, you wouldn't have a house anyway, it would have blown up and all you'd have been left with would be a heap of rubble.'

'What are you talking about now?'

'Nothing at all, Mrs Blackburn, nothing,' he muttered as he turned and went up a few more steps. 'You wouldn't have thanked me anyway.'

In the sitting room, Tom's two senior friends were quietly hoping to hear some of the loudly spoken words in the hall through the closed door. Then in walked Mrs Blackburn with a very red face. 'He must be quite mad!' she said. 'It really is intolerable. What is he talking about?'

'He's disturbed and perhaps we need to allow for that,' Mr Gallagher said.

'Yes, very agitated indeed, Mrs Blackburn. Would he let the house be blown up?'

'What do you mean? Mr Hunt said the same thing. You are all quite mad in this house! He's leaving us anyway.' And she swiftly left the room.

Some weeks later, after Tom had moved out of Stoneliegh house, he rang Gallagher at the shoe shop. He had unfortunately left a pile of music in the piano seat and couldn't face going back to get it. So he asked Gallagher if he would mind bringing it to the shop, and suggested he could meet him there one evening. He appeared overjoyed to oblige Tom and arranged to meet him the following Friday evening.

As Tom entered the shop he saw Gallagher at the far end talking to one of the girl assistants. When he spotted Tom, he burst into a smile, came straight over to him and they shook hands with vigour. Tom waited for him to shut up the shop at six and he brought the bundle of music from his office.

'That's a weighty parcel,' he said as he gave it to Tom. It was tied up with string. 'I hope they're all there,' he said as he locked the shop door.

'I'm surprised how much music I'd left there, just the books with my name on top.'

'Yes, I went through them carefully. Would it worry you if

you found I'd pinched a few by mistake?'

'Not really,' Tom laughed. 'Anyway, thank you very much.'

'You'll be coming over the road will you Tom?' Gallagher said as he started to the edge of the pavement.

'Yes, OK, but I can't stop long.'

There was the usual greeting from Elsa who had already poured him a Guinness. Tom insisted on paying and got himself a half of bitter.

'We'll sit over there if you like, Tom.' The pub was quiet at that time and they sat on a moulded ply seat with a pattern of holes and shiny from much use. As they sat before a dark wooden table, their conversation was affable though carefully not intimate. 'You've time for another now?'

Tom looked at his watch. 'No thank you very much, I really haven't got time.'

'Well now, that's a pity, but I can see time is pressing. By the way, Tom, I must tell you this: who do you think Mr Sheet's latest passion is?'

'I've no idea,' Tom said.

'It's Miss Betty Lovell. Now can you imagine that!'

'No. On the other hand, I suppose it's normal.' Tom grabbed his bundle of music, thinking how insensitive it was to tell him that last little bombshell of news. Gallagher remained seated. They gave each other a little wave as Tom left, and never saw each other again.

Chapter 18
Newburne, October 1950

Wakely sat in his dusty office, his lean figure crumpled over his desk as he wrote a carefully composed letter. It was a letter of resignation, for he was very much aware that his days at Fentons were numbered. There was an important question in his mind, but the wording did not come easy to his brusque nature. Should he get an official letter to the management before they informed him that he no longer had a job there? He had already screwed up several sheets of writing paper.

The grey-haired figure within a muddled setting of old blueprints in tatty rolls and folded bundles on the floor tied with string was a sad contrast to the once feared man. His power was broken. The windows that surrounded him where he would keep an eagle eye on the men operating the great number of machines were now grimy and the works were silent with many of the machines being dismantled and taken away. He looked up from his letter, and through the dingy glass, he saw the sturdy figure of Mr Wills approaching across the dusty and uneven factory floor.

Footsteps came quickly up the steep treads to the lookout office, then a sharp rap on the door.

'Good morning,' Mr Wills said, his white teeth contrasting with the black beard and moustache. He held a roll of prints which he banged rhythmically against his left hand, a habit he had never lost.

'Good morning, Wills, I presume you're keeping busy?'

'Yes, picking up orders,' Mr Wills said a little smugly.

'Glad to hear it for your sake. You know I can't say the same thing here in this place.'

'Yes.' Wills coughed. 'We know why the business has gone down – the management are to blame! They should have seen how things were going. They could have diversified. I sometimes wonder if they deliberately allowed the wind-down. Either that or they didn't know how to handle the situation – probably more likely!'

'That's your opinion, Wills. Whatever the reason, it's the end of the road for me, the end of the road,' Wakely repeated.

'Oh! I wouldn't say that. You're bound to...'

'I'll be out soon!'

'Uh - well... but have you made plans?'

'Plans? I'll retire, that's what I'll do, I've got some investments, so I could manage.'

'Not invested with Fentons I hope!'

'Well, yes and I will look into that,' Wakely muttered.

'Waste no time, Mr Wakely. Take my advice and go and see the management straight away.'

'I don't need your advice, Wills, but I will have it out with them. The worst thing would be if I have to take a job. Not easy for a man of my age. Almost thirty years I've been with Fentons, pretty well running this place – not easy to give up.'

'You won't! It's not in your nature'

'I'll sort something out,' Wakely said. 'All right for you, your place seems to be expanding. Nice little niche you've found yourself there, Wills.' Mr Wakely started to scribble again.

Mr Wills peered down through the grimy windows as he spoke.'I've built up a business which is now paying off. It's a matter of being able to produce something that people want, but you have to go out and find them. The rotary pumps are even doing well in the export market. I go away now as a rep, including trips abroad.' He turned away from the windows.

'Yes, I know you do, don't see you around so much.'

'No, of course. We're looking for new premises. This whole place will probably be demolished.'

'It's already dead!' Wakely said with a scowl, still leaning on his desk and looking up at Wills from behind his left shoulder.

Wills paced around Wakely's office, glancing at the untidy clutter. It all looked very depressing. Wakely scribbled a few more words of his letter, a solitary figure whose world was disintegrating around him. Wills gazed at the surrounding mess, at the dirty windows. The only sound came from Wakely's pen. In the midst of the decay, it was a place full of nostalgia.

Wills broke the silence: 'We've got a good order from an East London Company,' he said as he glanced down at Wakely, who had his pen poised over his rough scribbling. 'Don't let me disturb you!'

'No, you're not disturbing me, Wills.' Wakely looked up and turned in his office chair. 'What were you telling me?'

'I thought you might be interested. I went to procure the order in London a few months ago and stayed with a relative who lives at Wanstead and quite by chance I met a young chap who was an apprentice here.'

'Oh, who might that be then?'

'Do you remember Tom Hunt?' There was a short silence as Wakely's expression changed from one of boredom to a look of surprise.

'Yes, I do remember Hunt! He was trouble to me and going nowhere.'

'I think you're wrong, Mr Wakely. It was a coincidence that we should meet by the lake, quite remarkable really. Anyway, I'm glad to say he seems to be doing very well with a shipping firm.'

'You surprise me, Wills. I wonder how long that will last.'

'I think you were a bit hard on him, I must say that. He was good at his work, rather immature at the time, but he's going somewhere now in my opinion.'

'He needed to grow up – something to make a man out of him. I can't imagine it though. Could have been wrong, I suppose, but it's hard to believe.'

There was a lot of shouting going on down near the entrance.

'What's going on down there?' Wills said as he went to the

office door. A very large transporter lorry was being directed as it was slowly backing into the works. 'Another large machine about to be taken away, I think.'

'Yes!' Wakely said, 'I was expecting them, that's all I'm concerned with these days, dealing with the removal of machinery.'

'Keeps you occupied,' Wills said with a broad smile.

'If you think that's a joke, Wills, it's in poor taste.'

'It was just a remark, that's all.' He cleared his throat. 'Are you writing an epistle, Mr Wakely?'

'No concern of yours, Wills.'

'Oh! I didn't wish to pry.'

'I may as well tell you, I'm writing a letter of resignation. Thought I'd get in before the management tell me to push off!'

'Do you think that's wise?'

'Yes!' Wakely was very abrupt. 'Why not?'

'If you resign, they won't compensate you in any way – that's not a wise...'

'There's no chance,' he said with slow emphasis, 'they'd compensate me, I can tell you that. Anyway, I've made my own provisions long ago.'

'But I would have a talk with Meddows, just to get it straight where you stand – and especially as you have shares with Fentons.'

'I might.' Wakely screwed up what he'd written and threw it into the waste paper basket. 'Just leave me alone, Wills.'

'All right, I'm going.' Wakely looked at Wills, who was smiling broadly as he trotted quickly down the steps.

It was a chilly October day in Newburne and there were a few spots of rain starting. The large brown double doors were locked with no sign of recent use. The only thing new, was a heavy padlock securing the small access door set into one of the large doors. The office windows were dark and so dusty that the once bright gold lettering on the glass that spelt out the name 'FENTON AND SON' was scarcely visible. The whole impression was of a dismal and lifeless edifice. Tom sadly remembered that the cracked grey window was where Mildred once typed. A sudden feeling of nostalgia came over him as he thought of the happy laughter, and a wave of memories from the past flowed over him as he thought back to the violin lessons that he'd abandoned long ago. He stepped outwards on the pavement and looked up at the dark windows above, he had a futile thought of seeing a light up there but there was just blackness.

Beyond the derelict and boarded up cinema building, that the grammar school boys used to call the flea pit, a small side entrance wide enough for a car or a small lorry, lead to the back yard. The gate was open, and on it was fixed a new white sign board: 'MERTON PUMP COMPANY' and underneath in smaller letters, 'Directors, Jackson and Wills.'

The name on the sign amazed Tom: it had to be the Mr Wills he knew, who was now a partner in the small industry. He walked down the yard with a smile, thinking how well his old friendly and quite matter-of-fact colleague had succeeded. He was very curious to see how the place looked, after five years had passed. The yard had been cleared of the metal store and the old rusty castings. Even the welding shop and the toilets had gone. The fitting shop and smiths still stood, but locked and soundless, like disused warehouses.

The pump shop building showed little change, except for the new sign board, and the doors were newly painted. Tom opened the door and found himself in a cosy workshop. Four or five men were quietly working, and one man looked up as Tom closed the door.

'Good afternoon,' Tom said. 'Bit chilly out there!'

The man smiled and pointed to the office on the left. 'Do you want the reception?'

'Thank you!'

Behind the glass-fronted door with a drawn blind was the sound of typing. He hesitated before knocking and he placed his hand on the door handle, thinking he would see Mildred sitting there. He decided it was unlikely and he was having fantasies. It was a feeling familiar to him; of wanting though apprehensive. His strange feelings of panic were in a way, becoming mysteriously pleasurable. He turned the handle and looked in to see a bespectacled lady typing. She looked up at Tom and gave him a big smile.

'Oh, hello there!'Tom was speechless for an instant: he was looking at Mildred. The surprise knocked him back. She was just the same as far as he was concerned. She wore a pale pink woollen jumper which did nothing to hide the shape of her well formed bust, and a quiver went up his spine.

'You're still here,' he said clumsily. 'But in the Pump Shop. I meant to say, its... very nice to see you!'

'Well, this is a surprise!' Mildred said brightly and turned round on her stool, showing a shapely right knee. 'And how are you getting on now, Mr Hunt?'

'It's Tom – remember?'

'Yes, of course.' She paused. 'You've arranged to see...'

'Is Mr Wills in? I thought I would call as I am in Newburne, if he's not too busy.'

'If you don't mind hanging on a minute, he's got someone in his office at the moment, but I don't think he'll be long. It's nice of you to call in.'

'Oh, thank you.'

'Are you doing well?' she asked.

'All right!' Tom felt a warm glow as the old feelings came back. 'I think I may have to leave Brown and Saxon though. Not much future there as far as I can see.'

'That's a blow then!' She turned more, and faced him with both knees now showing.

'I don't really...' As he glanced at her knees, he faltered, embarrassed.

'Are you staying in Newburne, or is this a flying visit?'

'I'm staying with my parents for a few days. They've moved to Henley where my father's gone into partnership with a firm of builders. I've come to pay the old town a visit.' Tom thought of Mr Wills and instinctively glanced at Mildred's left hand. She was not wearing a ring!

'You've chosen an awful day.' She turned her head and looked at the window. 'Look at the rain now!'

'I did think to bring an umbrella,' he said with a smile.

'So I see, very wise.' There was a pause in the conversation as Mildred turned and typed a paragraph. She seemed very fast to Tom.

'Don't let me keep you from your work,' Tom said hesitantly.

'That's all right,' she said, turning back to Tom. 'I hope you're keeping up your music practice?'

'Well yes! But it's difficult in lodgings with the violin, which is frustrating, but I'm practising more on the piano.'

'I suppose it could be a problem. Some people are very unreasonable, but I'm glad you could use the piano.'

'Yes, though it's in a small room at the hotel where I'm staying, and a bit out of tune.' Mildred laughed. 'Better than nothing,' Tom continued. 'It would be nice if I had a flat or something, but I have to wait till I get settled. If I change my job...'

'So we'll see then. I do hope it works out right for you.'

'Yes, thank you, I have to do some thinking.'

'Of course,' Mildred paused. 'I enjoy the piano myself. Though the violin's my first instrument, I need the piano for accompaniment when I'm giving lessons.'

Tom felt they were continuing a talk he'd had with her years ago. 'I was wondering, I thought that... perhaps?'

'Well, this is a hesitating question,' she said with a smile. 'Come on!'

'I imagined you as a full-time musician by now.' Tom had an embarrassed grin as he thought he shouldn't have said that.

'I'd not be here typing if I could do music full-time!'

'No...' Tom was lost for words.

'I belong to the local orchestra and give more lessons now. You see, I don't do full-time. I'm not here on Friday afternoons or Saturday mornings. Frank is very helpful there.'

'Frank?'

'Frank Wills. You'll be seeing him in a minute.' She looked at her watch.

Tom had never known his first name, and he felt a twinge of jealousy. He hesitated. 'It's a pleasant surprise to see you!' She smiled broadly.

'I know Frank will be pleased to see you. You're in luck to find him in today.' There was a knock on the door and a man poked his head in.

'Thank you,' the man said. 'I'll be off now, make a dash for the car. What a morning!'

'Yes,' said Mildred. 'Bring some sunshine the next time you call! Cheerio, Mr Clerk.' Turning to Tom she said. 'I'll just ring up and tell Frank you're here.' She picked up the receiver and dialled one number. 'He'd have been disappointed if he'd missed you... Hello? There's a friend of yours here...Tom Hunt... yes, I'll tell him to come up right now then.' She was smiling as she replaced the receiver. 'Frank was surprised – he's looking forward to seeing you.'

Some men looked up as he walked to the stairs, but there was no one he could recognise from the past. As he went up the open wooden treads, he tried to dismiss any jealous thoughts, which were probably unfounded, yet still lingered, even after years had gone by. He wondered what kind of relationship Mildred now had with his old colleague. He was stunned at how the past had suddenly caught up with him, a strange feeling. He was sure he would never have felt that way if he had not met Mildred so unexpectedly. At the top there was a large room over the workshop where two draughtsmen and a lady tracer were busily working. Mr Wills came out from a door at the far corner with a beaming smile.

'A return visit is this Tom?' Mr Wills stood eyeing him with an amused expression, as if he'd only seen him a few hours before and had no intention of shaking his hand.

'Thought it about time I called.' Tom stretched out his hand, which Wills took. 'Happened to be this way – doing well I see.'

'As seemed with you, Tom, when our paths crossed a while ago.'

'No comparison!' Tom said, glancing around.

'Depends on what you want out of life. Anyway, come into my office.' Tom followed him in and Mr Wills sat behind his desk. 'Well sit down and feel free.'

'Thank you. This is a nice clean office!' Tom was glancing round at the cream walls, bare except for a large old framed photograph of an early steam ship.

'Yes, just been redecorated,' Wills explained. 'Hardly worth it though, we'll be out of here and in new premises in six weeks time.'

'Oh I see,' Tom smiled, still glancing round. 'Is it a bigger place then?'

'Correct! Though not a great deal larger. But the position is better, we're hidden away here. So we're moving to the Boltwood Industrial Park, just north of the river.'

'But this is almost in the centre of the town. Excuse me saying so, but I wouldn't say you were hidden away here'

'Well, to be honest with you, Tom, there are complications. If the decision was up to me, I would rather stay put!'

Mr Wills turned and looked out of the window, as if to check if there was any sudden change. He turned to Tom and spoke. 'The whole of this area has been bought up by a conglomerate with, it seems, unlimited capital. But we're still here and they want to get us out. I've been sticking it out as long as possible, as the bribe grew.' He smiled and hesitated. 'I have got to the point now, where I've given in. It's a deal I had to except. But the Boltwood isn't really out of the way. Almost everything is transported by road now, and there's plenty of room for lorries. No having to get through the town.' Tom wondered how much his old colleague had made on the deal.

'This whole place will be dead soon then?' Tom said.

'Could be completely cleared, but I don't know just what's being planned.'

'It's just that I don't like to see all this running down, it seems like a waste.'

'I think I understand how you are thinking Tom, but it's part of progress.

'It doesn't seem like progress to me,' Tom said anxiously.

Mr Wills got up and took a large book from a cabinet. 'See this, he said, weighing the book in both hands. 'This is our order book, and they're coming in more frequently as time goes by. There will come a time when I may have to take on some extra staff. We're not running down – just the opposite in fact.'

'Yes, of course, I see. I meant the old works, of course.'

'I know, it's a bit of a mess now!' Mr Wills said, with a wry smile.

'You've gone in with Mr Jackson?' Tom said hesitatingly.

'We're partners now, working out very well for us, not to say that anything is certain but we hope we have a reasonable future. You would have known our friend Jackson from the old days of course.'

'Yes, but I don't think he cared for me much!'

'He's not so bad when you get to know him.'

It all seemed a little unreal to Tom, for big changes made him feel unsettled. He looked at the picture of the steam boat, it seemed out of place there. 'That's an interesting old photograph of a steamship!' he said.

'Yes, it used to hang in old Mr Fenton's office.'

'Oh, so how...?'

'Did it come to be in my office?'

'I hope you don't mind me asking.'

'Of course not. It was given to me by his wife, she's a charming old lady, and still lives in the big house at the bottom of White Heath Hill. I keep in touch with her and call quite often, it makes her feel that there's still some link with the old firm. It's as if she can't accept that the place no longer exists.'

'I used to give the old fellow a lift to work some mornings, a long time ago. He always seemed sad to me.'

'I expect he could see all that he'd worked for falling apart and he could do nothing about it. He lost his only son in the Great War in 1914, you know.'

They sat in silence for a moment, then Mr Wills said, 'I'll be going to see Mrs Fenton tomorrow afternoon, I usually make it Friday if I can. You can come with me if you like and meet her.'

'I'd very much like that,' Tom said making a quick decision. 'Would she mind me coming?'

'No, I'm sure, because she likes visitors from the old firm. Are you staying in Newburne, Tom?'

'No, at my parents' place, a bit further away, but there's a good bus service.'

'Can you be here at quarter to three?'

'Yes, easily!'

'Good, that's arranged then, don't be late.'

'No I won't! I'll be on the dot.'

'You can find your way out, can't you? I have some phone calls I must make.'

'Yes, I'll see you tomorrow.' They shook hands.

Going down the steps, Tom was thankful that Mr Wills didn't come down to see him out. He was anxious to see Mildred again before he left. He walked through where the men were working and stood by the office door. One of the men, with straight blond hair, looked up and gave Tom such a serious look that he turned away quickly with a strange feeling, almost as if he was unwelcome there. He did not look back, preferring to think it was his imagination playing tricks with him.

He knocked and opened the door gently. Mildred, standing at an open filing cabinet, turned and gave him a warm smile. It rekindled a feeling that he'd left behind some years before, but he was much more self-assured than he'd been then. As he watched her sorting through files, a thrill went through him. He admired the perfection of her curves, no use trying not to think of sex. He wondered why such a normal part of nature should be a difficult subject. Surely love and sex were not necessarily the same, but he was a romantic. Astonishing how people, including good friends, (or were they?) would insist that romance only happened in stories and not in real life. The consequence was that he had to cope with frustration, which at times made concentration on his talents difficult. If there was some kind of special relationship between her and the now very much in charge Mr Wills, Tom felt he had to know.

Mildred shut the cabinet with a bit of a bang that took him

out of his deep thoughts. 'I'm... on my way out now,' Tom said.

Mildred locked up the filing cabinet. 'Did you have a good chat up there?'

'Yes we did. He was telling me about the new premises; will you be going there?'

'I think probably not, but I'm not sure at the moment. My position here helping out is only while I'm waiting to hear from someone in the music world.'

'Oh, I see.' Tom's emotions were tensing. 'Is that someone special?'

'No, nothing is special, but there's a possibility of getting into a theatre orchestra,' she said without showing much enthusiasm. 'Not really what I wanted, but at least it's music, and I'll do some teaching as well, that's all. It's difficult to get something permanent.'

'I hope it turns out all right for you, and I look forward to seeing you playing in... which theatre will it be then?'

'Thanks, Tom, but I can't say which theatre, the agent is dealing with it.' She moved some papers and put a book away on a shelf. 'Oh dear!' she said as she sat down in front of the type writer. 'It's not as if I'll be a solo player.'

'No!' Tom went silent for a moment. 'I'm coming here again tomorrow. I won't see you of course!'

'That's right. So you've arranged something with Frank have you?' Tom felt prickly as she called him by his first name.

'He's taking me along to meet Mrs Fenton in the afternoon.'

'Oh, that's good. I think you'll be very interested if you've not met her before.'

'No, that would hardly be likely. I used to sometimes give Mr Fenton a lift in the mornings, if I caught sight of him. He would be making his way with his stick very slowly, quite a long way for the old chap to walk, but I often saw him and he was always very grateful for the lift.'

'Yes, he would be.'

There was a silence as Tom glanced round the small office. 'Have you been to the house?'

'Yes, it's a large place. The garden's unfortunately rather neglected though.'

'That's a shame!'

'There are lots of model ships as well as pictures in the house, which should interest you. Mrs Fenton is an extremely knowledgeable lady. She's well over eighty.'

'Is she! She will have seen the firm grow and, well, finally crumble, for the want of a better word.'

'Yes, though she never seems to be downhearted. It was the old chap who would have felt it more, don't you think?'

'Yes, I think so, anyway I'm looking forward to tomorrow.'

'I'm sure you'll enjoy meeting Mrs Fenton,' Mildred fed a sheet of paper into the typewriter with carbon and copy paper underneath.

Tom felt he was distracting her from her work. He would rather have met her after work, and he paused for thought. He was too slow, for he was about to ask her to join him for lunch when he heard the voice of Mr Wills just outside the door. Tom was momentarily put off asking her the question. 'Your boss was outside, but I can't hear him now.'

'Yes, you mean Frank, my boss?' she said with a smile.

'Mr Wills, yes,' Tom smiled.

'I hardly look on him as my boss! I help him out, and that's what he pays me for.'

'I'm sorry... yes, of course.' Tom felt he'd said entirely the wrong thing.

'He doesn't worry you does he?'

'No, no! Not at all!' He joined in with her laughter.

'I don't think you need to worry.'

After that, Tom plucked up courage. 'Can you join me for lunch?'

'Oh dear,' Mildred said, 'I'm afraid today is out of the question. I really would like to, but I've got to rush off, I have an early pupil and will just have time for a quick sandwich. Perhaps some other time.'

'Yes, another time. Never mind... I'll see you again. It's been good meeting you.'

‘It’s been nice to see you again, Tom.’

He thought that Mr Wills might pop in and find him wasting her time, and it prompted him to get on his way. ‘I’d better be off now then,’ Tom said trying to appear bright and carefree. He had it on the tip of his tongue to say, ‘I’ll give you a call’, but it remained just a thought. As he took Midred’s soft hand in his, he thought for a moment of his last day at Fentons.

PART THREE

Chapter 19
Emily

The sun shone low in the sky as they drove along the tree-lined road that afternoon, with the light flashing onto their faces. Mr Wills was at the wheel of his small car with Tom, who was reminded of old Mr Fenton on his long and slow walk to work on this same road, always walking as he had done for many years. He would seldom miss being at his desk.

'I like this kind of day with winter approaching,' Tom said.

'Yes, sunny with a nip in the air.' They journeyed in silence for a minute.

'I was surprised to see Mildred West,' Tom said abruptly.

'In the reception office. Bowled over, were you?' smiled Mr Wills.

'Yes, I suppose I was, what with her musical ambitions...'

'She's invaluable to me, I'd be sorry to see her go.'

Such an answer sounded insensitive. Mildred's musical aspirations would always have been obvious to Tom. 'Highly reliable, I imagine; is she?'

'Yes, and she always knows what I want!'

Tom shuddered at the possibilities this suggested. 'In what way do you mean?'

'We can leave her to it and trust her to deal with most of the letters. She takes the weight off our shoulders. Knows how to keep the business going well. We make suggestions, and usually it just requires a signature from one of us – a working triangle. Believe me, she's almost indispensable.'

'Yes, I see.' Tom felt a little dispirited. Mr Wills had made it sound as if Mildred was almost running the small business. 'But

I was under the impression that she would rather be a full-time musician?' Tom was discreet enough not to divulge what she'd told him, but Mr Wills saved him worrying on that score.

'Yes of course! And she does take a long weekend which helps her with her music. If she left, we'd have to manage!'

They rounded a corner near the bottom of White Heath Hill. It was only a few more yards until Mr Wills pulled up just beyond a small gate on the left. 'This is it!' They got out of the car.

'A small entrance,' Tom said. He was looking at a wrought iron gate with a cast name plate that read 'OAKWOOD'.

'The main gates are farther along; always locked. This would be the gate Mr Fenton used, when he walked to work.

'I suppose it would be, it's a very attractive design.'

'Made by Fentons. The main gates match, but the railings have gone, like most of them in the town in the madness during the war. There's still a pile of them at the old foundry; rusting away!'

They walked between overgrown trees to the front of the house. An impressive red brick building, with a stone dated 1879 set into the wall above an impressive front door. There was a porch of decorative metalwork construction. Oakwood was the largest property in White Heath Hill with many trees and secluded by a small wood on the main gate side. Tom was very impressed but could see the garden was neglected. Mr Wills gave the bell pull a tug.

They waited on the doorstep for quite some time. Tom was about to suggest pulling the bell again when Mr Wills started coughing which worried Tom. Then a dog barked loudly behind the door, scratching wildly. Dogs didn't worry Tom, but he wondered how big it was.

'Are you okay?' Tom asked.

'All right.' Mr Wills cleared his throat. 'Don't worry about me.' The barking and scratching continued.

'Don't like the sound of that dog,' Tom said.

'He'll be all right when he sees me.'

'Do you think we should ring again.'

'No wait, Mrs Gilbert, the housekeeper will be in.'

'That dog will wear the door down if she's much longer.'

There was the sound of a key being turned and the door was opened by a smart woman aged about forty-five. Her fair hair was neatly drawn back with curved combs at the sides. She greeted them with a beaming smile, and held the dog by its collar as she pulled the door open. 'Hello, Mr Wills, nice to see you again.'

'Good afternoon, Mrs Gilbert.' At that point she let the dog loose, a large Labrador. 'Hello Skip.' Wills patted the dog. 'There you are, Tom, I said he'd be all right when he saw me!'

'Yes!' Tom patted the dog, who seemed equally pleased to see both of them.

'And you've brought a friend along?' Mrs Gilbert was looking at Tom with a smile.

'Yes, this is Thomas Hunt.'

'How do you do?' Tom said as he shook her hand. He looked at a cameo broach, pinned to one side of her cardigan.

'Nice to meet you. You work with Mr Wills?'

'No, I was with Fentons, and...'

'He was there for some time, Mrs Gilbert. He works in London now, but he's come down to see us.'

'Oh, that's nice. Do come in, both of you.' The dog scampered off into the trees somewhere. 'Don't worry about Skip, he's probably seen a squirrel. There are lots of them in the woods.'

They were in a square half panelled hall with a wide staircase. 'If you wouldn't mind waiting, I'll just go and tell Mrs Fenton you're here.'

'She seems very nice,' Tom said.

'Yes, she's been with the family for some years, so I believe, and she looks after Mrs Fenton's interests.'

'I see.' Tom's gaze fell on a large oil portrait that hung over the stairs, and he stepped forward to take a closer look. It was a painting of a beautiful woman with fair curls piled on top of her head. She wore a deep crimson velvet dress with a white lace collar. 'How beautiful!' Tom said. 'Who was Emily?' He was looking at the name on the bottom of the gilt frame.

'That's Mrs Fenton, probably painted about seventy years ago!'

Mrs Gilbert returned after a few minutes and beckoned them with both her hands. 'If you'd like to come into the drawing room and have tea: Mrs Fenton is so pleased you have called. They followed her through a dimly lit, panelled passage where on one side there were various models in glass cases of ships and engines. Tom only wished the light was better, but there was no time to linger anyway. He could not dispel the thought in his mind that he was about to see the lady who's portrait he had just been admiring, only she would be rather elderly.

They entered the large drawing room, where the furniture reminded Tom slightly of when he was staying at Forest Gate, though this was on a grander scale. There were many paintings, mostly of sea and harbour scenes but also a few landscapes. He also noticed a framed photograph on the wall, a little faded around the edges, of a family group sitting in the garden near the French windows.

Mrs Fenton was sitting in a comfortable armchair in front of a small table and silhouetted against the light from the French windows. She sat quite still and did not turn her head until they reached her. Then she turned suddenly, as if a little deaf.

'Ah, Mr Wills! It's good of you to call.' She moved her hand up gently and Mr Wills lightly held it. Tom moved in closer. 'And...?' She smiled as she looked at Tom and nodded. He was looking at a face that had worn the years well and showed great character. Though pale and wrinkled, Mr Fenton looked at him with bright eyes. Her hair was a little thin on top and as white as snow. He took her hand.

'I'm very pleased to meet you, Mrs Fenton.' Her eyes were almost hypnotic to Tom.

'It's good of you to come and see me,' she said, and in spite of her great age, he saw the likeness to the striking young woman in the painting. 'Please, both of you sit down. Mary will bring the tea in a moment.'

'Thank you,' Tom said.

'And what is your name young man?'

'Tom Hu—'

'Oh, I'm sorry!' Mr Wills intervened. This is Thomas Hunt, an old colleague.'

'Don't apologise, Mr Wills. There's no need for formalities. She smiled. 'And you work together, do you?'

'I work in London at the moment, but I was with the firm from my apprenticeship days.' He concealed his slight irritation at Mr Wills' intervention.

'You would have known my husband then, Charles...he was so very dedicated to his work'. She lowered her head in thought. 'He would never take a holiday you know. Poor old Charles. It wasn't easy for me at times but I miss him now he's gone!'

She rambled on about her late husband, and Tom listened to tales of long ago, a mixture of sadness and happiness. Just as he began to feel sorry for her, she would smile and look away in a dignified fashion. Mr Wills sat there surprisingly quiet, leaving Tom to listen and make the odd comment. As he did so, Tom noticed a small painting of a house in the country with patches of light on a tree-shaded lane, where hens were scratching. A Victorian lady carrying a basket was opening a gate while a dog looked up at her.

Mrs Gilbert came through the door bearing a large tray of tea and cakes, which she placed on the table.

'Thank you, Mary,' Mrs Fenton edged herself forward.

'Let me pour the tea, Emily?'

'If you wouldn't mind, Mary. You have a steady hand.' She had a white shawl which she started to pull up over her shoulders.

'Here, let me help you,' Mrs Gilbert said as she wrapped the shawl round her. 'You might find it chilly in front of the window, when we have a nice warm fire in the grate.'

'Don't fuss me, Mary; I wanted to enjoy the sunshine!' Mrs Gilbert sat with them and poured the tea.

'There you are, Emily.' She passed the tea to her with a smile.

'She's such a help to me you know,' Mrs Fenton said. 'Mary came to live with the family when she lost her husband.' There was a short silence.

'Do help yourselves to sugar,' Mrs Gilbert said. Tom could not help the feeling that the lady was trapped into a situation, almost as if she was a relative instead of a long-standing friend.

'Thank you,' Mr Wills said, speaking at last. Then he turned to Mrs Fenton. 'I can see you're well looked after.'

'Yes, of course.' Mrs Fenton said emphatically.

'Would you gentlemen like a nice home made rock cake?' Mrs Gilbert passed the plate to them both.

Tom was looking round the room, furnished in good solid mahogany, the paintings, prints and again at the old family group photograph that hung on the faded wallpaper. He was sure the room had been the same for many years. It had a presence. He thought of old Mr Fenton as a young man and head of the family. The room could tell so much!

'I sometimes used to give Mr Fenton a lift in the car, when I saw him walking in the mornings, Mrs Fenton.' Tom was not sure if she'd heard him, but then she turned her head.

'Yes, that's right, he would walk everywhere!'

'He was always very grateful for the lift,' Tom said loudly.

'In your car?'

'If I spotted him walking to work.' Tom leaned towards her with a smile.

'Oh, that was good of you, he would be grateful for that!'

Mr Wills sat quietly drinking his tea. Tom was still looking at the painting on the wall facing him.

'You're looking at the painting of my old house, Mr Hunt?'

'Yes,' Tom nodded. 'Your old house?'

'Many years ago, at Eastbrook.' She paused and looked out of the window. 'My father was a country doctor. He worked hard, but it was so peaceful out there in those days, so utterly peaceful.'

'Is the house still there?' Tom asked.

'Still there, did you say? It might be. But it is more than forty years since I was there!'

They stayed about an hour, and then Mrs Fenton thanked them for coming and hoped they would call again soon.

'She seems a very resilient old lady,' Tom said to Mrs Gilbert as she showed them out.

'Oh yes indeed, as strong-minded as ever. Thank you both for calling, I hope we'll see you again,' she said, addressing Tom. 'Mr Wills often comes to tea,' she said glancing up at him with a smile.

Emily silently gazed out of the windows onto the terrace. Early autumn leaves blew across the flagstones and the late sunlight shone low onto the unkempt garden. The tennis court was so neglected that it would only by chance be recognised as such by a newcomer.

'I don't want you to get cold there,' Mrs Gilbert said as she gathered up the tea things onto the tray. 'Why don't you come and sit by the fire where it's warmer?'

'No thank you, Mary. You do fuss so. I just want to sit here for a while.'

'All right Emily.' She took away the tray.

As Emily looked at the overgrown garden where once she was so proud to walk, she dwelt upon the past. The tennis court where the family loved to play, was always kept in immaculate condition. She thought she could hear the thwack of tennis rackets and balls, then peals of happy laughter...

In the summer of 1910, Emily's eldest daughter, Rachel, was aged twenty-eight and had just got engaged to Edward, the eldest son of a Colonel Pemberton. The happy couple finished a game and came rushing up to the terrace, and Rachel shouted, 'I won – I won!' There was such laughter, on that happy day, the last time that Emily could remember all the family being together and the maid bringing a tray of drinks.

'A toast to the future happiness of Rachel and Edward,'

Charles Fenton said as he stood up with his glass.

'Rachel and Edward,' they all said with glasses raised.

Dennis was the youngest in the family and only son, now aged twenty. Like his father he was a keen engineer, though he was mainly interested in cars. He had dreams of turning the whole business over to the making of cars, for it was a period of intensive development, especially during Dennis's teens when so many small works were starting to make them. He had visited the small Morris Cycle repair works in Oxford where they had begun to make cars. Dennis had built two beautiful models in the works to his own design by 1910, with the name 'Fenton,' cast into the shining brass radiators. He proudly motored around the town and into the country, sitting boldly up behind the wheel. People would look and say; 'there goes young Dennis Fenton!'

Progress was painfully slow, for he could not get his father interested in the new industry. The only far reaching future that Charles Fenton could see was to stick to the steam marine engine.

'Believe me, Dennis, I admire very much the work you've done, but marine engineering is our big business.'

'But, Father, cars are going to be the biggest thing ever created. I've talked to so many people on my visits, it's developing very fast now and surely we can't just be left behind.'

'I understand your enthusiasm, son, but look to the future.'

'I am thinking of the future father, I know you like the cars I've built and I have been highly praised.'

'Yes you've done remarkably well. You have your own workshop, where you can continue that work. But we are marine engineers and we have a full order book.'

'If only I could expand and build more motor cars, there is a big opportunity and it's not too late.'

'Well, I know how keen you are, but believe me son, the motor car market is expanding so fast, especially in America, that it is already too late for us. Believe me,' he repeated. 'But you must continue of course and I'll see if I can get you another man.'

'Yes.' Dennis knew he was up against it, but was encouraged by the offer. 'Thank you, Father.'

Emily was writing out invitations to her daughter's wedding, and she looked up as Dennis came in through the double doors from the conservatory.

'Hello, dear, I thought you were at the works.'

'I'm taking the afternoon off, Mother – I see you're busy.'

'Not really.' She smiled. He was her favourite, being the youngest and only son.

'Oh, I see you're working out the guest list for Rachel's wedding. What a bore it all is!'

'Be fair, Dennis, she seems very happy and...'

'I know, it's time she thought about getting married, I suppose. But all those guests, and the cost...'

'You know that's up to your father, and he's very happy about it. He gets on so well with Edward, because of his engineering interests.'

'I wish he was more interested in the Fenton car, Mother.'

'You know perfectly well, dear, that he's very keen on all your interests. You have your own workshop after all and two good engineers to help you. He really loves the splendid cars you've made, and you know I think you are doing remarkably well. Carry on with that work, I don't think your father would want you to do otherwise, do you?' She spoke quietly, wiggling her finger as she looked at him with a smile.

'Yes, of course you're right, it's just that there are so many surprisingly small workshops building them, and look at the size of mine!'

'I think that's the reason why we can't go in for making cars in a big way. Father must surely have made that perfectly clear to you. And well.' She laughed. 'I'm not the expert at all but even I can see that!'

'Yes, I do understand. Father did say I could have another man...' He went silent for a moment.

'What are you thinking about now, Dennis?'

'You know how well Father gets on with Edward!'

'Yes of course, dear. He likes him very much – fortunately, as he's marrying Rachel.'

'Did you know he's building an aeroplane?'

'Oh dear, I didn't know. They're so very dangerous! Does your father know what he's doing?'

'I've not discussed it with him, Mother. But they're not that dangerous, not if you know what you're doing.'

'And, *does* he know what he's doing?'

'Of course he does. He wouldn't be building it if he didn't know something about it, would he?'

'I still say it's dangerous. And Rachel knows all about this aeroplane, I presume?'

'I would think so, Mother, it's hardly a secret!'

'Motor cars are safer. At least one is on the ground, and not moving so fast.'

'They do go fast on the race circuit at Brooklands, but I'm not interested in racing. Fun to watch though!'

'I do really think they're mad.' Emily turned back to sorting out the wedding guests.

'I'll leave you to it, Mother.'

Charles and Emily were walking together on White Heath, such a rare pleasure for Emily. It was so difficult to get him alone these days. But with the children now grown up, she hoped to spend more time with Charles. But it took a lot of persuasion on her part to get him out on this sunny afternoon. She put her arm through his as they walked.

'This is so pleasant.' She held closely to him, as if they were newlyweds.

'Why yes, dear, I'm enjoying this walk.'

'I feel we should do this more often; don't you think?'

'There's no reason why we shouldn't, my dear.'

'Except that you're always so tied up with your work. Charles, I was thinking... isn't it time we had a holiday together?'

'It's difficult in my position, Emily' They walked in silent thought for a while. Then Charles said, 'We have three daughters, Dennis has gone into business on his own, and I have an under manager that I'm not sure I trust. How in God's name can I take a holiday?'

'What is it about William Bicknell that makes you feel you can't leave him in charge?'

'Well, for a start, we have no proper agreement. He's been with us for two years yet I hardly dare let him out of my sight.'

'You'll have to trust somebody soon. It's bad for you to work all the time.'

'It was different when Father was alive, but...'

'You still took no holiday; it was always work!'

'But Emily, dear, it's no hardship for me: I enjoy my work, you know that.'

'So I'm of no consequence then? Because you won't take a holiday, I must be satisfied to stay at home, even though the family are grown up.'

'Yes, I must apologise.' He patted Emily's hand. 'Of course you must have a change and get away from the house. You could go and stay with my sister Edith near Bath. You get on well with her and it's a very pleasant house not far from the town.'

'Yes, I'd like that, but it wasn't what I meant.'

'I know my dear, I promise I'll try to work something out, then perhaps I can come and join you and we can do a tour of the West Country.'

'That would be wonderful to look forward to,' Emily said as she clung to Charles while they walked down the steep path towards the house. Emily was thinking back to that wonderful Sunday over thirty years ago when they had walked down that same path to the new house, the day they'd announced their engagement. They were married the following year.

Emily went to stay with Charles's sister Edith and the family, where there was always an open invitation. A letter from Charles brought an immediate response, inviting Emily to come and stay as long as she wished. Edith had a large family, who were not all grown up and they were great company. Albert was very much the head of the household: he was always kind to Emily and made her feel very much one of the family. She went for long walks with Edith in the country and even into Bath to do some shopping. They would take a train for most of the way back. She enjoyed three weeks in that happy household, then returned home to Charles. They never did have that holiday together.

Dennis was still building cars in 1914, but progress was very slow, and he had only built six, including the two prototypes he kept for his own use. Although it was nearing the end of April, it was a gusty, wet morning and he was glad to be in his workshop. With his two faithful and very skilled helpers they made a good team, but there was little profit in the work, with an average of one car a year. The extra man his father had mentioned never materialised. However, Charles had allowed Dennis to continue on the chance that a few more orders would make it worthwhile expanding, but he was unable to compete. They were putting the finishing touches to the last motor car on order, although Dennis was hopeful that he had managed to procure a further two customers. They had to be wealthy to afford a Fenton.

A motor car drew up outside and Dennis recognised the sound of one of his. So he was not surprised when Edward came in and let the door slam behind him, in his usual exuberant flurry.

'Phew! Great day for flying!'

'What, in this weather?' Dennis said without looking up, for he was meticulously painting in a gold line on the car body. His two men looked up with a laugh.

'It will probably clear up later,' Edward said and he walked up to watch closely as Dennis finished the gold line.

'This is delicate work you know.' He looked up with the brush in his hand. 'I can't do this while I'm being watched. What brings you here on this blustery spring morning?'

'I happened to be passing this way and thought I...'

'Would come and annoy me?'

'You should take up flying, Dennis, there's really nothing like it. Better than being stuck in here all day!'

'I enjoy what I do, so I don't mind. Anyway, you were stuck

in your workshop for months working on that aeroplane.'

'Rewarding though,' Edward said with a light of excitement in his eyes. 'Anyway, you've only built... six motor cars, is it?'

'Yes, but you've only built one aeroplane.' They laughed.

'I know,' Edward said. These are fine cars of course, I love mine.' He smiled. 'And so does Rachel.'

'I'm sure she would rather you keep on the ground.'

'I don't think she minds me flying. She watches me often.'

'Yes but I do know she worries. Though she wouldn't say so!'

'She's never given me that impression, Dennis.'

'Don't forget I'm her brother. She used to worry about me when I was a youngster, she's a very caring person.'

'Yes, of course she is, but there's no way I could give up flying is there?' Edward stood looking at the newly painted car for a moment. 'Have you given more thought about joining the Royal Flying Corps? I could teach you to fly! And don't tell me you're not interested because I know perfectly well that you are.' There was a stunned silence.

'Don't be ridiculous,' Dennis said. 'You have to be an officer in the Royal Engineers.'

'That's what I came to tell you. I've already joined. You see, it happened quite quickly. As you know, my father is Colonel Pemberton, of the Royal Engineers.'

'Of course I know – don't tell me, I can guess!'

'I was persuasive and with his influence, and my interest in flying and engineering, he arranged a commission. If you could give it thought, I'm sure father would help.'

'I find that hard to believe, but I'll think about it!'

'I know you'll do that,' Edward shouted at Dennis from where he was about to open the door. He paused for a second, and walked slowly back to where Dennis stood holding the brush. 'Think, Dennis,' he spoke very softly, 'you and I could have a great time together. Can you get away this afternoon, we can go for a drive out into the country and discuss it?'

'What do you mean, a great time?' Dennis spoke in a whisper.

'You're a married man!'

'So? You'll be married yourself soon, I wouldn't wonder, and does that mean you cease to enjoy life?'

'No, I was only thinking of Rachel!'

'I'm responsible, Dennis, very much so, and now I have the best opportunity one could hope for, in the Flying Corps.'

'Yes, of course, although it *is* dangerous.'

'You're beginning to sound like... I don't know. But it's not that dangerous.'

'I'm sorry,Edward, I'll say no more.'

'So, what about this afternoon then? Look, it's starting to clear up now,' he said as he looked towards the window and there was a burst of sunshine.

'Yes all right then,' Dennis said with a sudden grin, 'but I have to finish up here first. Come round about two, I'll be at home then.'

'That means I'll have to meet your mother, She's always fussing about my flying, and now I've joined the...'

'I wouldn't have thought you would let that worry you,' Dennis interrupted.

'No, I don't suppose you would think that.' He smiled and walked to the door, 'I'll see you later then!' He went out quickly shutting the door with a slam.

The monkey puzzle tree that grew gradually taller each year, cast a shadow across one end of the tennis court, where a gardener was sweeping up a few dead leaves left there from the autumn. The court needed to be ready for the next season. The weather was becoming spring-like and Dennis liked to invite friends for a few games at the weekend. The wind had dropped and Emily walked in the garden; her escape. She sifted through memories, and thought of the house in the country where it was peaceful, and remembered especially the glorious summers, when she would often take the children in the trap, to see her father at Eastbrook. Especially after he decided to retire in 1906 at the age of seventy. It was a great sadness when she finally sold the old house after her father died. She had never known her mother, who had suffered from a strange illness. All her father had said was that she had gone into a decline, and died when Emily was not yet two years old. An aunt had come to live with them and brought her up till she was ten, and the Duckworths had been with them as long as she could remember.

There was a strong bond between Emily and her only son, for they confided in each other more than most mothers and sons normally would. Although Dennis was on good terms with his father, there was no real contact, in spite of how much Charles had wanted a son to carry on the business: after Emily had produced three daughters, he was overjoyed when a son came along. Dennis was very explicit when telling his mother about his friends, and his visits to the Morris works at Oxford. But especially about his friend Edward. Emily was wary about her daughter's marriage to him: she looked upon him as a wayward character and not to be trusted. Dennis told his mother that Edward was headstrong, for he often got bad ideas into his head, and stubbornly would not listen to advice from his best friend let alone anyone else.

Walking slowly across the lawn towards the house, Emily's thoughts turned to her family at present. Her eldest and married daughter Rachel had a little girl, so making Emily a grandmother. Rachel frequently confided in her mother that she was not very happy at times as Edward was often away, especially when he did so much flying. This worried Emily and also the fact that her own son Dennis was so friendly with him, for she thought he might also become interested in flying. Emily's other two daughters were still not married and one was now over thirty, which she was concerned about. She also thought Charles was sometimes not showing much interest in the family, or her for that matter, she could hardly ever get him away from his work.

It was twenty minutes to two when Dennis dragged himself away from his workshop, pulled up the starting handle of his car and drove off home. As he drove he was giving thought to

Edward's idea that he could get him into the Flying Corps. He knew he would never be able to get many orders for his motor cars: his were special. Not many people could really afford such craftsmanship. He wished he could expand, but it was too late.

Dennis had managed to produce a quiet running car: most of them were noisy. But how could he compete, when he was only known locally? The Morris works were building a small car, named The Morris Oxford. There were Hillmans and the Austin Works were producing about 1500 cars a year. The only car that ran more silently than his was the Rolls-Royce! His production of one car a year, no matter how good the Fenton was, made him feel it was a mere leisure pursuit.

Dennis had tried to tell his father that the steam turbine was replacing the reciprocating engine, but his father would not be persuaded. 'That's for the large ocean going liners, so we are not going to be competing there son.' As far as his father was concerned, the future lay with the industry that the firm was well established in; marine engines mainly for tugs and a few larger ships.

When Dennis arrived at Oakwood, where the main gate was usually left open during the day, he drove straight in. As he turned into the drive, he saw Edward's car parked in front of the house and he pulled up along side. The cars were identical except that Edward's was finished in red, and his was finished in a dignified black. Dennis walked round to the back of the house to the French windows, where he was about to enter, but stopped just in time. He saw the back view of an officer, his Sam Brown belt over his right shoulder and peak cap laying on the sofa. He was embracing Juliet, the younger of Dennis's two unmarried sisters. He recognised the profile, though half-turned away he would not have caught sight of Dennis for that instant at the window. Edward was absorbed, but Juliet's eyes met Dennis's for a split second, before he made a hasty retreat.

To catch Edward – Rachel's husband – and his best friend in a compromising position, gave him a shock. He knew Juliet had seen him, and he wished he'd not gone to the terrace. He quickly walked back round to the front, passing the parked cars and to the kitchen on the other side of the house. His mother was there with the cook and his sister Jane.

'I see Edward is here; I mean his car, Mother!'

'Yes.' She looked up from what she was doing. 'You didn't say you were seeing him this afternoon?'

'It was a last minute decision.'

'You didn't expect to find him in the kitchen did you?' Jane said smiling.

'No, of course not, I just feel hungry, that's all.'

'You've not eaten again, Dennis?' his mother said.

'No, had to finish up! Also leave my men busy.' He quickly helped himself to bread and a lump of cheese.

'You'll be surprised when you see Edward.'

'Yes,' Jane said, 'he's in uniform!'

'Oh, well, I'm not surprised. He has said he'd join the Royal Engineers, to get into the Flying corps.'

'Yes. I worry about Rachel. She's not...' Emily tailed off.

'Not happy, Mother?'

'It's hard to say. I think Edward can be a show-off!'

'Yes, I know!' Dennis said, quickly munching his bread and cheese.

'Are you very busy now, Dennis?'

'No, Mother. If we were going into the car business, we would have to expand, or give it up. Father never will.' Dennis hesitated. 'Can we leave it for now?' He finished eating. 'I must go and find Edward!' He rushed to the door.

'You'll give yourself indigestion! I think you'll find him in the drawing room with Juliet!' Emily shouted as he swiftly walked away.

'I hope he doesn't get it into his head to go in for this flying,' Emily said. 'He's so friendly with Edward you know.'

'Yes mother,' Jane replied, 'but there's nothing you or anyone can do to influence him, for he's already interested in flying, and the car business isn't...'

'You're right of course, Jane, I try not to think about it.'

Emily was never to forget that evening, both during the meal, or later in the drawing room, Dennis was in a strange mood. He and Juliet were not speaking to each other.

'Did you have a pleasant afternoon?' Jane said, looking at Dennis.

'Moderately,' he replied. 'We had some serious talking to do, that's all.'

'I thought you were enjoying Edward's company; you're still friends, I hope?'

'Yes, we are,' he snapped. 'He may be older than me, and he's taken a big step, but I don't think he's very mature.'

'He looks very smart in his uniform,' Jane said.

'I think he's very mature!' Juliet said sharply, having not spoken all that evening. Then she quickly walked out of the room.

'That's more than you are,' Dennis said, following her.

'What's the matter with those two?' Emily said.

'I wouldn't let it worry you, Mother,' Jane said with a modest smile.

Dennis and Juliet had disappeared into the study. Charles had been out all day, he was at a meeting in London and had said he would be returning on a late train that evening. He would often be late for a meal and his son Dennis was very similar. Emily and her daughter Jane sat quietly in the drawing room, Jane reading a book while her mother, a little agitated, flipped through the Daily Telegraph avoiding the political news. She found the Telegraph more entertaining, while Charles took the Times to the works every day. The door opened and Charles walked in.

'Hello, Father,' Jane said.

Emily put the paper down. 'You look tired, Charles.'

'I am a little, my dear.' He walked over and gave her a kiss.

'You had supper at the club, I hope?'

'Yes, of course!' He sat down. 'Is Dennis around?'

'He's in the study having a long talk with Juliet,' Emily said. 'Goodness knows what about!'

'Oh... I think I'll go and interrupt them then!' Jane slipped out without a word, leaving her mother on her own.

After some time, Charles came back into the room with Dennis.

'Ah, there you are,' said Emily. 'Where's Juliet?'

'She's gone to her room.'

'I hope she's all right, only...'

'There's no problem,' Dennis interrupted.

'Dennis has something to tell you,' Charles intervened.

'Yes, it's quite straightforward mother. I...'

'Come on, Dennis,' his father said, 'you've made up your mind, so spill it out:'

'I'll be joining Edward in the Flying Corps.'

Emily looked at her son with stunned silence. 'But... but your work.' She hesitated. 'On your cars!'

'What cars, Mother? It's not possible to compete. Anyway I've decided now, Edward's father is going to help me.'

'It's no good trying to change his mind, Emily.'

'I wasn't going to try,' Emily said, 'I know I'd be wasting my time.'

'It really is splendid. Mother,' Dennis said. 'I find it very exciting and I promise I won't take stupid risks.'

'I know how it is with you, Dennis, like your father in many ways... Determination!' She smiled, even though she was not happy.

The day Dennis came home in his officers uniform, Emily felt very proud of her son. He spoke excitedly about his flying and his enthusiasm somehow tempered her fears for his safety. Over the next few days he told her all he could about his flying experiences, until she felt she could not hear another word about flying. One day he flew very low over the house and frightened everybody. He pretended it was not him at first, but had to admit it after a while. On a sunny June afternoon, he sat with his mother on the terrace, speaking continuously while she tried to look interested. Jane and Juliet joined them with Rachel and her little daughter. Edward was not with her and he was not mentioned. Father came home and produced his full plate mahogany camera. With the sun glinting on their faces and by using a long rubber tube with a squeeze bulb, he was able to take a photograph of all the family together, himself included.

The following Saturday morning, Dennis told his mother about Sarah. He had met her on one of his trips to Oxford at the Morris workshops where her father was an engineer. Dennis had taken her out in his car, which had impressed her so much that she wondered why he had not gone into production in a big way. He had explained to her the difficulties. They started meeting quite often and he wanted to take her home to meet his parents, but not while Edward was around. He could not be trusted, even as a friend, and Dennis also had to consider Rachel.

When Dennis turned up with Sarah on Sunday afternoon, she made an immediate impression on his parents. She was a beautiful girl, tall with dark wavy hair, a lovely smile and deep brown eyes. When Dennis first told his mother of her, he spoke with great enthusiasm. She was twenty two, liked to go for long country walks as well as riding in the car, but was not so keen on his flying. She was very impressed by the garden and liked to play tennis, Emily found her easy to get on with and Charles liked her very much: he thought his son lucky to have met a young lady he could be so much in tune with. It made him think back over the years to when he first met Emily.

Only a few days later, after that pleasant weekend, the papers reported the assassination of the Crown Prince of Austria, the Archduke Francis Ferdinand at Sarajevo. Charles said the news was very grim indeed, but Emily did not bother her head with politics, so it was quite a few days later when she began to realise that it meant war. Six weeks later, in August, her son Dennis, along with many others, found themselves in France. His brother-in-law Edward was with them of course. Emily had not seen him for weeks, not since that strange evening, when Dennis and Juliet had that long discussion. She never did find out the truth, for in her mind she had almost guessed what it was about, and would rather not know the details.

Dennis wrote to his mother about once a week, but all letters were censored, with some bits cut out. Sarah, who received more letters, came over often. They were both equally worried and a friendship had sprung up which helped them to bear the burden together.

One dull afternoon in late November, Emily was in the drawing room and expecting Sarah for afternoon tea. The door opened and to her surprise, in walked Dennis with Sarah.

'Dennis!' Emily exclaimed, as she looked from one to the other. 'Such an unexpected surprise!'

'Yes,' he looked full of himself, 'I flew across, managed to wangle it.' Emily was looking at a happy couple, both with such a glint in their eyes, as they clutched each others hands.

'I don't know how you managed it, but...'

Dennis gave his mother a kiss. 'No details, Mother, please!'

Emily was always so afraid for her son's safety, but she had to dismiss the fear from her mind. They sat down to tea as if there was nothing to worry about. Dennis and Sarah sat close together on a settee. 'Before we start tea, Mother,' Dennis took Sarah's left hand in both of his, 'I wanted you to be the first to know.' Sarah looked at Dennis with a big smile. 'We want to get married!'

Emily was delighted, but tea on this occasion was quiet. She continually worried, and Dennis knew it.

'Is it very dangerous over there Dennis?' The question took him by surprise.

'You must try not to worry, Mother. It's less dangerous than the infantry digging themselves into trenches. Reconnaissance work is what we're concerned with, anyway. It will all be over in a few weeks, then we can get back to normality.'

'I see,' Emily said, 'well, I hope you're right.' She did not share Dennis's optimism.

Dennis left to take Sarah home in his car. She would usually walk down to the station and get a train. When Charles came in and Emily told him the news, he shook his head.

'Are you not pleased that they're getting married?'

'Yes, it's not that I think they shouldn't. Things are so unsettled and I find it difficult to think about weddings.'

'His quick visit concerns me,' Emily said, 'I was pleased to see him but I hope he's not doing anything silly.'

'No use worrying, you remember me at his age?'

'Yes, Charles, but things were so different then.'

That evening Emily left Dennis and his father to have a long discussion. They talked late into the night. Emily had difficulty in sleeping, and she left the lamp turned low. When Charles finally came to bed, they talked into the early hours. It was gone five when Charles turned the lamp off.

In the morning, Dennis had to have an early breakfast, then get on his way to catch a train. So he only briefly saw his parents and was not aware that they'd barely slept.

That terrible year was the most unhappy time Emily had ever known. The happy weekend only seemed to accentuate her final despair, which culminated with the arrival of the dreaded telegram. Her beloved son Dennis had been killed when his plane crashed behind enemy lines.

'You'll get cold sitting there Emily,' she heard Mrs Gilbert say.

'Oh dear, I was dreaming!'

'It's almost dark.' Mrs Gilbert switched on the standard light at the chair near the fire.

'Yes, I... I think I'll sit over there Mary, it *is* a little chilly!' Mrs Gilbert helped Emily Fenton into a comfortable position.

'Would you like the wireless on?'

'Not just now thank you, Mary, I'd like to sit here quietly until we have supper.'

Emily looked up at the framed photograph on the wall over the small table. The family were all there – her last happy day.

Chapter 20
A New Venture

As they drove away from the house, it was getting dark and the street lights had a misty glow round them. There was no conversation for a time. Deep thoughts were in Tom's mind, He was thinking of old Mrs Fenton, although she was comfortably off and well cared for, he was sure there must have been sadness in her life. All the signs were there, the neglected garden, a room that had not changed for many years, the pictures and family photographs that were all part of a past era. The portrait of Emily painted a great many years ago pervaded his mind. 'So beautiful,' Tom said thinking aloud.

'Been a nice day,' Mr Wills interrupted his thoughts. 'Can I drop you off somewhere?' he asked as they drove towards the town. 'Do you want the bus station?'

'I'm not in any hurry. Are you... going back to your office?'

'I have to call in,' he said. 'I think you would find the museum interesting.'

'I know it very well, it was one of my favourite haunts as a boy.'

Wills nodded with a smile. 'Yes, I don't doubt that, but have you been in recently?'

'No, not for some years! Has it changed at all?'

'There are some interesting additions to the local history.'

'I'm intrigued!' The car turned into the narrow drive, down to the old yard, dimly lit from the pump-shop windows where the men were still working.

'I won't be long! If you like, we'll walk down to the museum together. Coming up for a minute?'

Tom paused at the reception office and glanced at the door. 'She's not in this afternoon,' Mr Wills said, looking back at him, 'Mildred isn't here on Fridays.'

'Yes I know,' Tom said with slight embarrassment. Wills shot quickly up the stairs. Tom saw that he was being watched by the men working in the shop, so he was quick to follow Mr Wills to his office.

'Mrs Fenton's a very imposing and interesting old lady, isn't sh?' he said.

'Yes, she is.'

'I expect she has many stories to tell.'

'She doesn't talk about the past very much: there were family disasters. I know that the only son was killed in the Great War.'

'Yes... a sad story!' Tom was reminded of the gold lettering on the company office window: Fenton and Son.

'She just looks forward to me or any visitors, I don't pry at all; it's best that way.'

Later, they strolled down to the museum in the fading light. As they entered the old building, Tom remembered it well. There was still the same coolness and smell, a mixture of mustiness, and polish. They walked into a well lit room that was new to Tom, an exhibition of the history of the town and surrounding district.

'What do you think of that?' Wills said. He was looking at an old plough.

'That's interesting!' Although there was some corrosion, the restoration was good and the wording on the cast iron handle was clearly visible: 'Fenton and Son. Patent plough.'

'That was made by Mr Fenton's grandfather!'

There were many relics. Cast iron work included decorative railings. And parts of early cars, such as radiators large polished brass lamps, wheels and a horn among the exhibits, dating back to the early part of the Century. Tom looked long at a small steam engine that once propelled a river launch.

'This is certainly a very good exhibition! What a pity there isn't a complete car!'

'There is one I know of,' Wills said as he pointed at a photograph. 'The car is owned by Edward Pemberton, a retired RAF officer who married one of the Fenton daughters. They still take the car to meetings of vintage and veteran cars. That's them in the picture!' It was a large photograph, with the driver at the wheel and a lady passenger. Tom read the card under the frame: 'Edward Pemberton with his wife Rachel in their Fenton Car, 1935.'

'That looks marvellous. Is that the only one?' Tom asked.

'As far as I know, but there weren't many made. Our present business place was the old car workshop,'

'It's a wonder you don't see ghosts there!'

'Can't say it worries me, Tom,' Mr Wills said with a smile. 'That's where these bits and pieces came from. Parts of a car that never was!'

'I wonder what happened to the other cars?'

'Probably left to rot away in some farmyard.'

They wandered round the museum until the curator came and told them it was closing time. He was a man of character, and with his lined face, he seemed to blend in with the rest of the exhibits. Tom thought he remembered him from before the war, when he would sometimes visit the museum after school.

After some good-humoured banter with the man, Wills and Tom left. It was a dull and dreary evening outside.

'Fancy a cup of tea?' said Mr Wills.

'Yes, that's an idea. Where do you suggest?'

'Over there! The Little Tea Room, if they're still open.'

The lighted windows were inviting, and they were in luck. It was bright and warm inside, with floral patterned tablecloths. There was a pleasant smell of tea and cakes, and the urn made a loud hissing noise as it came up to the boil and filled the pot.

'Are you hungry?' Wills asked.

'Not really, after all those cakes we had earlier!'

'Two hours ago though!' Mr Wills ordered hot buttered toast and jam. 'So, you say business isn't booming at Brown and Saxon?' he asked, after the waitress had left them.

'It was, when I first went there,' replied Tom, 'but it seems to be falling off now, like it was at Fentons, I'm beginning to wonder about the future there, or engineering in general as things are.'

'How would you like to come and work for me, Tom?'

The question came as such a surprise, that at first Tom couldn't answer. Tom smiled at him in stunned silence for a moment, before speaking again. 'In your design office?'

'Yes, why not. Don't answer now; think about it!'

They continued to discuss the work and what it entailed. Tom always thought of obstacles. He was not sure how he would get on with Mr Jackson, the partner. He was remembering the old days when he'd had a few brushes with the man. Then there was Mildred... He was excited at the prospect of being near her, but at the same time he was concerned that she might distract him from his work.

Tom also pondered the relationship between him and Mr Wills, who could be his future boss. He wondered how he should address him. To call him Frank seemed far too familiar (he thought of Mildred)! Yet to address him as Mr Wills was too subservient.

'I need someone who can deal with presentation,' Wills interrupted his thoughts. 'I'm referring to art work!'

'Pictures?' Tom said.

'Illustrated manuals and perhaps brochures, if you think you could handle it. Also there are labels to be designed. This work is done by a printer at the moment. You would be an extra hand as I only have the one draughtsman. For I spend more time on business dealings now. I know you're good at artwork; how do you feel about it, Tom?'

'Yes... I'm interested. It sounds as if it would be just up my street. It's good of you to think of me.' Tom hesitated. 'I have to say, I've had a great deal more experience at drawing ships' plans, and just a little perspective work for the firm. Then I know I would miss the docks, there's such an atmosphere there. Though I'm studying three nights a week at an evening art school.'

Wills was listening quietly, and Tom was afraid he'd tell him to forget the whole thing. But he gave a quiet response. 'I think you should give it a go. Up to you, of course! Why not go back to Brown and Saxons, and I can give you a little work to have a go at: some designing. Then bring it back for me to see and we'll go on from there. How does that appeal to you?'

'Yes, I would certainly agree to that.'

'So if we call in to my office now, I'll find something for you to take away, then run you to the bus station. All right?'

'Yes, that's very good of you.' Mr Wills settled the bill and they stepped out into a cold dark night.

During the next four weeks, Tom spent most of his spare time at a table in his small room. He was determined he was going to impress, and borrowed books from the library to give him ideas. He realised he had a lot to learn. But with the books' help, plus his innate talent, he decided one Friday night that the illustrations were finished. He was not earning much money and the hotel where he was staying was costing him more than his previous lodgings. He had permission to take the following Monday off so he could visit Newburne, then found he hadn't enough money to go home that weekend. That put him in a pickle because he'd phoned Mr Wills the day before to check if it would be convenient, and it was all arranged.

Blow it! he thought. Perhaps someone might lend me enough money for the train fare. He went down to the bar, a place he avoided as he had to watch the pennies, but he dismissed the thought from his mind and walked in boldly.

'Hello, we have a new face,' said a fat man standing at the small bar, one of just four smart-looking drinkers. They all turned round and looked at Tom.

'Good evening,' Tom said, with an involuntary smile.

'And where have you been hiding yourself?' said the same man. He spoke with what Tom considered a contrived posh accent. 'We've not seen you in here before.'

'Well, I thought I would pop in,' Tom said.

'What will you have then?' Tom was not sure whether they all spoke together or one person asked him, as they were all slightly drunk. Four bachelors together, thought Tom.

'What is it to be?' said the lanky Irishman behind the bar. He and his sister ran the hotel at Blackheath.

'I'll have a light ale please.' They all tried to pay but the fat man got in first.

'Thank you very much.'

One of the four suave gentlemen was playing the one-armed bandit and had just lost again. 'This machine never pays out,' he said addressing the chap serving at the bar. 'You're making a lot of money out of us.'

'No! Not at all,' said the owner. 'He pays out if he likes you!' He laughed.

'We've been playing that machine all the evening,' said the fat man, 'and it's not paid out once. You have a go!' he said looking at Tom.

'Yes,' said another gent. 'See if you have any luck. He might favour you,' he said waggishly. 'He's not met you before!'

'I don't usually play those machines,' Tom said.

'Now's your chance to have a go.'

'How does it work?'

'Just put sixpence in and pull the lever,' said the owner.

There was lots of laughter as Tom went to the machine, with a feeling he was being pressurised. He put in the only sixpence he had, thinking he was throwing away money, and gave the lever a good pull.

Clonk, clonk clonk. The pictures stopped rolling, with Jackpot on each one. There was a loud tinkling as the coins poured out and Tom thought they would never stop.

Tom turned and looked at the amazed expressions on their faces, as the money poured out. They couldn't believe what they were witnessing. Tom made no attempt to suppress his emotions and burst into laughter.

'You seem to have cleaned them all out!' said the owner.

'Your lucky night, by God,' one said.

'Bring it all onto the bar,' said the owner. It took time to count and eventually he finished. 'That's four pounds, eighteen and sixpence,' he said. 'Now, how about that!'

'We've never seen you in here before and you've won the jolly old Jackpot,' someone said, amongst plenty of laughter.

'Calls for a round of drinks!'

'Yes, of course,' Tom said, and he treated them all. He was saved, for he'd just won more than half a week's salary! He could now afford to go home that weekend. The owner told a shaggy dog story while Tom made his drink last. It was getting late when he said, 'I have to go, I'm afraid.'

'Not going to have one for the road then?'

'No thanks, I have to get an early train in the morning.' Tom was feeling optimistic and told them he would be moving away from Blackheath.

'And just as we were getting to like you.' the fat gent said.

Tom went home that weekend. The Sunday was fine and sunny with a nip in the air. He and his father went for a long walk and called at a country pub with a river view where the landlord kept an excellent cellar.

'I hope you're luck is better than mine,' his father said, after Tom had told him about Mr Wills' offer.

'In what way, Dad?'

'It's this partnership of mine with Bolton.'

'Oh why, are things not going well then?'

'He's turned out to be a very tricky character to work with. Take my advice and don't make any hasty decisions.'

'No, of course not. It's hardly the same thing though. You're talking about a partnership, not like me: only working for Mr Wills if he likes my drawings. I might be lucky!'

'Yes, I know, Tom old boy.' His father paused and looked out upon the river scene. 'Be sure you have reasonable prospects for the future.'

'If he takes me on, Dad. It will be taking a chance anyway!'

'Yes... and I'm sure he will be impressed by your drawings.'

‘Well, he’s already seen quite a lot of my work. That’s why he asked me, and he’s certainly no fool.’

‘Yes of course, Tom.’ His father paused in thought. ‘You know I could introduce you into the Freemasonry.’

‘Yes, Dad, I’ll think about it. You asked me this before!’

‘It’s up to you, Tom. It’s not for me to press you, I could introduce you, but you have to make up your own mind and I’ll give you advice if you’re interested.’

‘Yes, I will give it some thought. What will you do about your partnership, Dad? Dare I ask if he’s a Freemason?’

‘Yes, he is, as it happens, but that had nothing to do with the unsatisfactory partnership.’

‘No, I wasn’t suggesting that. You never know how things will turn out. Will you be splitting up with Mr Bolton then?’

‘I think it’s very probable, Tom.’

They had a pleasant walk back through leafy woodland paths, where sunbeams glinted through the trees that were beginning to turn to autumnal shades. Although no more mention was made of business matters, Tom could not get away from thoughts of future uncertainties. But they joked a lot and Tom thought: *Dad is such a good friend*.

The next morning was damp and foggy as he walked down the hill towards the bus stop. Strangely, he enjoying the misty white blanket that narrowed the vista into a limited area. There were only two people at the stop when he arrived, but inevitably the bus was late, and as the number of people increased, he was concerned that it would not arrive at all. It was twenty minutes late. Tom sat at the front on the top deck where he could see the treetops more clearly than the driver could see the road as the bus steadily proceeded. The bus journeyed further from the river, and the fog began to clear, so normal speed was resumed, and he still got to Newburne before he was due to see Mr Wills.

A slightly sickly feeling of nervous excitement came over him as he entered the old workshop doorway of the Pump Company. Knowing Mildred would be there, he hesitated and glanced at the reception office door, then went quickly up the stairs, tightly clutching his folder of drawings.

Sitting in the office with Mr Wills, Tom watched as the man scrutinised the drawings, so meticulously prepared. There was just the glimmer of a smile as he took a long look at them, while Tom patiently waited for him to make a comment.

'You've gone to a lot of trouble,' Mr Wills suddenly said, without looking up. 'They're very good!'

'Are they what you had in mind?'

'Yes, and we'd work together on details of a brochure of this kind, regarding the form it would take and printing.' He looked up and gave Tom a hypnotic stare through his horn-rimmed spectacles. 'How are you placed with Brown and Saxon?'

'A difficult question to answer.' A feeling of uncertainty swept over Tom. There was a moments silence, and Mr Wills looked down again at the drawings. It was almost as if Tom's mood had an effect on the atmosphere. It had gone very dark and a feeling of unreality had quite suddenly overwhelmed him. Mr Wills seemed not to notice at first as he became a silhouette against the light of the window behind him.

Tom was wondering what to say next, when Mr Wills stood up.

'Gone very dark,' he said looking out of the window.

'Quite eerie!'

'Yes, we're in for a downpour I should think. Better have some light.' He flicked the switch, but no light came on. 'Well I'm damned! We seem to have a powercut.' He went out to where the staff were standing around in the strange darkness and spoke to them. He came back into the office grinning. 'What a time to have a powercut, just when it's so dark. We can't see a bloody thing!'

'It's gone very quiet,' Tom said.

'Machines not working downstairs!'

'No, of course not.'

Mr Wills stood with his back to Tom as he looked out of the

window. It was starting to rain. 'I'll be glad when we get into the new place!'

'Yes, how long before you move?'

'Next week. This place has an aura about it.'

'The old car workshops!' Tom said.

'As if young Fenton is paying us a visit.'

'Yes, it's gone so dark!' Tom felt as though the place *was* haunted.

'It's going to be a busy week.' Mr Wills said as he turned back from the window and grinned. 'To get back to the discussion, as far as I'm concerned, you can come and join the staff at our new place.' He paused and looked out of the window as it was raining heavily. 'If you really want to come back to Newburne Tom, but the choice is yours!'

'Thank you very much...I would miss the marine work.'

'We can't provide that, but business is good at present, and being a small firm, we're more like a family than these large companies.' For a moment, Tom thought of Mildred.

'Mr Jackson, my partner is quite willing to leave me to decide about taking you on. He agreed that the figure could be eight pounds five shillings a week to start with, to be reviewed after a period of six months. Does that sound agreeable to you?' The rain was roaring down on the roof and beating against the window panes.

'Yes... I should think so.'

'You don't sound too sure?' Wills looked up at the ceiling. 'Hope this roof doesn't leak.'

'No, it's not that, only I would have to talk to...'

'Your present employers?'

'Yes, at Brown and Saxon. I've not handed in my notice or anything like that.'

'You go back there and decide, see how you feel about it. You might change your mind.' Mr Wills chuckled. 'You can give me a ring during the week when you've decided.' Suddenly the lights came on. 'Ah; that's better!'

Tom went down the stairs with his mind in a turmoil.

Somehow, the thought of coming back to work in Newburne after a few years away disturbed him, even though it would be very different. As he approached the reception office door, the thought came into his mind that it was about seven years ago that he was having those violin lessons with Mildred, and at that moment, she came out of the door.

'Hello,' she said brightly, taking Tom by surprise.

'Oh, good morning... Mildred!'

'You're becoming quite a regular visitor all of a sudden!'

'Not really, I came to see Mr Wills. Just on my way now.'

'You can't go out in this. Go and sit in the office, I'll be down in a tick.' She went upstairs with some files, and Tom went into her office with a feeling of elation, and sat down by her little typing desk. He glanced around. There were two tall and old looking wooden filing cabinets, a leather music case laying on top of one. They sharply contrasted with the newly painted cream walls. The window was high with frosted glass and there was a small fern in a pot on the sill. A maroon coloured coat with a pink and yellow patterned scarf were on a hanger that was on a hook fixed to the side of one of the cabinets. He noticed there was a gold treble clef shaped brooch pinned to the coat on one of the lapels, and he was looking at it when Mildred came back into the office.

'I don't know,' Mildred said with a smile, 'you always bring rain when you're here.'

'Yes, you'll have to call me the rain man!' She laughed. 'But I've only called twice, I hope I don't carry the bad weather around with me.'

'I hardly think that's possible.' She chuckled. 'It really is grim.' She sat down at her desk and wound two sheets of paper with carbon between into the typewriter. 'How are you getting on then?'

'Well, there's a possibility that I may come and work here, I mean at the new place.' He was beginning to get that old dreamy-eyed feeling: the sexual warmth was so powerful when he was close to Mildred.

'Oh really, Tom! I thought you were well settled in London.'

'The trouble is, I like the work, especially the docks. But like Fentons, the future's not very hopeful, because they seem to be running down... umm. Anyway, that's the only reason for my having to think about a move.'

Mildred typed at what seemed to Tom a remarkably fast speed. He sat there entranced.

'So when will you start at the new place then?' she asked.

'Oh, there's nothing settled. I've not handed in my notice.'

'So you're not sure that you will be coming back to Newburne then?'

'No, but it's likely to work out that way I think, when I see how the land lies.' Mildred put some more paper into the typewriter. 'Will you be going to the new office?'

'That remains to be seen,' she said.

'I see... I was wondering if you've heard any more news about playing in a theatre orchestra?' Tom asked.

'Nothing definite as yet, no.' Mildred was typing another letter, while Tom tried to think how he could see her away from her work place. He was now much more at ease.

'Will you be here all day?'

'Yes until five.' She said as she turned to Tom, 'I break for dinner from half past twelve for an hour, just hope this rain leaves off.'

'Yes.' Tom looked at his watch. 'It's not twelve yet, it will probably clear up before then.' He was on the brink of asking her to join him, when the door opened and it was Mr Wills.

'You still here Tom?' he said with a big smile.

'Waiting for the rain to stop.'

'Yes, no point in getting wet, when you're nice and cosy in here is there? It seems to be leaving off now,' he said looking up at the high window.

'I don't relish getting soaked.'

'I'll leave these signed letters with you Mildred for the post. He's not disturbing you I hope, is he?'

'Not at all, Frank, you can't expect him to go out into this torrent.' Tom tried to hide his irritation at the intrusion. It did not bode well for the future, he felt.

'Humm!' Mr Wills exclaimed, and went out.

'Is he annoyed with me?' Tom said.

'No,' she laughed. 'It's his way.'

'Yes... er, you call him Frank. I only ever call him Mr Wills!'

'I've known him for a long time, don't forget.'

'Yes, of course,' Tom paused for thought, 'I was about to ask you if you'd join me for dinner, before I go back to London today. You could show me the best place?'

'Yes, I don't see why not!'

Tom felt a sudden sense of relief at her consent. 'Oh good. I hope this rain will soon stop, I'll just go and have a look outside.' Tom got up and went to the outside door. It looked very wet, with large puddles in the yard, but there were only a few light spots of rain. He returned to Mildred's office. 'Almost stopped now, just a little wet underfoot.'

'You may as well hang on here now for half an hour, then we can go together.' As she spoke, Tom was reminded of years ago, before his first violin lesson. Her words echoed the past: *'We can cycle up together.'*

Mildred took some letters upstairs and was soon back; she folded and slid them into the addressed envelopes and sealed them. 'That's it,' she said and took her scarf from the hanger. Tom looked at his watch as she put her coat on.

'It's only quarter past twelve.'

'That's all right, I've finished. Now we can go.'

'Oh good!'

She picked up the bundle of letters. 'I'll pop these into the general if you don't mind.'

'Of course not!'

They walked to the workshop doors, and Tom felt self-conscious as he glanced at the men who were staring at them as if they were about to whistle. Tom put his finger to his mouth, pursing his lips as if to dare them, and smiled. They just looked, but Tom was glad when he and Mildred were outside. 'I thought they were going to whistle or something, the way they were staring!'

'Not likely.' She laughed. 'They don't know who you are! You worry over things that don't matter.'

As they walked up the street, they were in tune with each other. It was strange, as if time had stood still for a few years. They laughed a lot and Tom felt proud to be with her. She dropped the letters into the post and they went to the little cafe near the museum. By chance they sat at the table where he and Mr Wills had had tea and that serious discussion.

'Do you always come here, Mildred?' Some emotional jealous feelings lingered in Tom's mind, whether founded or not.

'Quite regularly. It's reasonable, with good home cooking!'

'I came here with Mr Wills during my last visit. After we visited old Mrs Fenton, we went into the museum over the road, then came in here for tea.'

'Yes? I know Frank comes here a lot.'

'Oh, you.... come here with him do you?'

'I see, you think we're on those sort of terms. Believe me, he really is a loner, you know.' She laughed. 'He actually took me to the pictures once, but that was years ago, and that was the end of that.'

'But you call him Frank!'

'Most people know him as Frank. I expect you will when you get to know him.'

'I can't imagine that!'

'He's a funny old stick, you know. That beard and the horn-rimmed spectacles make him look quite stern, but don't let that put you off. He's a very kind man.' Tom felt suddenly relaxed.

The meal was very pleasant. Mildred insisted on paying for herself and afterwards, Tom walked her back to the pump works gate.

'Thank you for your company,' he said,' I hope we meet again soon.' He held her wool gloved hand and wished he could kiss her, but he remembered his experience with Betty and didn't dare. Still, he went away to catch his train with a warm feeling inside.

Chapter 21
Leaving London

Tom arrived back from Newburne late that night, Mildred on his mind in a mixture of nostalgia and imagined romance. He'd crept quietly up to his little room at the hotel and was sitting on the bed thinking. It seemed odd, for he'd not met her for so long, yet it felt so recent. He was recalling more clearly, how dismal he had felt when he said goodbye on her doorstep after his last day at Fentons, but there had seemed no way at the time he could have kept in touch with her.

Through the years he had allowed memories of her to fade into the back of his mind. Now the gap in time was suddenly and unexpectedly bridged. Together in the little cafe, the passage of time had not mattered. She was older but he had matured now, so the difference in their ages seemed to have narrowed, though not completely. The old feelings were rekindled. Tom was not surprised to find her unmarried, for he had not forgotten her disclosure during that violin lesson so long ago, that she could not get married and have a career in music at the same time. He was thinking now that perhaps her hopes had been too high; for she seemed no further forward, and he felt sad for her. He went to sleep that night, utterly lovesick.

The next day, back at Brown and Saxon, he awaited his opportunity to have a word with Guthrey. Waiting did nothing to steady his nerves, keyed up for what he felt might be a tricky interview. At half past ten, he knocked on the office door, and poked his head in.

'Good morning, Mr Guthrey, may I have a word with you?'

'Yes of course, come in and take a seat, Mr Hunt. What do you want to see me about?'

'About my position here.' Tom was bold. 'Do you mind me asking you what my chances are for the future with Brown and Saxon?' Tom said it rather fast, to get it over with.

Guthrey looked down and rubbed his brow. This needed some thought. Then he looked up and rubbed his hands together. 'Not much, if I'm frank.'

'Oh!'

'Look, Mr Hunt, the fact is that the future is in the balance at the moment. Men have been laid off already. It looks as if the boiler shop will have to close down – not at all rosy! There's been no mention of laying off staff, but if it happens, as looks likely, apart from those about to retire, the youngest or newer members of staff would be the first to go.'

'I see.' Tom hesitated. 'In that case, it makes this easier for me. I've been offered work in a small company owned by an old colleague of mine back in Newburne.'

'You're lucky then, though I'd be sorry to lose you.'

'I wouldn't commit myself till I'd spoken to you.'

'This would be a good time to accept; could be a wise move.'

'Yes, I'm giving it a lot of thought.'

'Good! Well, it's up to you Mr Hunt.'

'Yes, I think it's a chance I have to take!'

'If you've made up your mind, you should do well whatever you take up, if I can give you a word of encouragement.' He smiled.

'Thank you very much!'

'What is his line of business?'

'They make rotary pumps. He has a partner and they're about to move into new premises.'

'Very different work then?'

'Yes, I'm interested in illustrating, so I will be doing some art work in addition to design drawings.'

'I know you're interested in art, I've seen some of your work. But it's very specialised: have you had any training?'

'I've been attending art school in the evenings.'

'Oh,' Guthrey said. He seemed slightly amused. 'I thought you were studying the Higher National.'

'It's a conflict of interests but I'll never regret my engineering apprenticeship.' Tom started to tell him how his ambitions were divided but Guthrey didn't seem very interested, as he just nodded while Tom continued to talk.

'Take my advice and try not to spread your wings too wide,' Guthrey said. 'It sounds as though you could be on the right lines, though nothing is cast iron these days!'

'They're a small company but expanding. Only I will miss the ships.'

'Yes, I'm sure!' Guthrey paused for a few seconds. 'When do you want to leave then?'

After much thought, Tom phoned Mr Wills to accept his offer. He had agreed to give the usual notice to Brown and Saxon, so he could finish at the end of the following week. He was anxious to take a week off, and start on a Monday after a breathing space. Yet, having taken the plunge, a lingering feeling of uncertainty still haunted him. Such was the turmoil in his mind over the abrupt change in his life that would take him almost back to his original roots.

The time soon came for him to say goodbye to his colleagues. He knew he would miss the docks, and especially his friend Brian, just as he thought he was forming a good friendship with him – not easy to find. On that last day, he almost regretted his decisions, but he had thought deeply about it and there was little choice. He took a group photograph that they willingly posed for, standing behind one of the long boards for the drawing of ship's plans.

Tom went home to his parents and was restless, missing the life he'd become accustomed to in the East End of London. On the Friday, feeling a need for independence, he went to Newburne to find lodgings. Tom toyed with the thought of a small place all his own, but he was sure he could not afford the rent.

He went into the Dolphin public house, familiar to him from the past, where he got talking to a customer.

'We've not met before, have we?' The man spoke with a cultured voice, but was not well dressed, though he wore a waistcoat with a watch and chain. He thought of his father who proudly wore grandfather's watch and chain. The man was probably about fifty.

'It's not likely,' Tom said, 'It's some years since I was last in here.'

'This is my favourite haunt on Fridays, when I take a longer midday break.' He looked at his watch. 'I'll get back soon. They can manage without me for a while longer though!'

'You have a business nearby?' Tom asked.

'Yes, I have a photographic studio. I'm well known in the town!'

'I see.' Tom was slightly stuck for words as he thought of his old school pal, Henry Hayes. 'You wouldn't be...?'

'Blackett is the name!'

'Oh! It must be you who my old school pal worked for when he left school some years ago, during the war. Henry Hayes, you would remember him, I suppose?'

'Yes, nice fellow he was, joined the RAF.'

'That's right, I lost touch with him. Must see if I can look him up.'

'Oh dear, you won't have known then. Bad news, I'm afraid.' He hesitated and Tom anticipated what he was going to tell him. 'He was killed!'

'Oh!' Tom went into stunned silence, then recovered. 'Do you know how...?'

'Not in action, old chap. Plane crash on a practice flight.'

'How terrible!' Tom put his beer on the bar and said nothing.

'I'm very sorry,' Mr Blackett said as he leaned on the bar looking at Tom and swirling the beer in his glass.

'He was my best friend in my school days,' Tom confided. 'He had to join up and seemed to resent the fact that I was in a reserved occupation. That's how it was. Then when I got work in London, we went our separate ways!'

'That's the way of the world, I'm afraid.'

'It's such... bloody bad luck.'

'The world's full of that, old chap! Life is rough at times, like a game of chance and completely random,' Mr Blackett said.

'Yes, I know!'

'I was too young for the fourteen eighteen war, lucky enough to get a government contract for photographic work during this last lot, otherwise I would have been out of business most likely with the shortage of photographic materials. I won't bore you with the bad bits. Anyway, what brings you to Newburne today, are you working out here?'

'I used to when I served my apprenticeship at Fentons.'

'Oh, that's interesting. But they've gone out of business.'

'Yes, that's right.' Tom went silent, deep in thought as he took a sip of beer.

'Seems a dammed shame to me, old man. This town's not what it used to be! Why should a company that's been a part of this town for as long as anyone can remember close down?'

'They were old fashioned and didn't change, didn't advance with time. As steam engines were no longer needed, that was the end of the road for Fentons.'

'Sound's quite pathetic when you put it like that!'

'Yes,' Tom agreed. He picked up his beer glass, held it with both hands and looked into it as if contemplating its contents. Then he quickly drank up. 'I've got to go.'

He felt the sudden need to be alone. As he stepped out into the street he was conscious of the fact that he had just had a conversation with a man he'd never seen before, but it was as if he'd always known him. Mr Blackett was talking to a complete stranger; but Tom knew of him through his old school friend. The gloomy news imparted to him by a chance meeting in the pub gave him a feeling of emptiness as he walked down the street.

He walked past the old Fenton building, which appeared more dreary than ever that afternoon, as he looked up at the dark windows. It was now a lifeless edifice, doomed to extinction, including the old and boarded up cinema next door with broken windows and the now unused side entrance, with the sign removed that led to the back yard. Just waiting for the demolition boys.

It was getting foggy. 'Blast it!' Tom murmured to himself. He felt downcast by the news of his old friend, so he made his way to the bus station. He decided to give up his search for a place to stay, go home and leave it till Monday. As he travelled, sitting on the top deck, his thoughts were mainly of his old school pal. He somehow felt guilty, as if he was responsible for his death. He knew that it was not a logical thought, but it stuck in his mind as the bus swerved into village squares to drop passengers and pick up others in the cold darkening misty light.

The seats on the top deck were mostly unoccupied, but suddenly a man wearing a heavy mackintosh squeezed in beside him as the bus moved off. Tom felt stifled, mainly by the rubbery smell strangely mixed with a faint trace of perfume. He turned his head, and found himself looking into eyes that would never look at a woman in such a way. Although Tom was quite innocent of such facts of life, he knew instinctively that it was more than just a friendly smile beaming from that pale face. He felt trapped and wished he'd sat downstairs.

'It's such a foggy night, isn't it?' the man said.

'Very,' Tom said with a quick nod.

'I hope you don't mind me sitting next to you, but I think it's nice to have a companion, don't you?'

'Yes.' Tom forced a smile with a quick glance at him. The bus swayed on some bends as the route took in villages on the way.

'Whoops, I hope this driver's not going too fast in the fog.'

'Seems to be clearing in parts.'

'Going to stay the night somewhere, are you? I see you have a small case with you?'

'Going home, that's all.'

'Where would that be, somewhere interesting?' The man was

pushing closer to Tom, who was hard against the side of the bus. Tom needed to talk to someone, but this was the last straw for him that evening.

'Not far!' The bus was drawing up to another stop by a pub and a few houses. 'Excuse me, I've got to get out here,' Tom said as he struggled to get up with his case.

'You're not leaving me already!'

'Yes, I am!' He thought the man was not going to let him pass but he staggered back as Tom had to push past him.

'We must meet again!' The man quickly squeezed Tom's hips from behind as he made his escape to the back of the bus and almost fell down the stairs when the bus started to move off.

'Did you want to get out here?' the conductor asked.

'No, I want to sit downstairs,' Tom said and moved to a seat next to a middle-aged woman right at the front.

'Was anyone bothering you up there?' Tom looked up at the conductor, who had followed him.

'No, no really.' Tom was a bit flustered.

'Are you sure? I can turn anyone off the bus or put in a complaint.'

'No, that won't be necessary!' Tom didn't want any fuss.

'Suit yourself, but I've had trouble from a certain gentleman before.' The conductor walked away. Tom looked round and saw him go upstairs, so he guessed he was going up to see the man. No other passenger went up.

Tom glanced at the woman next to him. She had a shopping bag on her lap, and looked at him with a concerned expression.

'Sorry about that,' Tom said, and she smiled.

'Oh, that's all right, dear,' she said abruptly. 'I can see you're a bit bothered!'

'A man was annoying me, that's all.' Tom forced a smile.

'No need to apologise dear, it's no concern of mine.' She sounded like a Londoner.

'I think the conductor's more worried than necessary.' Tom was smiling. 'I'm not worried now!'

'Awkward customers usually go upstairs!'

‘Yes! I wanted a peaceful journey that’s all, so I came down here.’ Tom was beginning to think of the incident with amusement. ‘The conductor needn’t have interfered.’

‘Yes I know what you mean,’ she said cheerfully. ‘There are some funny people about, that’s why I sit down here in the front out of the way.’

‘Yes, it’s the best place; if you can find a seat!’

‘I get to the bus early dear. Always do my shopping on Fridays, I don’t like the Saturday crowds.’

The conductor was standing over Tom again. ‘I’ve had a word with Mr Funny Man up top.’

‘Oh! I don’t want to make a complaint.’

‘Would you excuse me please?’ the lady next to Tom said. ‘This is where I get out.’ Tom stood up and she squeezed by. ‘It’s been nice to talk to you. Tata,’ she said as she walked away along the bus.

‘Don’t think that gentleman will trouble you again,’ the conductor said with a cheeky smile. ‘He’s pretty harmless.’

‘Yes, I know! Thank you anyway.’ Tom sat down thinking he would far rather nobody else interfere with what seemed a minor irritation, though he hoped he would not bump into the man again.

The bus drew into the town square. As Tom got up, he caught sight of the man from upstairs getting out, so he made sure he was the last off the bus. He instinctively closed his eyes for a moment, as if that would prevent him from being seen – like the ostrich that buries its head in the sand. He smiled to himself at the thought and walked quickly on his way.

On the Saturday night Tom strolled into the town. He would have like to have a friend with him, but he had not got to know anyone there. He went into one of the pubs, there being nowhere else to go. The well formed lady behind the bar so diverted his attention that he was quite happy to stand there, taking his time over a beer, while trying to involve the busy lady in small talk. She awakened his basic instincts so that he stood there as if in a trance, pretending to himself that he was just enjoying a drink. *Now there is the perfect human body*, he thought. Although he was interested in her in an aesthetic sense, he could not separate that from the sexual stimulation he was feeling. Perhaps that was why so many successful and famous artists made love to their models, he pondered.

After a couple of beers, Tom came out into the cold night air. It was misty and the street lights faded into halos with the light spot in the centre. He put his hands in his pockets and walked towards the town hall, from which he could hear the sound of a dance band. It was the regular Saturday night hop. The sound of the band brought on the feeling that he often experienced, a mixture of excitement and nervousness which was strangely thrilling. He walked straight into the warm light and bought a ticket.

The young men packed the entrance, while the women sat on the chairs around the hall. Tom had taken a short course of ballroom dancing lessons while he was living at Forest Gate in view of his clumsy experiences a few times in the past. This gave him a little more confidence, though he found dancing difficult owing to a simple fact of nature. He was so turned on by his sexual drive that he had to use will power to concentrate on the dancing steps.

Tom enjoyed himself more as the evening wore on. A circle was formed for the Hokey-Cokey, and he did rather well. When the time came for the last waltz, he asked a girl he'd danced with during the evening to join him. She accepted and Tom was enchanted by the tall, attractive girl, who chatted and said she was a nurse. He escorted her back to where she had been sitting, a courtesy often sadly lacking in Tom's opinion. On impulse, he asked her if he could walk her home, but she replied with a smile, 'I'm with friends, thank you!' He wished he'd not asked.

He went to bed that night thinking how strange the day had been, and with the smell of perfume still in his nostrils, he slept well.

On the Sunday, Tom and his father went for a stroll. The wind was chilly so they soon ended up at their old pub having a quiet drink. But a few minutes later, Tom was shaken to see his unwelcome bus companion come in to the bar. He turned to his father and as he was whispering, 'Oh no, Dad!' his father looked up.

'Hello, Leonard, so you know the best pub then! Meet my son Tom.' Tom had to turn round and face the last man on Earth he wish to meet.

'How do you do?' the man said as if he'd never set eyes on Tom before. Tom shuddered as he shook a limp hand.

'My partner, Leonard Bolton.' Tom sat quietly, not wishing to enter into the conversation, although he knew he must seem petulant. When they left the pub, Tom decided to say nothing to his father about his bus ride encounter.

Chapter 22
The End of the Year

It was dark when Tom left the house on the first day at his new place of work, with a strange feeling of unreality. Going to his old town, to join his past colleague's Company, Mr Wills who had long ago helped and encouraged him in his apprenticeship days. The early bus journey was slow, but once on the double-decker, he sat upstairs at the front and enjoyed the long ride that began in darkness. He lit up a pipe and watched the dawn break as the sky gradually lightening in the East.

Tom walked into the Boltwood Industrial Park, a bleak place, on a misty morning. The buildings had no character and he even began to wonder if he'd made a terrible mistake. The area looked bleaker than the docks ever were on the dullest and coldest of days. He kept telling himself he had no choice, for the decision was made for him when he had that talk with Guthrey. Then, he was clinging to the hope that the rumours were wrong and that he would be offered an increase in salary, but they were only pipe dreams. He had to look upon this new work as the best break he'd ever had, so it was important to greet it with all the enthusiasm he could muster. He wondered if he would soon meet Mildred again.

Carrying his case, he walked briskly. The road was straight and seemed very long in the chilly air. The numbers on some of the buildings were larger than the names of the various small companies. There were buildings, that looked as if they dated from the Thirties for they were typical of the period. There were large storage blocks, with big doors and no windows, that probably dated from the war years. At last he reached the building he was looking for, right at the end. The number, twenty-five, was painted on the side in big square letters. Although the building probably dated from the mid-30s and was an improvement on some of the others, Tom was disappointed and would far rather have worked in the old familiar place they called the pump house. He was looking at a building that, to him, had little character.

The name over the entrance read: 'MERTON PUMP COMPANY', with Directors Jackson and Wills in small letters underneath, a little more impressive than the sign on the gate at the old place. Tom didn't know where the name Merton came from. He'd never asked. He just presumed it was the name of the original inventor of that type of pump.

The double outer doors were open, but glass panelled inner doors were kept closed. He entered an oak panelled foyer with a decorative floor of inlaid rubber. A large square white faced clock in a silver frame with cut in corners and black lettering faced the entrance. There was a small round low table on the right with brochures and magazines laid on it and two low chairs. To the far left, a passage led to a dark door, and to the immediate left was a door that opened in upper and lower halves. 'Reception' was written on the upper part and it was partly open. There was a narrow shelf on the lower door.

Tom imagined that Mildred would be in the reception as he gently knocked and the door swung open. But an efficient older woman faced him with a forced smile.

'Can I help you?' she snapped.

'Good morning, my name is Hunt, Thomas...'

'Good morning, Mr Hunt. We were expecting you.' Her smile became less forced. 'If you would like to go to the door round the corner,' she indicated pointing to her left, 'I'll come round and take you up to Mr Wills.'

'Right, thank you.' He walked round to the dark door, which was quickly unlocked. She was an attractive woman and quite short, very smart and neatly dressed in a black costume, white cashmere jumper and a string of pearls.

'We keep it locked for security.' She had a quiet whispering voice that varied little in tone. 'It's a precautionary measure. Mr Wills was insistent.'

'Really!'

'It's a bit out of the way here. You can't be too careful.'

'Yes I see,' Tom said, 'There must be another entrance?'

'The road down the side to the yard at the back,' she smiled.

Tom followed her towards the back, and he could see into the workshop area where three men were setting up machines. After a quick glance, he followed behind her up cold concrete steps with black iron railings. She had shapely legs with the seams of her stockings quite straight. He was impressed by this smart, businesslike woman and he thought that Mr Wills had chosen well to impress potential customers.

They neared the top of the stairs. 'May I ask, do you work here permanently... er Miss?'

'I'm Mrs Edwards, and at the moment I'm here full-time.'

'Oh,' Tom said quietly as if it was very confidential.

'A new set-up is interesting. We don't know how the future will go, do we?' She spoke even more quietly.

'That's always the case, but...'

'They'll do well, I'm sure,' she said as she led the way towards the front.

'They've been doing well for some years in the old place,' Tom said as they approached a door. 'By the way, did you know Miss West ?'

Mrs Edwards stopped and turned round. 'I've met her. I gather she was with them at the old Fenton building.'

'So she's not working here then?'

'No, not as far as I know.' She turned and opened the door which led into a small drawing office. Tom recognised the young draughtsman who'd been at the old place. There was also a lady tracer, but he did not remember seeing her. Tom said good morning as they walked through. Mrs Edwards knocked on an office door and opened it. 'Good morning Mr Wills, I have Mr Hunt here!'

Mr Wills greeted him with the usual beaming smile. As they shook hands, Tom quickly looked round the office. It was over the front entrance, larger than his old room, though decorated in the same modest way. A drawing board was near the window in addition to the same desk that Tom recognised. They stood there and Tom was waiting to be asked to sit down.

'If you'd like to put your case down there,' Mr Wills said indicating by his desk. 'I'll show you round!' Tom was glancing at the large photograph of the old steam ship that used to hang in Mr Fenton's office, and a wave of sadness came over him.

'Oh, sorry, I was just admiring the picture.'

'Yes Tom, so I see. That ship was broken up long ago!' Then Mr Jackson came into the office through an adjoining door.

'Good morning, Hunt,' he said in a brusque manner. Tom thought of the incident during his apprenticeship days when he'd sent some prints over to him untrimmed. Mr Jackson had brought them back and thrown them onto a table in a rage saying, 'You can trim those prints up, Sonny Jim!'

'Good morning!' Tom said and hoped he had not remembered the incident of years ago. He seemed to be a naturally blunt man.

As he was shown round, a strange and uncomfortable feeling came over Tom, as if he was not really supposed to be there, and he had to make an effort to throw off such thoughts. The new workshop, which was not a lot larger than the old one, was still being fitted out, as were stores and the despatching department. He was introduced to various people but didn't remember their names.

He finished up in a small spartan room on the first floor. There was only the one draughtsman and a tracer in the larger room. Tom thought he would rather have worked with them as he liked company, but space was limited and there were filing cabinets and plan chests crammed in. Also a printing machine was at the end near the door to Tom's little room. Mr Wills stood there with him.

'I think you should be all right in here, Tom.'

'Yes, it's cosy. I'm not used to having my own room though!'

'You don't mind do you?'

'No, of course... it's a nice large window, so the light is good, and I'm next to the larger office.'

'You'll be able to shut yourself in here and not be disrupted.' Little did he know that Tom would feel lonely!

'When do you think everything will be fitted up?'

'We should be all ship shape by the end of the week.'

'Yes, I see.'

'Where are you staying then?'

'I've not found anywhere yet, so I may have to go home on the bus tonight.'

'That's a bit of a journey!'

'Yes, and it means I have to make a very early start in the mornings. Time-consuming, so I need to find some digs soon.'

'I think I can help you, you could be lucky,' Mr Wills said with a big smile. He looked at his watch. 'Fetch your case, I'll just make a phone call and see if it's convenient and then we'll take a little trip in the car.'

Mr Wills drove Tom through the town to a small semi-detached house. 'The lady's name is Mrs Benson. Her husband is a policeman and a good friend of mine.'

'Oh really!' Tom said. 'I'll have to watch my behaviour then!'

'Have any doubts?' Mr Wills grinned, and Tom shook his head. 'She only takes one lodger, and has a vacancy, so you're in luck!'

The door was opened by an attractive woman in a pink overall. 'Hello Frank, you soon got here!'

'Yes, Mary,' he said smiling, 'Everything OK?'

'Yes!' She eyed Tom.

'This is Thomas Hunt.' Mr Wills gestured and Mary smiled warmly as Tom bid her good morning.

'Do come in, both of you.' The house had a nice clean smell. Tom instinctively wiped his shoes thoroughly on the doormat before entering the hall. 'Have you time for a cup of tea?'

'I think that would be very welcome, Mary, thank you.'

'I'll just put the kettle on then, and perhaps Mr Hunt would like to have a quick look at the room while it's brewing.'

Having spent three days in his new place of work, Tom found the work fulfilling, yet he had to throw off the niggling feeling that he had taken a step backwards, after all that time in the Dockland area of London.

At least Mr Wills had found him very good digs, and he was grateful. That night he lay in bed, going over old experiences again, still wondering if he had taken full advantage of his opportunities. He had ambition, and he decided that good things could come of his new position. The past few years drifted through his mind and he thought of the women he'd known. Not much luck there! But he had to stop having regrets about the past. He thought about Mildred, wondering how she was getting on and if he might meet her again. Perhaps a phone call...? Mixed up thoughts occupied his mind as he lay there and drifted into sleep.

Tom dreamed he was in a strange dimly lit room. He picked up a violin that lay on a sofa, but it broke at the finger board. As he looked at the pathetic instrument, a voice said, 'You broke it off, it's up to you to mend it!' He looked at a window and saw Mildred looking in at him with a sad expression. 'You've upset her again,' a voice said. There was a click and the door was opened. 'Cup of tea, sleepy head!'

Tom stirred. It was Mrs Benson. 'Good morning,' he said as he came out of his strange dream. 'Thank you very much...Oh dear!'

'Are you all right?'

'Yes, I was just having a dream, that's all.'

'A bad dream, was it?'

'No! I have funny recurring dreams.'

Mrs Benson always gave Tom his breakfast in the dinning room. When he got downstairs that morning, he met Sergeant Benson for the first time, as he was just about to go on duty at eight o'clock. Tom was strangely intimidated by men in uniform, which to him made them look larger than life.

'Good morning, Mr Hunt.'

'Oh, good morning,' Tom said, surprised by this pillar of the law.'

'We haven't met before. Been on duty.' Tom shook a large hand.

'Hello... er Sergeant.'

'Sergeant it is, glad to know you. I'll be off then, see you.' He went out by the front door.

Mrs Benson came into the dining room with a pot of tea as Tom tucked into a bowl of cornflakes. He was being looked after almost too well, an attention he had never experienced before, away from home. He had certainly never had a landlady who brought a cup of tea to his room in the morning!

'Thank you, Mrs Benson, I think you spoil me!'

'I do believe in looking after my guests properly. I never was one to take advantage of anybody, especially someone who is living away from home, Mr Hunt.'

'You're very kind, I do appreciate that.'

'And you're a good lodger too, you're so bright in the mornings!'

'Do you think so? I...'

'When I bring you tea, and wake you early, you always say good morning! And later when I make the bed, you've folded your pyjamas!' She repeated with emphasis, 'You say good morning and you fold your pyjamas.' She went out to the kitchen leaving Tom feeling a little embarrassed. She didn't realise the effort that went into his determination to make a good impression. Anyway, he always had folded his pyjamas, it was his way.

She soon came back with scrambled egg on toast. It was creamy and spiced with a light sprinkling of Paprika pepper.

'I met your husband as he was leaving this morning.'

'Yes, I heard Ron talking to you. He works various hours. It's according to his duty, you see. The police can never have set times.'

'No, I wouldn't think so.'

'My son's away on his National Service you know. He's got

another fourteen months to go yet.'

'I see!' Tom said. 'I suppose having to do National Service will end one of these days.'

'It's knocking some sense into him. The discipline, I mean. He's pretty bright but needs to grow up. Believe me, it's certainly done him a lot of good. It's made a man of him, it really has. I found a big difference in him when he last came home.'

'So it has its good points then!'

'Yes, it does. He used to be so untidy, and he was dreadful in the mornings. That's why I'm impressed by you being so bright in the mornings, Mr Hunt; and tidy too!'

'Well, I wasn't called up when I was old enough near the end of the war, because of the work I was doing at the time, but I've lived away from home for long periods.'

'Yes, I can see that would make a difference.'

'I like to be independent anyway.'

'Oh dear... Well, it's nice talking to you but I must let you finish your breakfast in peace.' She gave Tom a very big smile as she left the room.

On that Thursday morning of Tom's first week, he was quietly working on a brochure design. Not easy, so he was making rough sketches as he searched for inspiration. He was missing the company and the view of the docks. The new place was very quiet and lacked atmosphere; the change was too great. His view from the window was of the corner of a storehouse and trees with a few autumn leaves still resisting the breeze. Ideas did not come rapidly, and the more he tried the less inspired he became. He began to feel restless and was already worrying that he would not be able to stick it out for long.

He hoped to see Mildred again and wondered if Mr Wills was still in touch with her. It seemed unlikely, in view of what she had said at that last dinner time chat, even though she was on first name terms with him. Tom had never forgotten her words of years ago, divulging her most personal feelings: '*Music is my one ambition.*'

He opened the door to the adjoining office. 'Is there a local telephone directory around?' He addressed the room rather than the two working there. He'd been introduced, but was not yet on convivial terms with either the draughtsman or the tracing lady.

'Yes, here you are!' The lady, an older woman, handed it to him.

'Thank you very much, that's good of you.'

'Not at all, it's here on the side for general use.'

'Yes, of course,' Tom said with a smile. He looked at the tracing she was working on for a few seconds. 'Did I see you in the old office?'

'We were both there, so you probably did. We saw you!'

'Oh,' Tom said. 'I expect I was deep in thought, I'm sorry.'

'It doesn't matter!' she said smiling.

'I expect big Mr Wills was giving you a rough time,' the young draughtsman intervened jokingly.

'Not really.We were introduced, you're Terry, aren't you?'

'Yes, and it's Molly you're talking to.'

'Yes, of course.'

'Settling in all right are you?' Terry asked.

'Yes, OK thank you.' Tom was clutching the telephone book. 'If you'll excuse me now, I just want to look through this.'

Tom retreated back into his little office anxious to see if he could find a number to ring, as he was favoured with the luxury of a telephone. He flipped through the pages till he came to West; there were many! He couldn't see Mildred's old address, but he couldn't remember a phone there and in any case, she might have moved. He felt sure there would be a number he could call. But it would not necessarily be in the name of West anyway! Tom thought he'd have a wild try, so he picked six numbers out of the book to start with, all in or near Newburne and made a note of them.

He picked up the phone, and held his finger on the note pad where he'd written 'C M West'. The operator spoke and he recognised the voice of Mrs Edwards in the reception office.

'Good morning!'

'Oh, good morning. Mrs Edwards, I presume?'

'You presume correct, Mr Hunt.' *Curse it!* he thought. She most likely notes all the calls, and might even listen in. 'Do you wish to make a call?'

'Yes, Newburne two four eight six please.'

'Hold on...' At that moment the door opened and it was Mr Wills.

'Thank you very much,' Tom said and put the phone down quickly. Mr Wills stood silently for a few seconds, and a stupid guilty feeling came over Tom as he glanced up at that bulky character.

'The brochure can wait till next week if you don't mind, Tom. We've suddenly got a bit of a rush on,' he said as he put some rough sketches on Tom's board. 'Terry is busy and I won't be here tomorrow, so that leaves you. I'm sure you can handle it.'

'Yes, of course!'

'I want you to make a working drawing for me.' The phone rang and Mr Wills who was standing next to it, picked it up. 'Merton Pump Company... Yes, hold on, it's a Mr West for you, Tom, Mrs Edwards put him through.'

'I wonder what it's about,' Tom pretended.

'Hello,' a man's voice snapped.

'No there must have been a mistake... No, sorry you've been bothered...Yes, good bye.' Tom put the phone down, feeling he'd gone red in the face.

'Funny!' Mr Wills said and cleared his throat loudly. 'What was that all about?'

'I don't know,' Tom said, wishing he was somewhere else.

'I'll leave these details with you. All the dimensions are clearly marked.' Mr Wills went out, saying no more. Tom was left with an uncomfortable sickly feeling.

Later that day, Tom tried another number, but there was no reply. He didn't try again, for he thought of Mrs Edwards on the switchboard. He concentrated hard on his work in an endeavour to forget his stupid embarrassments. A walk into the town at one o'clock worked wonders. He visited the little cafe by the museum, where he and Mildred had dined together three weeks earlier. He had a vague idea that she might be there, but she wasn't. Tom resigned himself to the fact that he would have to think of another way to make contact with Mildred. Could he just call at her old home? But she could have left the area. It would be a waste of time if she was not living there any more. He thought of her laughing as she told him he worried too much. She was probably right.

One thing he was sure of: he was not going to ask Mr Wills where he might find her.

Chapter 23
Christmas Interlude

Christmas, that magical season, was only two weeks away. Tom was relieved when Mr Wills announced that the company would close on Christmas Eve, as he was planning to go away for the holiday period. When Christmas Eve came there was a small office party arranged by Mr Wills and Mr Jackson like a family get-together. Both the directors made speeches, thanking the staff and expressing great hopes for the future. They all left early in high spirits.

Tom went home to his parents; they were all to spend the holiday at his uncle's farm near Ipswich. Christmas Eve was cold but sunny, and the drive was very pleasant. As they turned into the farm drive, he had a feeling of excitement the way he had always felt when ever the family visited Birchwood Farm.

Uncle Horace came out of the old wagon shed and greeted them with a broad smile. 'Well, I'm blowed!' he said in his Suffolk drawl, as if he'd forgotten they were coming. His uncle's turned down, battered and stained old trilby appeared large on his short build. His round rugged face and kindly eyes showed much humour. Working his farm was his life, he was popular and at one with his farm hands.

In the kitchen, Agnes was busy preparing food. She was a widow before she'd married Horace, but Tom could not imagine calling her Auntie as he had always known her as Agnes. She was an attractive forty-year-old, tall with dark hair. Tom's mother had never liked Agnes, and he didn't understand why, unless she was jealous of her sister-in-law, whom she described her as a worldly woman with a common touch, and only after her brother's money. Tom did not let that bother him: he had shut away his own moody thoughts. Agnes was outgoing and Tom found her a good older woman friend, so he distanced himself from his mother's remarks.

Christmas day was wonderful: relatives and friends called at any time, and Tom could not remember happier days. On Boxing Day, many friends visited the farm. Tom especially liked a young couple, Stan and Christine, who arrived about ten o'clock that morning. Everybody went off in cars to where there was a hunt meeting, to see all the hounds and the riders in hunting pink take the stirrup cup before the start. Tom thought it was very colourful and exciting as they followed the hunt. They ran across the fields to see them chasing the fox. When he witnessed the dogs at the kill, he was suddenly quite distressed, but he said nothing. They might have wondered why he went quiet while the others were so vociferous.

Tom found himself in tune with Christine, so much so that he became conscious of Stan, her husband, throwing him jealous glances. Tom and Christine discussed the hunt: she felt the same way as he did, though they agreed it would be a problem if the countryside became overrun by foxes. Farmers looked upon them as pests, for they did so much damage, especially the indiscriminate killing of chickens, of which his uncle Horace had a great number. Christine was, if anything, more upset than Tom by the kill. After the colourful spectacle at the meeting before the hunt, it could perhaps almost be forgotten what it was all about.

That evening, Tom was with Christine in the kitchen, while the rest of the party were having a game in the sitting room. He and Christine were sitting by the warmth of the kitchen range. She was gentle, had a kindly nature and her large hazel eyes were hypnotic to Tom. He sat in a low armchair, while she sat on the floor and leaned back, resting her head between his legs.

'This is how I like to sit,' she said. Tom pushed his fingers into the strands of her soft brown hair.

'Yes, I...'

'That's lovely.' Christine was moving her head around.

'I hope no one comes in,' Tom said. She pushed her head back against his parted legs, which was stimulating. He looked down and kissed her forehead. 'Sorry!'

'Why sorry?'

'Stan might come in.'

'He won't!' Tom wasn't too sure.

They stayed there for some time, absorbed in a long discussion, mostly about her love life. She confided in him that she was not completely satisfied. As she went into details that Tom was no authority on, he was feeling sexually aroused and at the same time nervous that Stan would come through the door.

'Stan's just like a little boy in bed,' she said. 'He curls up like a baby!'

There were voices in the hall. Christine got up from the floor and sat in the chair opposite. Just then, Stan came in with uncle Horace.

'Hello, what's going on with you two in here?' his uncle said. Stan glared at Tom.

'We've been having a nice little chat,' Christine said. 'Haven't we, Tom?' She looked at him with a big smile.

'Yes, I see,' Stan said. He seemed piqued.

'Hello, Stan. I feel a bit guilty keeping your wife in conversation all evening.' Tom felt stupid and immediately regretted what he'd said.

'Don't be silly, Stan,' Christine said. 'You could have come and joined us any time if you wanted to.'

'We were having a game in there. You could have joined us anyway,' Stan said, with the glimmer of a smile, so Tom thought perhaps he wasn't really furious.

The next day, Tom and his parents were due to go home. Christine and Stan called early, just as Tom was off to collect some eggs to take home. As he was taking eggs from one of the nesting boxes, he was aware that Christine was standing near him. A tingling thrill went through him.

'Hello! Christine, it's nice to see you again before we go.'

'Oh, you're going back today, are you?'

'Yes, I'm afraid so, worse luck. It's been a good break.'

'I'm going to miss you, Tom.' She hugged his arm.

'You mustn't say that, Christine. Think of Stan!'

'I'm not feeling too pleased with him at the moment: I think he crept round and peeped through the window last night.'

'Why do you think that?'

'Just his attitude, something he said.'

'Would have looked a bit compromising, I suppose. Well, does Stan get jealous? Is it worrying you?

'No! Who cares!' They moved close to each other. Tom looked into her eyes. They kissed and he almost dropped the eggs.

'Why don't you put those eggs down, Tom?'

'Yes!' They went between two chicken houses, and she pulled him back against the chicken house wall. She trembled as he pressed against her warm body, between her legs. He was helpless for a minute as they were locked together. Then he was suddenly scared that someone would come and find them. She was quite red in the face.

'Another time, Tom! Don't forget the eggs.' Tom was still shaking as they strolled back to the house. Stan was chatting with Tom's father and uncle in the kitchen.

'We wondered where you'd got to,' Stan said.

'I was collecting eggs and met Christine.' Stan looked at Tom with a quizzical expression, but nothing more was said.

'Oh good,' Agnes said as she came into the kitchen. 'You've got some nice eggs to take back with you.'

'Yes thank you,' Tom said with a smile.

'Well, come and see us in the spring,' his uncle said.

'Yes, I always look forward to coming to Birchwood!'

When it came to leaving, Tom was fighting with his thoughts. He shook hands with Stan, who simply said, 'Have fun!'

'I try to,' he said, wondering if he'd said the right thing.

'Bye, Tom,' Christine said. He gave her hand a quick squeeze.

He dared not kiss her, even though Stan kissed Tom's mother as if he lusted after her. His father looked at Stan, then kissed Christine. Tom was anxious to get away at that moment.

'In the spring!' Tom whispered to Christine.

'Good bye, good bye.' They waved as they drove off.

Chapter 24
Mildred

It was New Year's Eve and Mrs Benson was extra cheerful when she brought in Tom's breakfast.

'Are you doing any celebrating this evening Mr Hunt?'

'I haven't planned anything,' he said thoughtfully.

'We're having a few friends in tonight, and if you haven't any other plans, we would be delighted if you would join us.'

'That's very kind of you.'

'It's nothing special, we usually do have a little private party to see in the New Year.'

'Thank you very much. I'll look forward to that.'

At work, Tom thought of the folks he would meet that evening, with curiosity. He had soon settled into his new lodgings, very different from those he'd known before. He felt as if he was one of the family, even though Mrs Benson addressed him formally as Mr Hunt. But when things were going well for Tom, he was sure it could not last!

There was already a party atmosphere when he got in that evening. Mrs Benson gave him a light meal and explained that there would be plenty of food later. He was always surprised how well she fed him, in spite of rationing. Mrs Benson explained that a few friends would be coming about eight o'clock but she was not sure if Ron would be able to make it very early, if at all, as his duties could be burdensome that night.

It was after eight o'clock, and Tom was in his room, quietly reading. He put the book down and Mildred was again in his thoughts, then he heard chatter downstairs. The sound of the gramophone started up, so he plucked up courage and went down to join the party. Mrs Benson was just letting some friends in.

'Hello, Helen,' she said, 'how are you?'

'Oh I'm fine.' They kissed. 'You're looking well, Mary!'

'Hello Jack,' Mrs Benson said.

'Hi! Mary,' he said with a very pronounced American accent, and gave her a big kiss. Mrs Benson was taking their coats and she turned to Tom as he arrived at the bottom of the stairs.

'Oh, this is Mr Hunt, my new lodger. Meet Helen and Jack.'

'Any friend of Mary's is a friend of mine,' said the big man in American Air force Officers uniform. He stuck out a large hand and shook Tom's with a firm grip.

'Good evening,' Tom said.

'Well, we can't just call you Mr Hunt,' he said with a broad smile, 'you must have a first name?'

'It's Tom!'

'You're lucky to have such a good home to stay in Tom, where are you from then?'

'I've been working in London till recently.'

'Fine, fine, I'm at the Air Base near here, lucky enough to have my lovely wife over here with me. I sure think this country is great, but we can't stay here for ever, unfortunately.'

'Do come into the sitting room, and meet the others,' Mrs Benson said. 'We can't stay in the hall all night!'

In the sitting room, Jack and Helen were told to help themselves to drinks. Tom was introduced to another married couple, about the same age as the Bensons, and he was immediately captivated by their attractive daughter. Her hair was a golden bronze, a straight silken swathe that fell softly to her shoulders.

'Meet Peter and Janet Brooks, and Doreen. This is Mr...'

'I'm Tom,' he quickly intervened.

'Hello, we've not met before, have we?' Peter said.

'Tom is our lodger,' Mrs Benson said.

'Nice to meet you, Tom; Mary feeds you well, I'll bet!'

'Yes, she does!' He wished people would stop referring to

the way he was looked after. Janet and her daughter were smiling in the background as they stood holding their drinks.

'Would you like a drink, Tom,' Mrs Benson said, dropping the formalities, and led him to a table. There was a row of two pint flagons of beer, some soft drinks and a large punchbowl. 'There's beer, orange or lemon; or would you like to try the punch?' She laughed. 'I don't think I made it too strong!'

'Can I try the punch?'

'That's a good start!' She ladled it into a wine glass.

'Thank you very much.'

'Just feel free to help yourself. Ah, that's the door bell, excuse me.'

Tom looked to where Doreen and her mother were standing and went over to join them. He guessed Doreen was a lot younger than he. He smiled, cleared his throat to conquer that old shyness.

'Do you work in Newburne?' Doreen asked breaking the silence.

'Yes, I do,' Tom said turning to her with a smile.

'What are you into?' She said, as she pushed her hair back with her fingers.

'Engineering mainly; what do you do?'

'Nothing really at the moment. I'm studying domestic science at a private finishing school near here.'

'Oh, I thought girls had to go abroad for that!' She laughed at Tom's suggestion. 'Or perhaps not these days. What does it involve then?'

'We learn how to be a good hostess, cook and run a home.'

'I see.' Tom smiled. 'Sounds useful!'

Mrs Benson returned chatting with a guest following her.

'I think you all know Frank!' Tom was startled, but of course, it was Mr Wills who had first introduced him to the Bensons. So it was hardly surprising that he should be invited. A slightly absurd thought that Mildred was with him flashed though his mind.

'I hope you're behaving yourself Tom,' he said.

'What a thing to say Frank!' Mrs Benson said indignantly.

'He's always the gentleman.'

'Hello Mr Wills,' Tom said. Wills gave him a quick nod and a smile, then turned and talked to the American couple who he obviously knew well, and Mrs Benson handed him a glass of punch.

'Here you are Frank, I know you always enjoy the punch.'

'Thank you Mary, that's nice; not alcoholic I hope!' She had already turned away as he raised his glass. He took one quick sip, shuddered and put it on the piano, then helped himself to a potato crisp. Tom was amused, as he knew Mr Wills' stance with the slightest hint of alcohol. The punch had quite a kick. As he turned to Doreen and smiled, he hoped he was not swaying:

Doreen helped Mrs Benson bring in the food: hot sausage rolls, mince pies and two large plates of sandwiches.

'Are we going to see Ron tonight?' asked Peter, addressing Mrs Benson.

'You know he can't say: it all depends if things get out of hand. We'll have to wait and see.'

Tom decided to avoid the punch. He tucked into some food and then poured himself a beer from a screw topped flagon.

The night wore on, and Peter sat at the piano and played some amazing 'Boogie Woogie.' Then Janet joined him on the long piano stool. They played in duet, popular songs, mainly of the thirties and some of the party joining in to sing. The atmosphere was stimulating and Tom had forgotten how many beers he'd had. As midnight drew near, Jack went out of the room and soon reappeared. Peter was putting a flash bulb on his camera. 'OK everybody,' Jack said, 'here's a special treat.' Mrs Benson and Helen stood on either side of him, 'All the way from across the ocean, real American Bourbon whisky.' He held up the bottle and Peter took a flash photograph, 'To see the New Year in.' There was a cheer, and Mrs Benson brought out some tumblers, and put them on the table.

'There we are, Jack.'

'Thank you, Mary.' He poured the whisky. 'I see we have eight glasses here, that will be Ron's. Well, I guess he'll be back sometime.' He charged the remaining glass. Mr Wills stood well away, clutching an orange drink.

'All help yourselves,' Mrs Benson said, and glanced at the clock. It started to strike as they picked up the drinks.

'Happy new year everybody,' Jack said while it was still striking. There was much kissing and when Tom instinctively gave Doreen a kiss, she seemed quite shy.

'Happy New Year... Happy New Year!'

The pianists struck up 'Auld Lang Syne', and the party continued for a while, then just before half past twelve Ron came in, wearing his uniform and there were exclamations of, 'Hello Sergeant!'

'Glad to see you Ron,' Jack said. 'There's a Bourbon already for you there on the table.'

'Which one is mine?' he said, for there were two remaining whiskies. 'Sorry I couldn't make it earlier. What a night; anyway I'm here now. Happy New Year everybody!'

They were starting to leave by the time Mr Wills came up to Tom and shook his hand.

'All the best for the new year Tom, I know you'll do your best for me. Don't worry if you're late in the morning.'

'I'll try not to be!' He hoped he didn't appear too tipsy.

'I don't know if you're interested, but Mildred West will be playing in a concert in Oxford on Saturday week. I thought you might like to know. I remember you had lessons from her once.' Those words seemed like a dream in the lingering party atmosphere.

'Yes, I am interested!' Tom said casually. He had been kidding himself for all those years that Mr Wills was not aware Mildred had ever given him lessons.

'She has great talent... I have special regard for her.' Tom felt a twinge of jealousy. 'She was always only really interested in music. Anyway, that's all water under the bridge.' His words were agonising. 'Anyway, I've got some details of the concert, I'll let you have them.'

The theatre had a magical atmosphere. A feeeling of unreality encompassed Tom as his heart pounded faster with anticipation. He often became very much aware of himself when in the midst of a crowd. He would feel alone. As he looked at the position the orchestra would occupy, he wondered if Mildred might see him. Would she be pleased? He took deep breaths as he tried to subdue his nervous excitement. As the seats were filling, he became overwhelmed with the thought that Mildred, his violin teacher of so long ago, was about to play within a large orchestra. Minutes seemed like hours, as he waited and glanced from side to side at the growing audience.

The musicians started to come in and take their places. Then he saw her get into position with the other violinists, and a warm feeling came over him. She was wearing a long red velvet dress with a white lace collar, a pale beauty and there were tiny flashes as the lights reflected on her spectacles. Her golden wavy shoulder length hair made her seem almost doll like. Tom instinctively tried not to keep his eyes on her too much, almost as if he imagined his attention would disturb her, and he looked at the other musicians as they tuned their instruments. Then the clapping as the conductor stepped onto the rostrum. Tom glanced at Mildred and imagined she saw him, but he was not sure.

Through the first half of the concert, he sat in complete ecstasy, captivated by Mozart and Elgar. With his eyes half closed, in a dreamlike state he watched the movements of the bows, aware of Mildred at one end of the string section. He contemplated the chance to see and speak to her, perhaps during the interval. Tom would go away unhappy if he did not try. He thrust this underlying thought aside until the final bar was played.

The musicians left the platform and Tom made a move towards the door through which they had all departed. He quite expected to be challenged, but no one did. He saw Mildred within a group taking refreshments. She had just got herself a cup of tea. He stood for a moment, transfixed and wondering if he should go over to her, but he wanted to speak to her alone. She looked up and saw him, and as she did so she appeared startled. Then she walked towards Tom carrying the tea cup and saucer, and smiled.

'Not as good as the tea you used to give me, Mildred, I'll bet,' Tom said.

'That's going back a long time,' she said with amusement. 'This is a surprise.'

'Yes, it must be. I hope you don't mind me just looking in to see you. I know I mustn't keep you, but....'

'It's OK!' She said. The warm feeling of long ago came over him, and there was a moment of silence.

'I just want to say how much I'm enjoying the concert. I had to try to see you.'

'It's a nice surprise.'

'I think you look super!'

'Thank you, nice of you to say so.' She smiled. 'Very glad that you came, Tom.'

'Yes... Can't keep you now, but... I was wondering if you would like to have tea with me one afternoon, perhaps?'

'That would be nice, yes,' she said thoughtfully.

'I can give you a ring if you like?'

'Yes, why not. I'll wait to hear from you, then.'

'I don't know your telephone number!'

'Just a minute,'she said, turning away. 'Something to write on?'

'Here,' Tom said, handing her his programme and a pencil. 'On the back of this.' She wrote quickly.

'I'll be playing a solo piece in the second half.' She gave him back the programme.

'Oh, that's marvellous, I'll enjoy that.'

'I hope so!' She smiled and turned to walk away, then looked back. 'Thank you for coming in to see me.'

'Good luck!'

'Thank you.' She seemed suddenly nervous. Tom feared that the challenge she faced in the future could end in forlorn frustration and even loneliness. He thrust those thoughts away and smiled.

When Tom got back to his seat, he was overjoyed with himself, relieved and happy, and forgot any reservations he had been fostering. As far as he was concerned then, she was the only woman for him. He hadn't even looked at what she had written on his programme. He turned it over to look just as the lights dimmed slightly, making it difficult to read her scribble. The audience clapped when a lady pianist with short dark hair, wearing a long black silk dress with a frilly collar, came onto the platform. She bowed and sat at the piano. Then applause as Mildred entered with her violin and bowed to the audience. The picture in Tom's mind of the so competent little figure in the red dress would remain with him always: he felt humbled at her talent. He remembered her saying, all those years ago, as she was about to give him his first lesson: 'They say that music and art go together!'

He was still in a dream, as he left the theatre, and he kept on looking back as if he expected to see her running to join him. It was not until he was in the bus on his way home that he thought to look at the back of his programme. He experienced a moment's panic as he had the awful thought that he had mislaid it, but it was in his pocket. She had simply written an Oxford telephone number. So he still didn't know her address, but he guessed she had moved.

Tom entered the Phoenix Restaurant in Oxford, where he had arranged to meet Mildred the following Saturday afternoon. His heart beats increased as he stood inside the entrance, looking across the room. He spotted her in a far corner and she gave a little wave, as if she were the Queen.

'Very good timing,' she said, looking at her watch.

'Oh, bang on.' Tom looked at a wall clock.

'You've been shopping I see, and bought some books.'

'Yes... a couple of art books. Get me into a book shop and I'm liable to forget the time.'

'Not this time though!'

A waitress in a black dress, white frilly apron and cap came to the table.

'Do you like crumpets?' Tom asked, looking at Mildred.

'That would be very nice, if they have them.'

'Yes we have, Madam,' the waitress said. 'And a pot of tea for two is it?'

Mildred poured the tea and they were enjoying the crumpets.

'Are you living in Oxford now?' Tom asked.

'I found some rooms in part of a house, two weeks before Christmas.'

'That's not a good time to move!'

'There were problems; I wouldn't worry you over them anyway.'

'I hope the other people in the house appreciate music.'

'Absolutely: they're all musicians. We get on well!'

'Oh good – so that's not a problem.'

'I had to sort myself out and... well, Dad died last year.'

'Oh, I'm sorry, it must have been...'

'He'd been ill for a while.'

'I see. So... your mother?'

'We don't get on. She can be awkward at times. I couldn't live with her.' There was a moment of silence. 'She'll get over it.' Mildred sounded determined.

'Yes,' Tom nodded. 'So Oxford is...?'

'My music is very important for me.'

'Yes, I know.' He suddenly saw her as a different person.

'And there are better opportunities here.'

They sat over a last cup of tea. 'I dare say you've heard, I'm working with Mr Wills now?' Tom said.

'With Frank. Yes, I thought you would be.' She was slightly hesitant.

'I haven't got round to calling him Frank.' Tom forced a smile.

'I suppose that's natural as you've just started working with him.' She smiled. 'I don't think he'd worry though.'

'We get on very well, as a matter of fact, and I think I have a better future now.' Tom rubbed his hands together and looked down at the table. 'That's not to say I'm always going to be satisfied to work for someone else. Like you, I have artistic and creative ambitions.'

'Yes, I understand of course.'

'Yours is music, which I enjoy listening to of course. Well, let's face it, I only enjoy playing the violin or piano myself for fun. I mean, I am not good enough to entertain by a long way.' Tom smiled. 'I can create more in art; painting, or even writing!' They sat in silence for a while. Tom feared in his heart that they could drift away from each other, and he shuddered at the thought.

'It's getting late!' she said, looking at her watch.

'Are you doing anything special this evening?' There was a pause as she looked at him with an inquisitive halfsmile, and Tom felt uncomfortable. 'Or shouldn't I ask that?' Again, he wanted to bite his words.

'That's all right. Actually, I have to be at a rehearsal at seven tonight.'

'On a Saturday?' Tom said clumsily.

'I'm playing in a charity concert on Sunday afternoon.'

'Of course, that's good, but you have to relax sometime.'

'I enjoy it anyway: it's my life!' Her expression was indignant. 'Your art is important for you, Tom.' He thought she sounded patronising, which he didn't like.

'Yes of course... I'm sorry.' He paused for thought. 'But it doesn't stop me enjoying your company. I have to get away from it sometimes. We all have to have a time to relax. Oh, what more can I say?' He could find no more applicable words to add without sounding condescending. So he settled the bill.

As they were walking out, Tom was quite suddenly aware that there seemed to be a barrier between them. He was not sure whether it was true or cynical conjecture on his part. He dismissed the disturbing, dull, sickening thought as they were reaching the door. They looked at each other and suddenly she gave Tom a big smile, which immediately reassured him, and he almost laughed.

'I have enjoyed our conversation, Tom.'

'Yes, so have I.'

'And thank you for the tea, it was very nice.'

'It's a good place,' Tom said as they went through the door.

'Ooh! a bit chilly out,' she said.

'Yes. Have you far to go, Mildred?'

'No, it's easy: there are plenty of buses.'

'Can I see you home; get you a taxi?'

She burst out laughing. 'Of course not Tom, I'd much rather find my own way.'

'I still don't know your address, by the way?'

'You can always ring me sometime, if you like.' She squeezed his hand, then gave him a quick peck on the cheek. 'Thank you again,' she said, and walked quickly away along the pavement. Tom just stood there and watched. She turned and waved.

'Bye!' Tom shouted with a pathetic note in his voice.

Watching Mildred walk quickly away, Tom was dolefully aware that he might never see her again. As he wandered around the town, he felt happy for her yet sad. She was still the same country girl who had talent. But although he found her slightly more sophisticated, her hopes for the future could end in loneliness. He thought she was wrong to give up her life for an ambition that might never be fulfilled. Then again that might not be true: perhaps he was being selfish. For why fear for her future? Was it that he feared he'd somehow blown his own chances?

A couple of beers did little to cheer him before he got on a train for Newburne. Two young girls sat opposite him in the compartment, chatting away to each other. Their enthusiasm and cheerfulness made him feel more relaxed, but they got out at the first stop, leaving Tom with his own brooding company. *Perhaps I'll ring her*, he thought. *Just give her time to think about it, then a surprise phone call.*

But he never did.

Chapter 25
Doreen

The night was full of strange dreams. Tom suddenly woke and it was dark, a clock downstairs, just faintly heard, struck five. He had spent a restless night, and lay there for some time. The pale light of dawn gradually crept into the room, while he dwelt upon the previous day with an exaggerated feeling of loss. He knew he had to stop lingering over circumstances beyond his control, and as the light grew, he thought of his unknown future stretching out like a long secret road.

Tom had come in the previous evening about eight and met Mrs Benson in the hall. 'Have you had a good day?' she said.

'Well, I...'

'You don't look very happy.'

'I'm all right, just a little tired, that's all.'

'You go into the sitting room, Mr Hunt, and I'll bring you a cup of tea.' She had called him Tom at the New Years Eve party. Tom thought she feared sounding too familiar, though she remained very affable as always.

'Thank you... you are good to me.'

'Now, we've had supper, so let me find you something to eat.'

'No, please don't bother, I'm really not hungry.'

'Oh... well if you're sure.' Mrs Benson had cheered him up a little. She would often talk with Tom till late in the evenings when Sergeant Benson was on duty, but after his disconcerting date with Mildred, he went to his room, keeping his thoughts to himself.

Sunday morning, he lay not sleeping for what seemed hours.

'A cup of tea for you, Mr Hunt.' Tom had dozed off again.

'Oh dear, thank you, Mrs Benson. What time is it?'

'Gone half past eight!'

'I'm sorry, I had a restless night.'

'I wonder why that was? 'I don't know.' He yawned.

'Breakfast will be ready when you are,' she said as she left the room.

'Would you like to come into the kitchen Mr Hunt,' Mrs Benson called as he came downstairs. Ron was at the kitchen table, reading the Sunday paper. 'I hope you don't mind having breakfast with us this morning. It's cold in the dining room as the fire's not been lit.'

'Yes of course, that's all right... makes a change,' Tom said.

'Good morning,' Ron said, and he put the paper on one side. 'Sit yourself down then.'

'I expect you'd like porridge,' Mrs Benson said, 'on this cold morning.' She had just placed fried egg and bacon before the sergeant. Tom would have liked that, but he thought he'd had his ration.

'Oh! Yes, thank you.'

'What are your plans for the day then?' Ron asked.

'I've not made any plans.'

'Don't be so nosy, Ron, it's really none of our business,' Mrs Benson said.

'That's all right, I don't mind, Ron, er I mean Sergeant Benson.'

'Look, why not cut the Sergeant when I'm off duty? Just call me Ron, OK?'

'Yes, if you don't mind.... Ron then.'

'Of course I don't mind, Tom.' He smiled.

'And when you're in uniform... on duty?'

'Makes no difference in private, but sarge would do otherwise.'

'Now isn't that splendid,' Mrs Benson said with a laugh. 'He won't know whether he's coming or going.'

Ron pointed quickly at his wife with his fork. 'I'm sure she won't mind you calling her Mary. Will you, dear?'

'You're embarrassing the poor man,' she said as she gave Tom his porridge and sat down with hers, 'you'll put him off his porridge.'

'No it won't! Enjoying it aren't you, Tom?' Ron was tucking into his egg and bacon. 'Never eat porridge myself. Gives me indigestion.'

After breakfast, Tom spent most of the morning practising the piano in the cold sitting room. He had asked Mrs Benson if she minded and she was very encouraging.

'Just help yourself, any time,' she said. 'I like a little music.'

'I'm not an expert I'm afraid.'

'As long as you enjoy it, go ahead. I hope you don't get too cold in there though.'

'Thank you.' Tom did find it cold and he played badly. Then his mind drifted onto the way things went for him the day before. His playing got worse and he stopped, rested his elbows on the keys and buried his head in his hands.

'Are you all right?' Mrs Benson said as she came into the room.

'Yes thank you,' Tom said, looking up. 'I was just thinking!'

'You must be frozen! You'd better go into the kitchen, where it's warm.' She put a match to the already made up fire. 'There we are, that will soon get going now.'

'Yes... and you're right, I am a bit cold in here.' Tom stood up and clenched his hands.

'Dinner will be ready shortly. It will be a nice warm fire in here by this afternoon.'

Ron was sitting by the kitchen grate still reading the paper.

'Come and warm your hands, Tom.'

'That's better.' Tom held his hands near the fire bars.

'Well, twelve o'clock.' The dining room clock was striking and Ron put down the paper. 'I'm going to walk up the road for a quick one at the King's; like to join me Tom?'

'Oh, yes I would like that!' Tom rubbed his hands together.

'You're not still cold, are you?'

'I'm warmer now thank you.'

'You'll need a coat. It's a cold day and looks as if it's going to snow.

'I'll just go and get my coat.' Tom thrust away his brooding thoughts.

'The walk will do you both good,' Mrs Benson said.

They walked about a quarter of a mile: the King's Head was on the corner at the end of the road. Ron was given a warm welcome: evidently he was a regular customer. Pays them to be on good terms with the law, Tom was thinking. They stood at the bar drinking mild and bitter.

'Peter and Janet are coming to tea this afternoon,' Ron said. 'You remember the Brooks, and their daughter Doreen at the New Year's Eve party.'

'I certainly do! Will Doreen be coming?'

'Yes, her parents are picking her up from Claremount.'

'Oh good, I think she's a very nice girl.'

'Yes, Tom, and she's grown into an attractive young woman!'

'I agree... her father's good on the piano.'

'Yes and Doreen has a fine soprano voice. We often finish up with a musical evening on Sundays.'

'That's very enjoyable.'

'Well, it should cheer you up, Tom. I hope you don't mind me saying so, but you don't seem too happy at the moment.'

'Oh, what makes you say that?'

'I can always tell. I tend to read moods – part of my job.'

'It's OK now.' Tom felt as if he was being interrogated.

'Girl let you down or something?'

'Yes, well something like that.'

'You'll soon get over it, plenty of pebbles on the beach.'

'Yes, but not many special ones.'

'They always seem special at the time.'

'It was someone I'd known for a long time.' Tom felt he'd said too much already. He had to keep his secret.

'Someone local?' Ron asked.

'No, a very long way from here.' Tom was fearfully thinking of the fact that Mr Wills was well acquainted with her and at the same time, a friend of Ron's. 'Can we get off the subject please.'

'Yes, of course. We'd better get back for dinner, Tom.'

The subject of Tom's tender love life was not mentioned again. They consumed an enormous meal, and Tom helped after with the washing up. Then they flopped out in the sitting room. There were a few books in there and Tom spotted an interesting old volume to peruse on engineering with many engraved illustrations including beam engines and paddle steamers. He felt nostalgic about his old firm that had so disastrously declined.

It was soon after four o'clock, when the door bell rang. 'That's probably them,' Ron said, getting up. Tom always felt emotionally stimulated at such moments. He hoped Doreen would be with them. There were voices and laughter in the hall, and he heard Peter Brooks having a joke with Ron. 'A policeman's lot is not a happy one.' Doreen's laughter was predominant. Tom stood up as they entered the room and shook hands.

'We've met of course,' Peter said.

'New Year's Eve,' Tom said as he took Doreen's hand and they smiled at each other. Strands of soft hair veiled her cheeks.

'Yes, that was a lovely party,' Doreen said, and Tom was mesmerised by her bright eyes.

'It certainly was!' Janet said.

They had tea in the sitting room by the warmth of the fire; plenty of cakes and sandwiches. Tom was not hungry, but he enjoyed a cup of tea. He sat next to Doreen, not knowing what to say. Then she broke the silence. 'Can I pass you a rock cake, Tom?'

'Oh, no thanks, I'm full up, so don't tempt me.'

'Go on, be tempted, I'm sure you can manage one.'

'I do like them.' Tom took one. 'But I had such a big dinner!'

'I think Mary makes the finest rock cakes,' Peter said. 'You must be the best fed lodger in the town, Tom.'

'I'm not complaining.' He hid his slight irritation at the familiar comment.

'I should think not,' Ron said, and Tom thought he'd said the wrong thing. But there was a lot of laughter, so he soon forgot his absurd bashful feelings.

'You're still at the good cook school, are you, Doreen?' Tom asked a little clumsily.

'I'm at the Claremount,' she said with a laugh. 'We don't just learn cooking you know!'

'No, of course not. How long will you be there then?'

'Until May, that's at the end of the course. Then we give a party and practise being good hostesses.'

'Very good, I would imagine.'

'Well, we try to be,' she said.

It was getting dark and Ron got up from where he was sitting. 'I'll light the gas,' he said and he pulled the chain of the gas light that hung at the centre of the ceiling. The light was surprisingly bright, and made a gentle hissing sound. There was an electric standard light behind the sofa where Tom and Doreen were sitting. Tom had wondered why there were gas lights as well as electric.

'You have alternative lighting!' Tom said.

'Yes, we had sockets put in but we thought we would keep the old gas in case the electricity is cut off.

'Oh I see, it's a good light,' Tom remarked.

The evening wore on and the despair that lingered in Tom's mind from the previous day had fallen away, though it was not forgotten. As he sat with Doreen, their conversation became more animated. Ron stood up and sang some old songs, while Peter played the piano.

'East and West, North and South, from Bristol to Peru... Drake is in his hammock and a thousand miles away... On the road to Manderlay... and the dawn comes up like thunder out of China, cross the bay,' Ron ended on a strong vibrato note. Everybody clapped and Tom was very impressed. They managed to persuade Doreen to sing, for she was shy about it at first. Tom felt quite emotional as he listened to her clear tones. She sang 'Cherry Ripe, Cherry Ripe' and other old fashioned songs that Tom enjoyed. She finished up with, 'We'll gather Lilacs' of recent war time memories, and there was another good clap.

'That was wonderful,' Tom said as she came back beside him on the sofa. 'Do you sing with a choir?'

'I used to, but not now.'

'That seems a pity!'

'I know I would never be that good, so I just sing if I'm asked by friends.'

'Well, I thought you were very good!'

'Nice of you to say that, Tom,' She spoke quietly, cupping her mouth with one hand. But there's lots of good singers and I'm never likely to get anywhere, though I enjoy it when I'm asked. But I do get a bit nervous though.' Tom thought of Mildred and was momentarily lost for words.

'Yes, I think I understand,' he said, coming to life.

It was an evening he would always remember. It seemed for him to mark a small step from one era into another. He started meeting Doreen regularly, and they went for long walks together through wooded countryside. They shared many common interests like visiting historical sites, and would finish up having tea out somewhere in the afternoon. The weather was getting more Spring-like and they would sometimes sketch together, though she admitted that art was not her best subject. They were by a lake, sitting on a fallen tree when they kissed. Their companionship had been very slow in changing from one of friendship to a sexual relationship.

They walked along a footpath in conversation.

'The course at Claremount finishes next week,' Doreen said.

'Oh! So then what will you do?'

'I don't know yet!' she said as if it were a joke.

'Out into the wide world, not knowing what to do?'

'I won't get lost!' she laughed. 'We lived in at Claremount, but I'll live at home for a while. Would you like to be my guest at our end of term host night?' she suddenly asked.

'Well thank you for asking me, yes!'

'Of course I'd ask you first, Tom.'

'Oh!' he hesitated. 'What does it involve then?'

'Nothing, silly thing. You'll just be expected to wear a dinner suit, that's all.'

'That's all!' Tom exclaimed. 'But I don't own one!'

'Don't worry; you can hire that.'

A few days later, she had arranged everything, and they went together to where she had made an appointment for him at a hire shop. He looked at himself in the mirror and felt a little odd at what he saw.

'Like some other fellow!' Tom uttered.

'Don't be silly, you look very nice and smart.'

'I suppose I do look rather distinguished.'

'How does it feel? It looks a good fit!'

'Well, it feels OK.'

Tom arrived at Claremount House dressed in his finery, where he was greeted by one of the girls at the door.

'Hello. I'm Cynthia, and you are?'

'I'm Thomas Hunt, how do you do.'

She opened the door wide. 'Come in,' she said, looking him up and down. 'Who's guest are you then,' she asked with a haughty chortle.

'Doreen Brooks,' he said.

'Good, let me take your coat then, Thomas.'

'My friends just call me Tom,' he said as she was helping him off with his coat.

'Right then, Tom!' she said as she put his coat in the cloak room. She was so tall that she made him feel quite small. She had straight, shoulder-length black hair and was wearing a full length low cut black dress. Very sexy, he thought as he followed her into a large room full of young men all wearing the same uniform – like a lot of waiters, Tom thought.

Doreen emerged from somewhere behind the scenes wearing a light blue dress with a finely pleated skirt. She greeted Tom and squeezed his hand as they kissed, then led him to a long table and gave him a glass of Champagne.

'Help yourself to eats, there's plenty for everyone.'

'Thank you, it looks marvellous, Doreen.'

'It's a sort of cocktail party-cum-lots-of-grub do.'

'Oh yes, I can see that.' Tom had difficulty in understanding why he'd had to go to the expense of dressing up. He thought a smart suit would have done, but it was all part of the decorum that mattered for those who ran the finishing school.

They stood around holding glasses and food with difficulty. All the young men were talking to each other like cut-out figures, such was the formality. Even Tom found himself feeling like a cut-out figure, as if they were taking part in some sort of play, where nobody quite knew their lines.

'Tom, meet Bonzo.' Doreen introduced him to a tall lanky chap who looked down at him from aloft.

'Charles Bonson.' They shook hands. 'And what do you do?'

'Engineering mostly.'

'That sounds frightfully interesting.' They had nothing in common and the small talk soon petered out.

After a while, and quite by surprise, Doreen took Tom by the hand and led him up the stairs. He'd had a few glasses of champagne and felt a little woozy.

'Where are we going?' Tom asked.

'To my abode!'

'Oh, that's interesting.'

'In here,' she said, opening an oak door. 'My room!'

'This is nice and cosy,' Tom said with a trembling voice.

'Not for long now though,' she said. He was looking into her eyes and she surprised him by putting her arms round his waist, then rubbed her head against his chest. 'I do like men in dinner suits,' she said.

He instinctively put his arms round her shoulders. 'Oh well, we all look alike!'

'Does something to me.' He felt her trembling. She edged Tom towards the bed and put one hand on the counterpane. Is this the shy young girl I used to know? Tom thought.

'It's a very comfortable bed,' she said.

'Is it! That's good.' With his limited experience of the ways of women, he was in a confused state of mind, and didn't know what she expected. He was putty in her hands, and was trembling himself with sexual feelings. Was the next move up to him? As she was so young, he became fearful of losing control of himself. He was for a moment thinking of his friendship with her family and friends, and the trust they had placed in him.

'Have a lay down. She gestured as she looked towards the bed then looked back at him.

'OK then, I'll test it.' He lay back on the bed. 'Yes, most comfortable.'

'Just relax,' she said. Tom wondered how much Champagne she'd had. Without another word, she got up on the bed and kneeled astride him. She pulled up her skirts and moved up to his middle. Tom did nothing more than lie there while she looked down at him, smiling. She rocked forward and back, her long hair dangling as her expression became radiant and her complexion quite red. Tom was suddenly swirling helplessly in a pink cloud.

When they went down to join the party again, he felt neither really satisfied nor dissatisfied. Doreen introduced him to the lady of the house with complete calmness, but Tom felt self-conscious. Silly guilt, he thought, for he was sure the lady would not have approved of their conduct, even though nothing had really happened. Doreen kept close to him all the evening and there was much conversation, though the atmosphere was now one of polite restraint.

PART FOUR

Chapter 26
Birchwood

Tom asked Doreen if she would like to come with him to his Uncle's farm near Ipswich. He phoned his Uncle who was pleased to hear from him and said, 'You will always be welcome any time at Birchwood, stay for a long weekend. Agnes and I look forward to meeting Doreen!'

It was a beautiful spring day. They journeyed to London, and got on an Ipswich train at Liverpool Street station.

'I think you'll love Birchwood, Doreen, it's an open house for friends and relations. We have lots of fun and the farm has always been magic for me with many happy childhood memories. My Uncle Horace has only recently married... to his housekeeper, I mean Agnes. So now I have another aunt, but I still call her Agnes.'

'Yes, of course, Tom, I'm looking forward to meeting them.' Doreen cuddled up closely to him.

Uncle Horace came to meet them at the station. He had just arrived in his reliable old Morris Oxford, and greeted them with his Suffolk drawl, as he stepped out of the car. 'The train came in on time! Good to see you, Tom.' He turned to Doreen with a big smile. 'And...?'

'Meet Doreen,' Tom said gesturing.

'I've been looking forward to meeting you. I reckon Tom's got rare good taste for beauty.'

'Oh!' Doreen smiled and shook her head with embarrassment. 'Tom's been telling me about you.'

'Well, the truth will out in the end!'

'He talked about life on the farm.' Her words turned to laughter as she looked at his uncle, who was putting on his usual amused expression.

'Well, look at that,' he said. 'What a lovely laugh!'

'Don't worry, Doreen, he always makes me laugh.'

'This is a fine thing. Come on, the pair of you, let's get on the way.' He helped with their cases and they got in the car.

It was strange, but just when Tom thought he would find excitement, as he always did in the past, he was at odds. For as they motored up the approach drive to Birchwood Farm, he turned to Doreen and saw that she had a faraway look. He had intended to say something about how wonderful he felt, but now those words seemed inappropriate.

'Are you all right, Doreen?' he asked instead.

'Yes,' was all she said, the words coming from a thousand miles away. He was puzzled at her sudden distance, as she'd been so cheerful and loving up to that point.

'This is the farmhouse, Birchwood. Lots of land, chickens and an orchard of many apple trees.' But Doreen just nodded and said nothing, and he thought perhaps she was unwell.

'It's gone all quiet,' Tom's uncle said. 'Are you two OK in the back there?'

'Yes, all right ,Uncle,' Tom said loudly. He turned to Doreen and mouthed, 'What's the matter?'

'Nothing! Absolutely nothing!' she snapped.

Women are a strange breed, was all he could think. Or was it something he'd said? Could there be something wrong that he didn't know about? He had known her to go quiet before, a strange moodiness that he was unable to understand or deal with. He just had to hope it would wear off soon.

'Here we are,' his Uncle said as he swerved round a circular lawn and pulled up at the front of the Edwardian house. 'I expect you two could do with some tea now.'

'Yes rather,' Tom said.

The front door was not generally used. They always went through a laurel hedge arch, leading to the back yard, where a few chickens clucked and pecked at the ground. Tom carried their cases as he and Doreen followed Uncle Horace through the lobby and into the large kitchen. Agnes's face lit up as they entered. 'Lovely to see you!' she said, as Tom gave her a kiss.

'Yes, I always love coming to Birchwood. This is Doreen!' He turned his head quickly to see if she'd cheered up.

'Oh, I have been looking forward to meeting you,' Agnes said. 'You look tireds dear.'

'Hello,' Doreen said with the glimmer of a smile. 'I'm not a good traveller. I'll be all right soon.' Tom noticed she looked pale. Strange, she'd always seemed all right in other cars.

'Would you like to lie down a while, my dear?' Agnes asked.

'No really, it's nothing.'

'I was going to say, you're in nice time for tea, but I don't expect you feel... Well, sit down for a while.'

'Just relax, Doreen,' Tom said. 'I'll go and find Uncle Horace.'

'I'm sorry, Tom,' she said looking up at him from where she was sitting with a pathetic expression.

'Don't worry. I'll see you in a moment.' He squeezed her hand.

He found his uncle out in the big old wagon shed, preparing pig food. He liked to chat with him while he made up the various mixtures that looked like sawdust and large cornflakes, then walk round with his Uncle, who carried two buckets. The pigs squealed loudly as the swill was poured into the troughs and they snorted as they lapped it up. Tom liked to scratch their coarse bristly backs while he chatted with his Uncle, who looked at him from under that same old battered trilby hat.

'Is Doreen all right, Tom?'

'I hope so. She's resting in the kitchen. She seems OK.'

'Strange how some people – especially women – get car sick.'

'Oh, do you think that's all it is?'

'I would think so. We can go in and have tea now. She'll probably be as right as rain.'

'Hope so!'

Back in the kitchen, he found Doreen smiling again, and the colour had come back into her cheeks. 'You look better now,' he said. 'I was quite worried. Was it the car journey?'

'Yes, I think so, but I'm all right now.'

'You don't always get ill in a car do you?'

'No, it's worse sitting in the back,' Agnes put in. 'Do you feel like tea now, Doreen?'

'I'm starving,' Tom said, 'but Doreen...'

'I'm better now, I told you, Tom.'

'Yes, sorry.' The kettle whistled on the kitchen range.

'You're not a bit sorry,' she said, and actually smiled.

Agnes put the teapot on the table, then she brought in some sandwiches and a large cake. 'There we are,' she said. 'Horace won't be a minute – he's just washing.' She cut some slices of cake. 'Now, help yourself to whatever you want.' Doreen took a sandwich and Tom had some cake.

'This is very good!' he said.

'Baked it yesterday, when I knew you were coming.'

'And I can only manage a sandwich,' Doreen said. .

'Stan and Christine are coming over tomorrow,' Horace said as he came in to join them.

'Yes,' Agnes said. 'We thought we would all go down to the beach hut at Felixstowe.'

'That's if the weather's still good of course,' said Horace. 'I reckon it'll be all right though.'

'Fingers crossed!' Agnes said.

'Yes, um... that would be nice,' said Tom, thinking of his little encounter with Christine at Christmas time.

The weather was good the next day. Tom was still anxious at the thought of meeting Christine again. It might be like being in the middle of a triangle, with Christine at one corner, Doreen at another, and Stan looking daggers at them from the third corner. *That's to be ridiculous*, he thought.

When Stan and Christine arrived soon after ten o'clock, it was all smiles. Tom thought Stan gave him a funny old look when he introduced Doreen, but he dismissed it from his mind. Agnes had prepared sandwiches and cakes for the day's outing.

'Why don't you come in our car?' Stan suggested.

'Yes, why not!' Tom had to agree. He hoped a different car might be better for Doreen. 'But go steady, Stan. Doreen gets car sick sometimes.'

'I'm always steady, Tom,' Stan said. 'Not like some people.' Tom hoped he was referring to driving.

Stan suggested it would be better if Doreen rode in the front passenger seat, which Tom had to allow whether he liked it or not. And Christine rode with him in the back. Stan did drive very steadily and Doreen had no trouble coping with the journey. In fact, she laughed at Stan's jokes most of the way. Tom had to avoid showing his irritation with Stan, for he was sure Stan was being deliberately provocative. He glanced at Christine, and she shook her head, to show she did not approve.

The beach hut was one of a row along a quiet stretch of shore. The cooking facilities were just barely enough to make tea. There were several assorted folding chairs and a camp bed. Steps led down from the door onto the sand where they set out the chairs. After they had partially stripped off, there was general agreement that it was a bit cold for swimming, but Tom was determined to test the water. Wearing his trunks and with a towel round his shoulders, he ran quickly down the sand, then gingerly over the shingles. He came back, having got wet up to above the knees.

'That's a bit too cold for me,' he said, drying himself, and there was a laugh. 'Well, at least I tried it.'

'You're shivering, Tom,' Doreen said.

'This will warm you up.' Agnes handed him a cup of tea.

'Thank you, that's welcome.' They sat round enjoying tea.

Later, Tom and Uncle Horace sat on the sea wall, having a philosophical discussion. 'You know, of course, that Agnes and I have only been married just over a year. I nearly finished up as a bachelor.'

'I see...' Tom lapsed into silent thought.

'She's been married twice before; did you know?'

'No, I didn't know!'

'Doesn't bother me. She's a fine woman – wouldn't you say?'

'Yes, I've always thought so. It must be five years since I first met Agn... I mean Auntie Agnes.'

'Yes, yes... I suppose it must be. It was a quite wedding.'

'Yes I know, Uncle. Don't you think life is like a game of chance... um, for most of us?'

'Oh... I reckon if you say so, Tom.'

They had been sitting there for more than an hour when Tom realised everyone was gone. 'It's getting chilly Uncle. Where have they all got to?'

'It seems as if we've been deserted.'

'There's not a soul to be seen,' Tom said with concern.

'I think Christine and Agnes have gone for a walk.'

'You mean just the two of them? Where has Doreen got to?' He hesitated. 'And Stan, for that matter?'

'Here they are!' Horace was looking behind them. Christine and Aunt Agnes were coming down the sandy bank.

'Hello you two,' Christine said. 'Where are the others?'

'That's what I was wondering,' Tom said.

Tom got up from where he was sitting and walked towards the beach hut. As he neared the hut, Doreen came out.

'There you are, Doreen.' He tried to appear unconcerned.

'It was getting chilly outside,' she said. He thought she looked a bit flushed.

'I expect we'll be going back soon. Where's Stan?' As he spoke, Stan came from behind the hut. Tom said nothing, he just stared at him. Then the others came to the hut.

'I think it's time to go, don't you?' Horace said.

Agnes agreed, and they put the chairs away and locked up.

'Nice having a beach hut to go to, Agnes... a good hideaway!' Tom found himself saying.

'Hideaway?' she said. 'Well it's nice to get down to the seaside at times.'

As they walked back to the cars, Stan sidled up to Tom. 'Tit for tat!' he sneered, and Tom knew what he meant. Stan had been in the hut for some time alone with Doreen. Tom suddenly thought of that End of Term party at Clearmount and he felt angered, but there was nothing he could do or say about it, other than give Stan a cold look. But Tom's expression of annoyance said more than words. Stan could have been merely antagonising him. Had he just had a friendly little chat with Doreen, or was it something more? Tom's imagination tormented him, for he would never know. The words 'Tit for tat' rankled in his mind for a long time afterwards.

Chapter 27
The Ring

The weekend was too disappointing for Tom to dwell on, especially when he recalled those happier days spent with Uncle Horace and Agnes. A grey cloud had blemished what should have been a joyful time. Tom blamed himself for blindly letting a happy day be so spoiled. There were doubts that overshadowed the day. Could he trust Doreen? Stan's loathsome remark had been intentionally provocative, but did it mean what Tom imagined? Doreen had once told him she got into trouble at her old school, when she was discovered with a boy she called Mickey in her room. But Tom hadn't given it much thought.

He took Doreen to meet his parents one weekend. His father liked her; he was not sure if his mother took to her, but she was slow to get to know people, so he didn't let that worry him. They all went to a restaurant on the Saturday evening, and the conversation was very convivial. .

'What will you do now then, Doreen, having finished at the special school?' asked Tom's father.

'Temporary work in the kitchens of the Checkers Hotel. I have a special interest in cooking.'

'She's got a good voice as well as being a good cook, Dad.'

'Yes, so I understand. I've yet to hear you sing, Doreen.'

'We all enjoy a musical get-together at home, Mr Hunt.'

'What's all that about?' Tom's mother intervened. She had trouble with her hearing, which made it difficult for her to join in conversations.

'We were saying that Doreen has a good singing voice, Mum.'

'Has she! Is she taking it up professionally?'

'I don't think so,' Tom said loudly. 'Mind you, I think she's very good.'

Doreen shook her head. 'I don't think I'm that good!'

'Many of us underestimate our talents,' his father said.

'You can say that again! But I think it's usually others who underestimate our talents surely, Dad.'

'Could well be, Tom, but remember, you need to have self confidence and self discipline. It's how we make use of the ability we have that counts. So you have to make a personal effort; others won't do it for you.'

'Lecture over, Dad? I'm enjoying my meal now!'

On the Sunday morning Tom and Doreen went for a walk by the river. 'Fancy a drink?' he offered. 'One of my favourite pubs over there.'

They crossed the road, and Tom thought of the unfortunate encounter with his father's old business partner. He knew he wouldn't be in there, for Leonard Bolton had been forced to sell his side of the business and move away, after being charged with a sordid offence. Tom felt quite sorry for Bolton. He did not condone his conduct but thought him a pathetic man, unable to control the urges within him.

They found a corner seat by a window with small panes and a very solid well polished oak table.

'You've gone quiet,' Doreen said. 'What are you thinking about?'

'Oh sorry, I was looking at those old horse brasses on the oak beams. In bygone days they would only be seen attached to a harness. They're not always genuine but I'm sure those are.'

'They're attractive, aren't they?'

'Yes, and I prefer originals of course!'

'What time is your mother expecting us for dinner?'

'Oh, they eat about half past one on a Sunday, there's no rush!'

'Oh good, this is nice.'

'You mean the ginger wine?'

'As well, yes! I mean this is a pleasant little pub.'

'Yes, Dad and I like it, nice and quiet.' They sat in silence for a while. 'Umm...We do get on well, Doreen, don't we?'

'Like a house on fire!' she said in a casual way.

'Oh, well I presume by that you mean, OK!'

'Yes of course, silly thing.' They looked at each other and she gave Tom a funny little smile.

'As long as the house doesn't burn down.'

'You are an old pessimist!'

'Am I?' He looked at his watch. 'Twenty past one. I think we'd better go home. Dinner will be almost ready.' Dark clouds were rolling up as they walked back.

After the meal, Doreen helped with the washing up and Tom was very impressed, but he thought his mother's thanks meagre, which was discouraging. His feelings matched the darkening sky. The time for them to get the bus back to Newburne was fast approaching.

'We better go down in the car,' his father said.

'OK, Dad. Looks as if it's going to rain anyway.'

Doreen was talking with Mrs Hunt, but it sounded more like an argument than a conversation. 'I do have a mind of my own, Mrs Hunt.' Doreen said tersely.

'Come on, Doreen, we're taking the car. We haven't got much time,' Tom said with agitation. He was wondering what the argument was about. They said a quick goodbye.

'We don't see much of you,' his mother called. 'It was five weeks this time.'

'Stop worrying, Mum. Suppose I was in the Air Force, which I almost joined, remember? I would be lucky to see you in six months or more.'

At last she gave a slight smile.

'Come on, we might miss the bus. I'll drive,' Tom said. 'I could get out of practice.'

'I didn't know you had a licence, Tom.'

'Yes, I've kept up my licence since near the end of the war, so I won't have to pass a test. I don't get much chance to drive these days though, as I can't afford a car of my own.'

'You've got five minutes, Tom,' his father said.

'We'll make it. It's usually a bit late.' They pulled up near the bus stop. 'No bus there look. Not in sight, and there are people waiting.'

'It's been good meeting you, Doreen,' said Mr Hunt. 'You know, I think Tom's very lucky to meet a girl like you.' He moved into the driver's seat and waved as he drove off.

The bus was late, and the journey seemed endless. They could have got off and taken a train, but the bus was more convenient because it passed Doreen's house.

'Was Mum being awkward?'

'I think she thought I was too young for you.'

'So she *was* being difficult. I know she can be strong minded. Her deafness makes her appear unreasonable at times,' he said speaking in a slightly irritated tone.

'Don't be annoyed, Tom. She'll be all right with me, once I get to know her. I like your father very much, by the way.'

'Oh good. Dad and I are great friends. We go sailing together sometimes.'

'That sounds fun. I'd like to go sailing.'

'I'll take you one day.' The thought of married life sometime in the distant future flashed through his mind, but it wasn't Doreen he pictured himself with. *Mustn't think of Doreen as second best*, he told himself. How unfair that would be!

'What are you thinking about?'

'Nothing much, just enjoying your company.'

'Is that all?'

'You must know that I'm very fond of you!' He felt a little awkward, as if he was testing his own thoughts. 'Do you think we're getting too involved? Well... not that I'm worried.'

'Are you sure?' she smiled.

'Of course I'm sure. I mean, it's not a game, is it? On a bus is not the ideal place to say it but of course I do like you very much.' He was quite unable to say the word 'love'.

'Yes... I know! Silly thing,' she cuddled closely to him. A wave of doubt passed through Tom's mind. She seemed so young. For an instant he thought of Mildred. She was very mature, but she was in love with music! That all seemed a long time ago now. Suddenly he felt lonely, afraid he was going to hurt Doreen. It was a thought that would haunt him for some time to come. Back in his room that night, Tom opened the little Victorian box and looked at the ring his mother had given him. It was very valuable, with three diamonds that sparkled under the light. He kept it hidden at the back of the top drawer in his bedroom. He remembered his mother's words when she gave it to him; 'This ring is very precious, it was your grandmother's engagement ring. Do you understand, Tom?'

'Yes, of course, Mum. Grandfather gave it to her when they got engaged.'

'Yes! They were very happy. Not all marriages are happy.'

'No, Mum, I know.'

'So I want you to keep this and only give it to someone you love, that is, when you're quite sure she's the right one.'

'Yes, but how could I be sure?'

'That won't be easy. You'll have to judge that for yourself.' His mother gazed at the ring. 'See how it sparkles, and think of the girl of your choice. Try to think if she's worthy of the value of this ring, not just the material value, but the emotional worth to the previous wearer.'

'Grandmother?'

'Think of her happiness, her happy family; my brothers and sisters.'

'But there must have been hard times, Mum?'

'Yes, there were, but Father was a very successful man, an engineer and a businessman, before he started farming.'

'I can't imagine myself ever being so successful though.'

'Just think of the family background when you look at the ring. I can probably help you choose a good wife.'

His mother's words stayed with him as he fixed his eyes on the sparkling gems. The last thing Tom wanted was for his mother to intervene with his choice of a wife. The diamonds flashed as he moved the ring in its box. He had once had a vision of the ring on the D string of a violin, a fading fantasy. As he looked at the ring, which had seen a whole family grow up, Tom was emotionally overcome as his thoughts swung from Mildred to Doreen. He was seeing her on Wednesday, and he was now asking himself the question; was she worthy of the ring, a precious family heirloom? He had to make his own mind up. She was very young, just eighteen. Should he propose to her, and would she say yes? Then her parents might not agree anyway. He spent a restless night.

For the next two days at work, he thought of Doreen as if she was some kind of distant vision. He knew he had to make the biggest decision of his life. Was he just trying to forget Mildred? He sometimes felt he wanted to run away somewhere. That wouldn't help, for he would be running away from a good job. No, he had to take hold of himself and dismiss those thoughts. He was suddenly happy again and looking forward to seeing Doreen the following evening.

In the morning when he had just finished breakfast, Mrs Benson came into the room as he got up from the table.

'You're just leaving of course?'

'Yes. On a nice morning like this I quite enjoy my stroll to work.' Tom wondered why she should ask such an obvious question, as he left at about the same time each morning. So he expected that she wanted to say something special.

'Tell me if I'm being nosy?' He had to smile. 'You're fond of Doreen, aren't you?'

'Yes!' He hesitated. 'And I don't think you're being nosy.'

'I've known her since she was only a little girl. Peter and Janet Brooks are very old friends. In fact Ron and Peter were at school together.'

'Oh, here in Newburne?'

'Yes, at St.Barts.'

'My old school!' Tom smiled. 'Before my time though.'

'Frank Wills was also there, but after Ron.'

'And just before me!' he said with a smile. 'Better not hang about, otherwise I'll tell Mr Wills it was your fault, if he should see me come in late!'

'That would never do!' Mrs Benson laughed.

'I may be late for supper tonight, or if I don't come back for the meal at all, would you mind?'

'Why should I mind? You will be seeing Doreen, of course?'

'Yes. How did you guess?'

'Doesn't take much guesswork. If you're going for a walk, why don't you bring her back here?'

'Thank you, we might pop in then. Now I really must go!'

At work, he was thinking of seeing Doreen that evening, but he could not get Mildred out of his mind. She kept coming back into his thoughts. It was a strange dilemma for Tom, who fell in love too easily. It played on his mind to such an extent, that he felt almost as if he owned any woman he fell for. His groundless fantasies all too easily assumed reality. He suddenly remembered back to the words of Mr Sheet, when he was at Forest Gate: *'I think you're in love with love!'*

During the day, he got into conversation with Mr Wills, not about the work he was involved in, but about the old school. They talked about the same masters that were still at the school during Tom's time.

'I've not seen you at any of the Old Boy's Conventions,' Mr Wills said. 'Do you keep in touch at all?' He cleared his nostrils loudly.

'Not at all now. I lost touch with my friend Henry Hayes.' He paused as his throat caught. 'He was... killed in a flying accident on a training flight in the RAF!'

'Sorry... that was bad luck!'

'Yes... Do you still see old Mrs Fenton, by the way?'

'Emily Fenton died last year!' Wills said bluntly. 'She was very old, you know.'

'Yes! She seemed a sad old lady.'

And Tom thought of the engineering works that now stood silent.

Chapter 28
Crucial Decision

It was a warm day as Tom and Doreen walked in the cool of a winding woodland path. He had walked along that same pathway many times with his father in his boyhood days.Clumps of primroses grew in high mossy banks on either side, and the woods were full of bluebells. A pheasant flew off with a loud cry, startling them.

'Come on, I'll race you,' Doreen said, as she suddenly ran. He was not in the mood for running, but gave chase.

'I'm right behind you!' he shouted, but let her win. She leaned back against an old oak and panted while Tom landed with his arms on the tree, on each side of her body.

'I won!' she said breathlessly.

'Now I've captured you and you can't get away.'

'I don't want to get away,' she laughed impulsively.

As they kissed, her family and their trust in him flashed through his mind, but she seemed so much in command.

Mr Wills was so pleased with the way Tom had adapted himself to the work that he gave him a pay increase. Tom did a deal with Molly, the tracer. She sold him her old 1936 Morris Minor car for twenty five pounds, which he managed to scrape together. His Father lent him fifteen pounds which was regarded as a permanent loan. The car was not in use during the war years and was in good condition for its age. He took pride in doing it up, and he enjoyed driving, specially at weekends. They went on outings, sometimes down to the sea, often enjoying a picnic, or they would have tea in a cottage tea room.

One Saturday, they hired a skiff. He enjoyed rowing with vigour while Doreen steered and he was admiring her legs as well as the river scenery. They tied the boat by a field. An ideal place to sit in the gentle breeze, with a view across the river where it was wooded and to some distant hills, through a gap in the trees. After the picnic, they lay back on the grass very close to each other. But the tranquillity of the setting ended abruptly when a man who came towards them waving a large walking stick.

'I know what you people are up to, get off my land!' he cried.

'What do you mean?' Tom said. 'We're not doing any harm.'

'Go on, off my land with you both!' the man shouted as they threw the remains of the picnic into the boat. They clambered in and pulled away, while the farmer stood on the bank, red-faced, puffing with anger and a defiant expression. He vibrated his stick, pushed hard to the ground as if he was trying to bore a hole in the turf! They laughed heartily afterwards, during their row back, and it didn't spoil a wonderful day.

That evening at her place, they enjoyed making their own music. Doreen chose some popular songs of the day, while Peter accompanied on the piano, and Tom dared to play the violin. Doreen's mother Janet had less musical talent. She joined in when they were all singing, but Tom thought her enthusiasm exceeded her ability.

Doreen had been at The Checkers Hotel for a few weeks, and was happy there. Her domestic science course had paid off. She was quite an expert in the kitchen, which Tom regarded as a boon. He would often meet her there. They arranged to go to the pictures, as there was a good film showing. That evening after work he went to the back of the hotel, knocked on the kitchen door and poked his head in. Doreen was just cleaning down a working surface and the chef was busy at the hot stove.

'I've just finished,' Doreen said as she looked up with a beaming smile.

'Am I a bit early?'

'No, we had a busy time this afternoon, there was a wedding reception!' He was reminded of that nagging question again.

'Yes, I see!'

'Don't stand at the door, Tom, I'm sure Roy will let you into the kitchen.'

He stepped inside and Roy turned. 'Be my guest!' he said. He was a plump middle-aged man with a pink face, and balding. He took his work seriously. 'Would you like an omelette?'

Tom looked at Doreen and she nodded with a smile. 'Well thank you very much.'

'That's what Doreen likes, she's a good girl you know. I'll make two, sit yourselves down then,' He sat where there was room at the end of the table.

'All right if I sit here?'

'I'll move some of these things,' Doreen said.

Tom never forgot that tasty omelette, filled with bacon and mushrooms.

Tom and Doreen went to see a film that evening, but afterwards, she sank into one of her faraway moods that he found hard to cope with. That night, he talked with the Bensons till late, about life in general. Tom had one of his troubled dreams. There was a girl in a wedding dress, but as she turned round, she had no face! Then there was a very tall wedding cake on a table in the centre of a large bare room. Mildred came into the room dressed in office clothes and stood by the cake. Tom held the ring with three diamonds and showed it to her. She looked closely at it. 'That's very beautiful,' she said, and the cake fell to pieces.

He was woken by Mrs Benson, and the faint rattle of a teacup and saucer. There was the sound of rain beating against the window as he came to and turned over. 'It's almost nine o'clock,' she said quietly.

'Oh dear! Is it as late as that, and do I hear rain?'

'Yes, it's a wet morning. I thought I'd let you sleep on as we were all late last night.

'Thank you, I'll be as quick as I can.'

‘Don’t worry, I’m about to cook breakfast. Take your time.’

He was soon down, and there was the delicious smell of bacon cooking in the kitchen.

‘That was quick!’ Mrs Benson said. He had got used to having his breakfast in the kitchen with the Bensons at the weekend, which he found an enjoyable change from the rest of the week.

‘Where’s Ron? Not on duty in this weather, is he?’

‘Yes, I’m afraid so, he went off at six!’

‘I would hate that, especially on a wet Sunday morning.’

‘He’s used to it, but a wet morning is not so good.’

Such a morning had the effect of making breakfast more enjoyable, Tom thought, as a gust of rain beat against the window.

‘Poor Ron!’ he said.

‘In the station! Could be having a snooze.’ And she laughed.

‘Well, we were late last night, so he didn’t have much sleep!’

‘More tea, Tom?’

‘Thank you. Um... I was worried last night,’ he began.

‘Worried? What about?

‘When we came out of the cinema, Doreen went quiet on me. I don’t know why?’

‘Went quiet on you? I wouldn’t let it worry you, she may not have been well!’

‘She didn’t say so. She seemed distant somehow.’ He thought he’d better change the subject. ‘Looks as if the rain is leaving off!’

At half past eleven, Doreen arrived. The Bensons had invited her to Sunday dinner as a surprise. Tom got up and gave her a kiss. Her face felt cool and slightly damp.

‘This is an unexpected pleasure, Doreen.’ He looked round at Mary, who eyed him with a puckish expression.

‘I like surprises,’ Doreen said as she removed her coat.

‘Yes but... on such a wet morning! How did you get here?’

‘On the new Sunday morning bus service, I got off at the end of the road. It’s not raining hard now anyway.’

‘Well that’s good. Lucky I’ve shaved and look respectable.’

‘Wouldn’t worry me either way!’ she said with a smile.

'But it might worry me, you wouldn't like to kiss a bristly chin, would you?' She just smiled and shook her head, and they sat on two kitchen chairs sharing the Sunday paper. He thought of the night before: he was still feeling a little ill at ease when she turned up, but now she seemed back to normal. He certainly didn't wish to dwell upon the reason for her moodiness the previous night.

Ron came in at one o'clock. Tom saw him like two separate personalities: the normal Ron, then the Ron in uniform.

'What a morning!' Ron said. 'How are you, Doreen?'

'Fine thanks,' she said brightly.

'Has the rain left off, sergeant?' Tom asked.

'Clearing up, damp and misty though.' He smiled. 'I'm off duty now, remember!'

'Yes of course, it's the uniform, sorry.'

They enjoyed their meal, then afterwards, Ron had to go out again.

'I'll help with the washing up,' Doreen said to Mary.

'No, I'll manage. Why don't you two go into the sitting room? You can be quiet and undisturbed there.'

'But, all that washing up,' Doreen protested.

'No, don't be silly, I insist: you've come to see Tom, not to work.'

It seemed obvious that Mary Benson was doing her best to encourage them to be alone. Tom quickly slipped up to his room and put the ring in his pocket. It was an instinctive action, like the next move in a game. He had the feeling that his world was slipping away, out of control.

Those worries went away as they sat together on the sofa, and Tom was overcome by a strong sense of responsibility. It was as if the ring in his pocket had a power: indeed he was extremely conscious of the fact that it was there. He looked at her, and as he did so, a voice within him seemed to be arguing with his mother, making him think of the words, 'be sure; are you sure?' He thought of his grandmother. Even though she was only faintly remembered from his childhood days, she was an important figure in the fantasy that was in his mind.

'You look far away,' Doreen said.

'Sorry, I think you're mesmerising me.'

'Don't be silly, we haven't only just met.'

'You always do...' He was looking into her eyes. He drew her close to him, and they kissed. They said nothing for a while and at that moment he felt sure he loved her. But even so, 'I think I love you' was all he could bring himself to say. 'I've got something to show you, Doreen.' He took the ring from his pocket, and opened the box. 'There! My grandmother's diamond engagement ring.'

'That's very beautiful,' she said as she looked at it for a long time. 'How brilliant the diamonds are!'

'I wonder...' He was temporarily lost for words.

'Can I take it out of the box?' She removed it with care.

'It's very precious, of course you know that!'

'Oh, Tom,' she simply said as she held it. She surprised him then, as she slid it onto her engagement finger. She had taken the initiative. 'You do want us to get married?' she pleaded.

'Yes... of course.' She cuddled up close to him.

Later, when Ron got back home, they were having tea in the kitchen. Mary Benson was talking, then she suddenly stopped.

'Doreen!' she squealed, looking at the ring. 'You two have got engaged!' She looked from one to the other.

'Yes!' they said together

'Well I never! And such a lovely ring! Let me look.' She bent and held Doreen's hand. 'Isn't that beautiful!'

'My Grandmother's diamonds!' Tom said.

'Congratulations!' Ron said, and all their faces lit up.

Soon after tea, Tom took Doreen home in his proudly owned old Morris. The important consideration, which he was anxious about though he had not given much thought to it, was how Doreen's parents would take to the idea of their marriage. He was very friendly with them, but she was still under the age of consent. Her father opened the door before Doreen could get her key out. 'Hello you two,' he chuckled. Tom hoped he would still be smiling when he asked him for his daughter's hand in marriage.

'You must have been listening out for us, Dad.'

'No, I was just in the hall and heard the car.'

'It is a bit noisy I suppose!' Doreen said.

'Hey, not that noisy,' Tom said. 'Anyway I've brought Doreen back home safe and sound.' She stepped into the house.

'Come in Tom, I wasn't expecting you back quite so early.'

'Thank you, Mr Brooks.'

'We wanted to talk to you and mother,' Doreen said excitedly. They went into the sitting room where Janet was busy knitting.

'Hello Mrs Brooks.'

She looked up and smiled. 'How are you, Tom?'

'Very well thank you!' He noticed that Doreen was hiding the ring, covering it with her right hand. Then Tom and Doreen stood together and smiled, as if they were trying to convey thought waves.

'What's up with you two?' Janet said. Then Doreen showed her parents the ring, and her mother was struck dumb as she looked at the sparkling diamonds. 'Well this is a surprise! It's beautiful, but...'

'They're real diamonds mother!'

'My grandmother's,' Tom said. 'Her engagement ring and it's very special.'

'Yes, I can see that! I'll go and make a cup of tea.'

'I'll help you,' Doreen said, and Tom knew they would be going to have a chat. He was left alone with Peter Brooks, whom he thought he knew so well; but now it was as if he was a different person and Tom could not help feeling a little intimidated.

'Sit down then, Tom, and we'll have a talk.' He'd never seen Peter look so stern. 'Please forgive Janet: this has come as a surprise. As Doreen's our only daughter, she's naturally very precious to us. I hope you're sure, absolutely sure that you really want to marry Doreen?'

'Yes, I... we love each other very much!'

'She's under age, you know, of course.'

'Yes.'

'We all get on well together and you seem to be in a job with a future. That's a feather in your cap.' They both smiled.

'Yes, I've just received a rise in salary, and I have ambition.'

'Give it thought and don't rush in too quickly. I think that's the best advice I can give you. Doreen isn't perfect, you know.'

'No one's perfect, Mr Brooks. I wouldn't like to say I was!'

Peter Brooks smiled. 'I'm quite pleased really, Tom. Fathers are always very protective towards their daughters, I suppose. Just give us time to get used to the idea. Such a step has to be well considered.'

'Yes, of course... I do understand,' Tom said with a confidence he did not entirely feel.

The following weekend Tom took Doreen to stay with his parents. His father was delighted at their news but Tom was not so sure that his mother shared that enthusiasm.

Over the next months, Tom remained unsure how their courtship had changed. The crucial difference, as far as he was concerned, was the ring. Whenever he thought of his mother's warning, he drove the thought away out of his mind as quickly as it had appeared. His and Doreen's parents also looked upon their relationship in a different way. Now it was time to make preparations, not time to contemplate. Strangely, he had felt happier before the engagement.

He reflected on all the ideas he'd had in his mind about how one should tackle the business of living. Past uncertainties and disappointments he'd experienced quite naturally meant that he would always have doubts about any change. This was a watershed, the one big chance that had to be a success. He involved himself with a variety of activities as if he was about to lose his freedom forever. He had always hoped he would be happily married at the age of twenty-five, but his ideas of romance seemed to belong in the realms of fantasy. Yet Doreen had become a part of those fantasies. He dreamed about his coming marriage as if he was going into a great new world of complete bliss. He kept on saying to himself: *she's such a lovely girl*, and sometimes a great sadness would sweep over him. *She must not be let down*, he thought; *she is worthy of that ring.*

They spent time looking for somewhere to live. Tom wanted a house. Could he ever find enough money? But he would rather pay a mortgage than rent. They found a semi-detached that they both liked, on the outskirts of the town, for two and a half thousand pounds. Tom's father put down the deposit and a twenty-five year mortgage was arranged.

One dreary evening, while he and Doreen sat together at her parents' house' there seemed an uneasy tension between them. Tom could not understand why. They had gone out for a meal in a little restaurant and had been talking away quite cheerfully. Then she'd gone into one of her distant spells, and remained that way while he drove her home. It was late and her parents had turned in. Sitting together on the sofa, he found conversation strangely difficult and there followed a period of silence. The seconds seemed like long minutes, till she spoke.

'I've been thinking,' she said.

'I can see that!'

'Yes well, do you think we really should rush into marriage?'

Tom was speechless for a few seconds, then: 'So that's what you've had on your mind, and only a week before the wedding! What is everybody going to think!' It came as a surprise, and he felt confused and didn't know what he should say. 'I don't like fickle women!' was all he said. There were no goodnight kisses.

Another sleepless night followed. Now there were doubts. 'Why now?' he thought, and he went over and over it many times, all the things they had done together since that first meeting on New Year's Eve. He could hardly imagine her as the same person. He had just been struck a bitter blow. Her words had put fear into his mind, for he wondered if he would be able to trust her. He was in fact at a loss to know his next move. He thought so hard for an answer. Would it be wrong to just do nothing?

On the Monday morning, Tom had a little chat with Terry, the young draughtsman, who was always friendly. He asked him to join him for a drink during the dinner break, and was determined not to appear in a gloomy mood. 'You might be able to give me some advice.' Terry had only recently married and he was at least three years younger than Tom.

'What advice?' Terry said.They were sitting in a shabby pub where the tables and chairs should have been replaced years before, but the beer was good. 'I can only stop for a quick one, my dinner will be waiting for me at home.'

'Yes, well, I need to talk, it's just that...'

'Don't say you need advice from me!'

'Well, you might have some ideas.'

'Not long now, and you'll be a happily married man.'

'Yes well... engagements are difficult, aren't they?'

'There are problems with finding somewhere to live and all that. My Dad had a friend with a cottage to rent.'

'That's not the problem!' Tom paused. 'You see, when we were just going out, not courting. I mean, before we got engaged, not that I think there's much difference...' He was getting himself tied in knots. 'Anyway, it's all changed. Now she's said she's not sure she wants to get married.'

'Oh dear, perhaps you should call it off then.'

'I don't know what to do.'

'You have got a problem, if she's jilted you!'

'No, not exactly. She's said she's sorry.'

'So, are you going to marry her then?'

'It hasn't been cancelled, and the arrangements are still going ahead.'

'All I can say, Tom, is, I think it is only natural. I remember having those sort of doubts myself, just before the wedding. But now I'm settled and happy with such a wonderful wife and a nipper on the way.'

'Oh, that's good!'

'I wouldn't let it worry you. I don't know if I've been a lot of help. Sorry, but I have to go now, or I'll have marriage problems! Good luck, Tom, and don't forget the stag party!'

'Oh yes!' Tom gave a smile as Terry quickly shot out. He sat there for a while, slowly finishing his drink, then he got himself another one.

Waves of depression washed over Tom during that week and he put on a brave face. Then in the end, only two days before the wedding, he went over to stay at his parents' house. It was difficult to talk to them about his real feelings for it was as if he didn't know himself. His mind somehow felt numb.

'I'm having serious thoughts!' Tom said, addressing them both.

'What about?' his father asked. There was a silence. 'Well?'

'About the wedding. Should I be marrying Doreen?' Tom lowered his head to his hands.'There are uncertainties. Something Doreen said: it's not just me. Doreen's not sure. She spoke about it last weekend and it's been on my mind ever since.'

'Oh dear!' his mother said. 'You shouldn't go through with it then, if you're not sure.'

'What, at this late stage?' his father said. 'Those worries are only natural. You'll be all right.' He dismissed the idea.

'Oh, I don't think he should marry her if there is doubt,' Mrs Hunt insisted. But his father would not hear of it and refused to discuss the question any further, so the plans went ahead.

The night before the wedding, Tom didn't want a stag party, but just a drink with Terry. If only to steady his apprehensive feelings. They went to The King's Arms at the end of the road, he had insisted on staying in Newburne at the Bensons that night, and his parents would come down in the morning. Tom had asked Ron to join them, but he was on duty. So he had a couple of pints with Terry. But other customers joined them, and they all wanted to buy Tom a drink. Terry had to go at eight, which left Tom at the mercy of those well-meaning, friendly customers. He soon got talking to a friendly German, who told Tom he'd been a prisoner of war in England through most of the war and had not been back to Germany since.

'I hear it will be a happy day for you tomorrow – I'm Karl.' They shook hands. 'Let me buy you a drink.'

'That is kind of you, but I'd really better not.'

'I insist,' Karl said, pointing at Tom's empty glass. He had already ordered him another pint and there it was, on the bar.

'This must be the last one.' A wave of guilt rolled over him. 'I have to be at the church tomorrow.'

'I have an English wife, she is fifteen years older than me. You must come back to my house for a coffee and meet her.' The offer of coffee tempted Tom, as he felt he needed sobering up. His insistent companion had a bicycle, and wheeled it as they walked in the cold foggy night air.

'My wife's name is Angela. I like the English and I would not like to go back to Germany.' Tom soon lost count of how many times Karl said how much he liked the English. 'Hitler was bad, a very bad man,' he repeated several times. They had crossed the road and walked about two hundred yards to his house.

The house was in a terrace. As he left his bicycle in the hall, he called out 'Angela!' Then he led Tom into the kitchen and they sat at the table. He was a small man with a round red face, small blue eyes and blond hair and Tom thought he was aged about forty. 'There you are,' he said as a much older woman came through the door. 'You can now say hello to my wife. This is Tom and shall we have coffee.' Tom was surprised at how old she seemed, with greying hair. She looked more like his mother than his wife. She was pale and thin, and wore a light blue dressing gown. She only nodded, then made coffee. All the time, Karl spoke a lot of nonsense and Tom thought it was a strange set up. No one else could get a word in.

Then Karl said, 'You can stay the night if you like, we would like you to stay.'

But it was getting very late. Tom was already worried that he would not be popular with the Bensons, though Mary Benson had said, 'Enjoy your stag do.' It was almost midnight as he walked back to his lodgings in the cold foggy air. He was feeling very confused and kept thinking of what lay ahead of him. It was his wedding day, yet it felt strangely like an ordeal to be faced.

It was a bleak December wedding in the local church, a quiet family affair with only enough guests to fit round the large dining table at Doreen's parents' house. They went off to a hotel in Lowestoft for a few days. The weather was so cold that all they could do apart from stay in the hotel was to go for a brisk walk, well wrapped up. He noticed more than ever the change in Doreen; she was no longer the girl he had first met what now seemed so long ago. But he kept saying to himself. 'It has to work' as he thought of the years stretching out before him.

He felt as if he had walked through a heavy door that had slammed behind him with an almighty bang, and through which there was no exit. As he held his new bride's hand across the dining room table, and looked at the wedding ring and the sparkling diamond engagement ring, he thought of his mother's words. For the ring was a symbol that reminded him of his grandparents' happiness, and all those aunts and uncles on his mother's side. It seemed as though it had a special power. '*This must not fail,*' he thought through gritted teeth, until his marriage had assumed the proportions of a mammoth task, rather than a joyous union of two people.

Chapter 29
Neighbour

The ground was white with frost on a bitter December Sunday morning, and Tom was struggling to dig up parsnips that the previous owner had left in the ground for him.

'Good Morning!' said a voice, spoken quickly with a local brogue. Tom turned to see his neighbour, a tall man with strong features with his cap pulled well down over his head and hands stuffed into a duffel coat. 'It looks as if you've got a hard job on there, I hope you find it worthwhile,' he said with wisps of breath in the cold air.

'Oh yes, the ground is pretty solid with frost.'

'We've met before!' the man said and came close to the fence. 'I'm Bob Denham: remember me at Fentons?' He took his right hand from his pocket. 'We're neighbours now.' They shook hands.

'Excuse the glove,' Tom said and Bob laughed.

'That don't matter! You're Tom Hunt aren't you, used to work on that noisy old lathe. Tom recognised the man, though older. He started filling a pipe, Tom thought he looked about sixty or so, or in his late fifties. 'How are you getting on then?'

'OK! Just settling in. Funny, you living next door now.'

'Yes !'

'You used to give me good advice. It seems a long time ago. How are things with you?'

'All right I suppose,' he said thoughtfully. 'A lot has happened since the old firm closed. I thought you'd moved up to London.'

'Yes, for quite a time, and it was interesting. The firm was not getting the orders. So as things worked out, I'm now back with Mr Wills, Merton Pumps.'

'Oh yes, sounds a bit like Fentons in a way! I remember old Frank Wills. That's good then. I hear he's doing well in the pump business.' Bob lit up his pipe. 'Those parsnips will be good now with this frost.'

'So I'm told.'

'Yes... well, you're going to have a busy time settling in,' Bob said as if it were a major exercise. 'Let me know if I can be of help in any way.'

'Yes, thanks. Well, I am having trouble with the boiler!'

'That's a nuisance! No hot water?'

'Hmm,' Tom nodded, 'it's just coming out warm.'

'I'll come and have a look at it for you if you like. It's probably the same as the one in this house.' He turned and pointed back with his pipe. 'We had some trouble with ours when we first moved in. I might be able to do some adjustments.'

'When did you move in then?'

'Last winter, after Christmas. I'll just let you get those parsnips out and pop round in about half an hour, if it's all right with you.'

'Thank you very much. I can do with an expert hand.'

'Funny you should say that Tom; plumbing is what I do now.'

'Oh, that's handy!'

'Brrr, mind that fork!' Bob said as he went up to the house.

Having dug up five large parsnips, Tom decided to make it six. He raised the fork, and as he brought it down hard, a prong went though his shoe and between his big toe and the next. The pain was extreme and he instinctively cried out. He hobbled back to the house with just the five parsnips.

Doreen was in the kitchen. 'What's the matter with you then?'

'Oh dear! Ouch... I was going to get six, but I've just jabbed my foot with the fork and it hurts like hell.'

'That was silly of you,' she said, while Tom struggled to get his shoe off. She seemed not to care. He limped up to the bathroom and washed the wound gently between his toes in tepid water. He was afraid he had broken a toe as he administered first aid, which consisted of cotton wool and iodine. That smarted, but nothing seemed broken.

The front door bell rang, and there were voices in the hall when Doreen answered. Tom stayed in the bathroom, and pulled on a sock, but the shoe was unbearable, so he went into the bedroom and put on his slippers.

'What are you doing up there all this time?' Doreen shouted.

'Dealing with a painful foot.'

'Well Bob from next door has fixed the boiler.'

'Good, thank him for me, I'll see him later.'

'I have, and he's gone!' she snapped. 'It was very kind of him to call, don't you think! He put it right in no time, that's more than you could do.'

'He told me he would put it right, he's a plumber!'

'Oh! He didn't say.'

'He's a useful man to have as a neighbour anyway. I knew him years ago at Fentons.'

'It was nice to have someone interesting to talk to. He didn't say you knew each other.'

Doreen sat in the lounge all the afternoon. Tom found her writing in a notebook.

'What are you writing?'

'Just thoughts!'

'Good thoughts, I hope.'

'I don't have bad thoughts,' she said indignantly, with a disdainful smile.

Later, when Doreen went into the kitchen, she left her notebook on a chair in the lounge. Tom took a quick look, but the pages she'd written were in pencil and heavily scribbled out, so not a word could be read. They must have been very secret, Tom thought.

One evening, Tom came home from work to find a young man in the house he had never met before. He was drinking Tom's malt whisky.

'This is Mickey,' Doreen said. We were at school together.

He's come to have tea with us: I thought it would be nice for you to meet him.' As Tom shook hands with him, he remembered that Doreen had been in trouble at school with this very same young man. Tom spent an evening of controlled politeness.

As the weeks passed, their relationship did not improve. He often wondered if there was such a thing as married bliss. There must be lucky ones! He thought of his mother's words, and believed she was probably right. But how could one be sure! Nothing he could do could improve his marriage. He often thought back to when he'd first met Doreen at that New Years Eve party, with her long blond hair. It was now cut quite short and artificially waved, which disappointed him. When he told her he preferred her hair as it was before, she just said, 'Oh really!' Thoughts from the past punished him. He had got on so well with her parents. He did his best to wave those thoughts aside and make believe how lucky he was, to have such a good wife, telling himself it would all be fine in the end.

Christmas was almost a disaster, as far as Tom was concerned. In fact, the worst he could ever remember. The respective parents were all invited to spend Christmas day together, but they barely tolerated each other. It was all very strange, for Tom had always got on so well with Doreen's parents. They parted politely, but after they had all left, Doreen burst into floods of tears. He tried to comfort her, but did not understand why she was so upset. Perhaps she felt that the great effort she had put into the food was not appreciated.

'What's wrong Doreen, was it something I said?'

'It was your mother! You remind me of her sometimes.'

'I don't see how; I often don't agree with her anyway.'

Silence descended between them as they spent a long time washing up and putting everything away.

In the New Year, he spent time in the garden, in a way more to show willing, which he hoped would impress Doreen, than for the joy of gardening. It was an optimistic thought, for she didn't seem very impressed. Though as he carried on doing the work, he became a little more interested, and aware of the importance of growing vegetables. He had always had hobbies and pursuits that were now only in the back of his active mind. But he would enjoy a chat with Bob who gave him gardening hints.

On a warm day with the feeling of spring in the air, Bob was busy digging a hole to make a pond, while Tom was just digging. Bob's wife, Joyce, walked down the garden. A beautiful woman, so much younger than Bob, she could have been his daughter. Tom's attention was diverted as he pretended to carry on digging, while making frequent glances at Joyce. She was smart and looked very slender in a well fitting skirt. The thin belt round her small waist accentuated her shapely figure, tall and slim with wavy jet black hair and curls that surrounded small features on a lovely ivory pale face. Her smile was sunny and her voice lyrical and feminine. She suddenly surprised Tom and greeted him over the garden fence.

'Hello,' she said. 'Everybody's busy gardening.'

'Oh yes,' he said looking up. 'Hard work!'

Bob left his hole in the ground and joined them. 'Yes, I need a break,' he said while filling his pipe. 'Enjoying your digging Tom?'

'Not much!'

Weeks went by and they became friendly, with invitations to each other's houses. Joyce played the piano, she was talented and enjoyed entertaining, so she was often asked to play. Tom and Bob would go to the local pub to get away from gardening, or whatever job they were doing. Bob never wanted the women with them. Tom pondered over Bob's young wife, and the difference in their ages. Bob had told him he'd lost his first wife, and bored him with the details of her illness. So the subject had to be avoided. Fortune had come his way, Bob said, when he met Joyce. He'd been a widower for three years. Joyce had hinted to Tom that Bob had a brother in Australia who was much older than him and was quite well off, and Bob's son had his own printing business. It made sense. Tom felt a little disloyal for wondering what else such an attractive woman could see in Bob, and he dismissed the thought.

It was a different world; he had almost forgotten what it was like to be free. His uncertain marriage had stifled him, as if in a ravine with no escape. The rot had already set in. So he wanted to have it out with Doreen, but it was hard to know the right moment. One day he braced himself to confront her. But it was only a brief conversation in the kitchen.

'Can we talk?' Tom asked.

'What about?'

'Our marriage!' he blurted awkwardly. 'Any thoughts about the future?'

'What makes you think we'll still be together in two years time?'

Her remark was out of the blue. Dumfounded, Tom went out to the garden. He talked with Bob, who spent most of his spare time gardening.

The Pump Company was doing well and Tom went down to have a look round the works, very small when compared with the old Fenton factory. He liked to get away from his little room where he felt quite remote at times with no colleagues to talk and work with. The work was rewarding though, and he concentrated with determination, dismissing the niggling thoughts of his uncertain home life. The small workshop was very pristine and tidy compared with Fentons. He often thought back to those old days and apart from Bob his neighbour, he wondered what had become of all the skilled men.

A lorry backed into the despatching area where crates containing finished Merton Pumps were ready for loading. He stood watching when he was startled by a voice from behind.

'Wasting time?' It was Frank Wills.

'Oh, sorry.' He was thinking that he'd caught him standing with his hands in his pockets.

'Don't worry Tom.' Wills gave a little chuckle, 'I want us to have a talk, come to my office.' He was looking at his watch, 'in about twenty minutes.'

'Yes, OK, Frank.' Must be important, he thought.

He had been with the Merton Company for a year, and the staff were on first name terms with Frank Wills, but not with Mr Jackson, who was not popular. The environment was new to Tom, but he was now used to the friendly atmosphere and he enjoyed the creative work.

'Sit yourself down then.' Mr Wills cleared his throat. 'Anything special you would like to say about the work?'

'Well.' Tom hesitated. 'I like the freedom here... I mean, you trust me, I presume, in how I tackle the designs.'

'Yes, of course, especially the booklets for advertising. Anything else?'

'No, I find it all interesting, I hope I'm doing all right!'

'Yes – I must say I'm very impressed with the way you interpret what I require. You come up with good ideas, excellent work!' He was looking at Tom, straight in the eye with a thoughtful expression.

'Thank you very much... that's reassuring.'

'Would you like something in the way of more responsibility? I could put you in charge of the department. How does that grab you?'

'You mean the department as a whole, Terry and Molly, with me in charge?'

'Yes, I don't like a fragmented set-up, so what do you think?'

Tom was astounded at the unexpected proposal. 'Oh, I can't see how they would like that, it might cause problems.' It seemed a strange suggestion. 'I hope you don't mind – but I feel I would rather leave things as they are, for the time being anyway. But thank you for asking.'

'It would result in an increase in salary of course, but just leave it for now then.' Mr Wills paused for thought. 'As you know, I go away at times, and I would like you to accompany me on my next trip.' He smiled. 'Well?'

'Yes of course, if I could be of help.' Tom was wondering how he would get on with his old colleague. He had always considered him a little bizarre, though independent, but a character with strong convictions. So those words of encouragement were very uplifting.

They were travelling first class, an unusual luxury for Tom.

'We'll be doing some business in the dockland area near Wapping,' Mr Wills told him.

'Oh!' Tom paused with the memory of a small archaic boat building yard. 'Yes, I know the area from the past...'

'I know you do,' Frank said abruptly.

'What's the name of the people?' Tom said brightly as he thrust aside old memories.

'I shouldn't think you would know them: Rogers and Cooper Marine, a small company. They're well established though.'

The revelation was a completely unforeseen bombshell. 'Yes, I see,' he said, and wondered if he might meet Rogers again. 'Has he finished his prison sentence and back in business?'

'What was that?' Frank said.

'Oh, sorry, I was thinking out loud – yes, I did, um have heard of the people.'

'What did you mean, get back into business again?'

'Well.' He was almost lost for words. 'When I was with Brown and Saxon's, I met Mr Rogers. He came about some drawings, and I thought I heard him say he was going out of business, that's all. But it was a long time ago.' Tom was not happy with his explanation. He was trying to avoid telling Frank Wills what he knew about the kind of man Rogers was, but he didn't know much about it anyway, apart from what he was told and had read in the paper. He thought it could be embarrassing if he met the man himself.

Frank took Tom to a lodgings off Whitechapel Road where he told him he had often stayed and had booked them in for the night. They had travelled light, packing just the minimum requirements in their brief cases for one night. He was introduced to a very cheerful lady with an East London accent who greeted Frank like an old friend.

'I expect you two are hungry,' she said. 'Dinner won't be long.'

'I'm sure I told you, Mrs Wentworth, we're being picked up here by a firm's car and taken out for a meal by one of the partners.'

'Yes, of course you told me,' she said with a quiet laugh. 'I forgot for a minute.'

'He said he would call for us at half past twelve,' Frank said looking at his watch. They went into the sitting room.

'Does your uncle still live in Leytonstone?' Tom asked.

'Yes, I call on him occasionally.'

'You stay there?'

'He's a bit of a loner, I wouldn't trouble him anyway.' He looked at his watch again. 'Time's getting on, nearly one! – and I think that's probably the car!' he was looking out of the window. Could it be Rogers, in his old SS Jaguar after all this time, Tom couldn't help thinking.

It was Mr Cooper who met them, in a large black Austin saloon. 'I'm Charles,' he said as they shook hands. He was a jolly Yorkshire fellow with a red face, thick white hair and large moustache. 'My partner is joining us, he may be there first.' Tom instantly thought of Rogers and felt uneasy. It could be awkward to explain, if there was any mention of their meeting of some years ago. They were taken to a very smart French restaurant with dark red decor, where they were introduced to his partner Bill Bailey, a tall slim man with thinning blond hair. Tom was relieved not to be faced with his old crony from the past. Charles Cooper put on thin gold framed spectacles as he looked at the over sized menu. 'We'll have a bottle of wine,' he said with a broad Yorkshire accent. A waiter swiftly put a napkin on Tom's lap. The meal was excellent and took far too long. The wine was very good, but Frank Wills sipped an orange juice.

After that, they ended up in a small first floor office not far from the restaurant, but no where near the old dock.

'This is quite a way from the yard then.' Tom suddenly remembered he was not supposed to know where the yard was. 'I suppose, isn't it?' he continued.

'My original office,' Bill Bailey said.

'Did you know... um, a Mr Rogers?' Tom asked with hesitation. He was curious and even wondered if it would have been better not to ask.

'He was a bloody rogue,' Charles Cooper said. 'Less said the better.'

'Yes, he's gone,' Bill Bailey said. 'He's no longer with the firm – though he wasn't all bad really Charles. Part of the old set-up, wasn't he? And a good designer by all accounts.'

'You gentlemen don't want to hear all this history I'm sure,' Charles said. Tom was glad, and kept quiet.

'But you've kept the name!' Frank said.

'That's about to be changed,' Charles explained. 'Lets get down to business.'

Getting down to the business of ordering the pumps they required after pouring over drawings was surprisingly swift. Their requirement for six specially designed bilge pumps was secured and a cheque for the deposit was handed to Frank Wills with a handshake and smiles. Then Charles Cooper drove them back to the lodgings.

'We've finished up earlier than I expected,' Frank said, addressing Mrs Wentworth. 'So I think we may as well make our way back to Newburne now; no point in staying the night.' Tom was disappointed.

'It's a bit late to get a train back now, surely, haven't you arranged with this lady.....'

'Mrs Wentworth doesn't mind; I never have to worry, do I' he said with an amused expression. But Tom thought he was taking liberties. She would be too polite to say so. Frank telephoned for a taxi.

On the train, Frank Wills had his head buried in the evening paper, while Tom was turning things over in his mind. He had been secretly looking forward to getting away for a night. Doreen wouldn't be expecting him home that night and now he mistrusted her to the extent that the last thing he wanted was to catch her in a compromising position at their home.

Frank folded up the paper. 'Same old rubbish, read about it last night.'

'What's that?' Tom said.

'Talking about abolishing hanging, public outcry, various opinions for and against.'

'I find the whole subject very depressing.'

'Yes, I know.'

'I was thinking, it was very good of them to take us out to that restaurant today.'

'Well, they are clients, aren't they!'

'Yes, but they are customers and shouldn't we have treated them.'

'No, why should we?' Frank said abruptly, and Tom wished he'd not mentioned it.

Back in Newburne, Tom phoned home from the station and Doreen was a long time answering.

'Oh, it's you,' she said. 'Where are you staying then?'

'I'm not staying anywhere, I'm at the station.' There was the sound of a kiss, as if she was being fondled as she was speaking on the phone. 'Just thought I'd let you know. Should see you in about half an hour; I'll get a bus.'

'Well, I wasn't expecting you, that's all... Bye!' She ended abruptly. He was sure he was not mistaken about the kiss, especially as she was very cold and distant with him when he got home and he felt as if he was an intruder.

Tom got his violin out one day, to practise. He wasn't doing very well when Doreen came into the room and said, 'Why don't you stop that awful row!' He knew his playing on that day left much to be desired. But she had so completely changed from the girl he thought he knew so well, and he was very puzzled. 'I thought you liked me to play,' he replied. 'Don't you remember when we all used to join in? Have you given up singing?' He had to calm his anger.

One day he clumsily tried to have sex with her, and she accused him of trying to rape her. He was in a state of confusion, for he was at a loss to know what was wrong. Was it her, or was he at fault? But no reason came to his mind.

Enough was enough, so one day when Doreen was in a very cold and reticent mood, he decided he had to have it out with her.

'Are you seeing someone?' he asked rather too abruptly.

'What do you mean someone? Of course I see someone. I like to see my mother!'

'I mean a man friend – OK, lover if you like. Sorry if it's blunt.'

'What a silly question.' She laughed unkindly. 'It's all in your mind.'

'I only want us to be open with each other.' He was beginning to wonder if he was making a terrible mistake.

'I thought I have always been open with you. You've met my friend Mickey.'

'Are you seeing him then?'

'Not really! It's just that we've kept in touch, you must know that. We were close friends in our school days. We write to each other. He's very kind and he understands me. When we were together at school, I especially enjoyed the companionable silence, which I never get with you.'

Tom did not argue. Strangely, they never quarrelled. Tom felt abandoned, but he clung to the hope that he would not lose her. He was willing to forgive, for he felt sure he still loved her in spite of her obvious infidelity.

One Saturday he was on his own while Doreen was away visiting her mother, and he met Joyce in the garden.

'Hello, Tom,' she said and a warm feeling came over him.

'Oh, hello, Joyce.' As she stood with her hands in the pockets of her skirt, an erotic feeling swept over him.

'On your own this morning?'

'Yes, Doreen's visiting her mother.'

'Bob's away all day up in London,' she said 'Gone to Lords to watch cricket. He often goes there'

'Oh,' Tom hesitated. 'And you don't go as well?'

'No fear, it bores me to tears. Would you like coffee, Tom?'

'Thank you.'

'Come round and join me then,' she beckoned. 'I'll be in the kitchen.'

He walked round with mixed feelings. Was she just being friendly? Or luring him in while Bob was away. Whichever way it was, he was not going to worry that morning; she had cheered him up. He wondered if she'd noticed that things were not all well between him and Doreen. He opened the kitchen door, and there was the smell of coffee.

'Come and sit down Tom. So... Doreen has gone to see her mother. Is that far?'

'No, just a bus ride.'

'Does she ever drive the car?'

'No, she doesn't. She'll be back late this afternoon.'

'There we are.' She put two cups of coffee on the table. 'Why don't we go into the sitting room where it's more comfortable and we can have a nice chat.'

The sitting room was like the room in his house but a mirror image as they were semi-detached. The room captured the morning sunshine.

'This is nice, Tom, and we have the house to ourselves.'

'Yes. While the cat's away...'

'The mice will play!' she said, going into shrieks of laughter.

'Well, it's a funny situation.' Tom thought he shouldn't have said that, and felt embarrassed. But she was still laughing.

'Does Doreen see a lot of her mother?'

'Oh, yes she does, and her mother comes to us. Not to see me, but to talk to Doreen, and they talk for hours sometimes, but I don't know what about. Seems to be secret!'

'Perhaps you should ask her!'

'It's not something I can do somehow.'

'You should enjoy married life, and not have secrets.'

'Yes, I know!'

'Marriage isn't easy. Bob and I often don't see eye to eye.'

'I wish I could get on with my hobbies more.'

'What do you like to do?'

'Well, I used to paint, and even play the violin at one time, but I've had to give that up. It's strange, but we used to have fun, I mean before we got engaged. Oh dear, I feel I shouldn't be telling you all this.'

'You can talk to me about anything. I'm older than you, I'm sure – thirty four!'

'Oh, I'm twenty nine, so...'

'Not that much difference, five years, that's all.'

'Yes...You see, Doreen has a good singing voice, but she's given that up now, and she even hates me playing the violin.'

'Oh, I'm sorry, that is a shame!'

'Would you play the piano for me?'

'You mean now?'

'Yes now; would you play for me now?'

'Of course Tom! What would you like me to play?'

'You choose. I like to hear you play.' Joyce got up, sat at the piano and turned over pages of music. Then she got more music from the piano stool.

'I'm not all that good,' she said as she started to play some selections from Gilbert and Sullivan.

'No, that's not true, you play very well.'

'I do my best,' she said as she played.

As he listened and watched her play, he was becoming very sexually aroused. At that moment, he didn't even care if he had a close relationship with her. After all, what was Doreen up to. Waves of erotic feelings and fantasies gripped and held him spellbound, as he listened and studied her shapely buttocks that stretched her skirt as she was seated on the piano stool. She suddenly stopped playing and turned round, as if she could read his mind.

'We were talking about hobbies,' she said. Her eyes were sparkling with excitement.

'Yes...'

'I like to make lampshades.'

'That's interesting,' he said thinking he would rather she continue playing.

'Yes it is, I'll show you some I've made.' She walked over to the corner, and switched on a tall table lamp. 'Do you like this one?' It was a cylindrical shape and pale green. 'Bob makes the wire frames for me and I sew on the fabric. This is made from waxed cartridge and painted.'

'Yes it's... it goes well with the room. Have you made many?'

'A few, I've made a nice long curved one to go over the bed, come upstairs and see it.' Erotic thoughts flashed through his mind as he followed her up to the bedroom.

The lamp over the bed was about eighteen inches long, on a quarter circle wire frame, fixed to the wall above the bed head, and the same green as the one he'd seen downstairs.

'Do you like it?' she said.

'Yes, I think you're very ingenious, it's a good shape.'

'Let me switch it on.' She bent over in front of Tom. 'There you are, isn't that nice,' she said brightly.

'Lovely!' he said a little breathlessly. They stood facing each other, not speaking for a few seconds. He dare not say the words that were in his mind. Lured into the nest, he was thinking, what does she expect. He wondered if he should say 'thanks for showing me,' and walk downstairs. But he felt transfixed.

Who should speak first? Still facing each other, he wanted to touch her.

'It's a nice warm morning,' she said. 'Why don't you relax.' There was another short silence. 'It's no good pretending, Tom.'

He only saw her sparkling eyes, then he spoke. 'You're very... um, lovely!' She did not speak, they moved close together and kissed. 'Oh Joyce; what am I doing?'

'Don't be silly, you know very well what you're doing.'

'Sorry!'

'Don't be sorry,' she said, 'come on, it's all right:'

'But... but what about Bob?' Tom's conscience bothered him.

'He doesn't make love to me.' She undid the top button of his shirt.

'But I...'

'No buts.' And she continued to undo his shirt, then he didn't care any more.

The spell was cast, any restraint he'd ever had was forgotten while he was in her hands. What was happening with Joyce was completely unexpected. He had at one time believed the man was supposed to take the initiative, although he had thought that it was often the other way round. When he looked back at his experiences with women, he had always been too shy and retiring. So while there were missed opportunities for him, it was usually the woman that led him on. Too often, it would all go wrong or end in bitter disappointment.

He lay back on the bed while she sat astride, it was she who was doing it all. As he felt her heat, and looked up at her beautiful black hair bouncing, her mouth open as she panted, nothing else mattered. They were as one, joined by the powerful force of nature. He was in an ecstatic cloud. 'You're lovely... Oh, lovely!' he shouted.

Things were never the same after that. His marriage was never going to work out anyway. Feelings of guilt lingered, especially whenever he met Bob. Even though Joyce had lured him, he could not be sure if she was being truthful when she told him Bob didn't make love to her. In spite of doubts, he still clung to the faint hope that his marriage might be saved in the end, but Doreen never came back to him. It was as if she was a hundred miles away, even though they were living in the same house. When she moved into the spare room, he could hardly bear it, and he tried to reason with her, but she seemed to be nurturing a secret.

One day, he arrived home to find she had gone. He came home from work and the house was empty. As he sat in the deserted house, he felt a terrible mixture of remorse and anger. In his mind, he drifted back in time to when he and Doreen had first met, and he started to cry. It was deeply depressing, and in spite of her strange aloofness and secrecy, he looked back at happier days. Again, he was blaming himself and thinking he should have been more forthright. He had a meeting with her father, Peter Brooks, but he was almost as distraught as Tom, and he did not blame him in any way.

The marriage ended in divorce after only eighteen months. The hardest thing of all was that Doreen divorced him, citing incompatibility. Tom dared not contest it for fear that his own infidelity would be found out; it would have ruined two marriages instead of one. He was sure she had no knowledge of his yielding to temptation, which he certainly didn't want aired in court. Having to bear the legal procedure was fearful for Tom. He would never forget the men in black gowns and wigs, who made a great deal of money from other people's unhappiness.

Tom went away on a lone holiday to find himself after it was all over. But there were no forgiving words from either side, and the ring was lost for ever.

Chapter 30
The Last Movement

He wanted to make this trip on his own. Much had changed, but the old stone bridge over the river was still there. Tom looked over the wall and down into the water at his reflection, his white hair blowing in the wind against a blue sky. It was a warm day now, but for a moment he remembered a cold wintry night more than fifty years before, when his friend and colleague from Fenton's had met him at that very same place. He wondered what had become of David. Would he have made a success of his life in every way? There can be no one way of looking at the meaning of success. A close and happy family had become most important to Tom. He often asked himself how could he have made so many wrong turnings long ago. He wondered what kind of life Doreen had made for herself. He had stumbled and fallen. But he had somehow clambered back, and luck had come his way, two years after his divorce. It pained him to think of that episode in his life, when the mean men in black cloaks and wigs sometimes haunted him. But time could never erode all the happy memories, and he tried to forget the unhappy days and wasted years.

He crossed the road to The Dolphin where he'd had that last drink with David. It looked the same from the outside except for a large sign on either side of the doorway that read 'Good Bar Food, and Karaoke Nights'. 'Worth a try!' thought Tom. But he was met by a deafening sound, flashing lights and the *thump bang bang bang!* from an electronic game machine, as if a fierce battle was raging. It was the kind of boozer he never used. He turned abruptly away with a feeling of anger at what had been done to the old friendly pub; it would be impossible to have a conversation without shouting.

He found a little pub in a back street hidden away behind a large barricaded building site. It was The Magpie, he vaguely remembered. In the past, it was run by two very cheerful elderly ladies, popular with the locals and especially with dart players. It was now very run down, the walls inside were brown and it was bare. The only redeeming feature was the original engraved glass in the doors and windows, and the sturdy old mahogany bar. There was only one other customer, who was putting money into a Jukebox and selecting tunes. Tom wondered what kind of noise might hit him. Behind the bar a middle-aged woman wearing jeans put a half-smoked cigarette on an ashtray. She had a miserable expression.

'Hello,' Tom said, pretending to sound cheerful. There was no reply. 'A pint of bitter please, in a glass with a handle if you don't mind.' She gave him a straight glass. 'Oh never mind; it should all taste the same by rights.' He was just making conversation, but he didn't think she'd heard him. He gave her the exact money for the beer.

'Lovely, thank you,' she said, and coughed.

The music started and it was quite subdued. The man had chosen some old favourites, to Tom's relief.

'Do you do sandwiches please?' Tom asked the miserable woman.

'Ham, cheese and onion, or pickle?'

'I'll have a ham sandwich please.'

The woman had a puff on her cigarette before she went over and made the single sandwich, divided it into four, threw in some lettuce and cut up tomato.

'One forty please.'

Tom was worried by the lack of hygiene. 'It's quiet in here!' He said.

'We've been hidden away by all this demolition and building.'

'Bloody disgrace it is, they're wrecking this town.' It was the only other customer, suddenly speaking up in anger.

'This pub's coming down you know, we're closing next month,' the woman said.

'Spoils the character of the town!' Tom said.

'It's already gone too far,' the man said, and he went on at length.

Tom walked on through the town. There were too many changes; he couldn't even vaguely remember where some of his favourite old haunts were. The main cinema was now a bingo hall and it looked as if it had been that way for a long time. Glancing into the butchers where his mother had once bought her weekly supply, he saw the old shop was miraculously still there. The mahogany pay booth stood in the corner like a shrine, a reminder of the past. The meat was being served by a young girl and an older man, but the cutting, serving and taking the money was all done by the same hands. *Whatever had happened to butchers' shop standards?* Tom thought as he walked on. These big spotlessly clean supermarkets were taking their business away.

His favourite music shop was alas no more. The friendly man who kept the shop was a local character who liked a joke and Tom had enjoyed many a laugh with him during his frequent visits to buy music books. His mother had purchased his violin from the same shop. But now it was long gone, and a characterless building occupied the site.

A sickening coldness swept over him, for so much had been blotted out. He had his memories, but there was much sadness there for him. He thought of Doreen, and she was like a ghost that sometimes haunted his mind. He saw her smiling face and long fair hair as it used to be, and he wondered what she was doing now. His grandmother's diamond ring was just a picture in his mind. He had to forget such thoughts, for he had made a new life long since.

He walked into the gigantic shopping centre where the works had once stood. Passion swept over him; it was an outrage that so much had been destroyed. What was the importance of heavy engineering now; are there any craftsmen? Steam engines were long gone and could only be seen in museums. Small steam river craft and some railways were kept going only by those who loved to run them for pleasure.

There was a new music shop where the instruments were mainly electronic. Tom spotted among the guitars a violin and thought of his own. It lay in the loft at home, unplayed for a very long time. A feeling of nostalgia enveloped him as he remembered so clearly that concert in Oxford many years ago. He thought of Mildred playing in the orchestra. He was almost overcome by sadness and wondered what had become of her. Slowly he turned and walked away from the awful place.

The pain he'd felt when he was in love so many years ago was just a faint memory now. For him at the time, it was his whole world, the helplessness of the mere apprentice with no money. His mobile rang, and it was his eldest son, John.

'Hi, Dad.'

'Oh, hello, John, I'm just on my way to the station. I won't be late for the opening.'

'Had a good day?'

He hesitated. 'Just walking down memory lane; the old place has changed. See you at seven.'

Walking to the station, he rather wished he had not made the nostalgic journey. He hadn't forgotten the opening of the model reconstruction of the old docks, and as he settled in his first class compartment, he was thinking very much about the opening party. They had worked on the models for months. He turned his mind to the reunion dinner that had been arranged to follow by some fellow colleagues. He wondered what they had in store for his seventieth birthday.

The train sped on its way to London.